Charles Raymond Booth Barrett

Battles and Battlefields in England

Charles Raymond Booth Barrett

Battles and Battlefields in England

ISBN/EAN: 9783743333475

Manufactured in Europe, USA, Canada, Australia, Japa

Cover: Foto ©ninafisch / pixelio.de

Manufactured and distributed by brebook publishing software (www.brebook.com)

Charles Raymond Booth Barrett

Battles and Battlefields in England

INTRODUCTION.

"THIS England," exclaims Shakspeare's Faulconbridge in that stirring boast which will ring for ever in the ears of Englishmen,

> "never did nor never shall
> Lie at the proud foot of a conqueror
> But when it first did help to wound itself."

The Bastard generalised from a single instance; for only once, from the time when the Angles gave the island its name down to King John's day, or for that matter down to our own, has England undergone a "conquest" in the strict sense of the term, and no doubt on that one occasion it had first helped in the person of its ill-fated ruler to wound itself. But in the strife of "malice domestic" as distinguished from "foreign levy,"—in the civil broils which have led to no conquests save those of political factions, and have left behind them no conquerors save the English prince who vanquished a kinsman, or the English rebel leader who overthrew his king, "this England" has given itself many a wound. One wonders whether those who have made no reckoning of their own will be prepared for or surprised by Mr. Barrett's statistics of English battles—that is to say, battles of the first rank in military or political importance—from Fulford to Sedgemoor. Fulford, the first in his list, was fought on September 20, 1066, and Sedgemoor, fought on July 6, 1685, is the thirty-seventh. That means an average of one battle about every seventeen years for a period of a little over six centuries. It is a pretty long and a fairly lively tale, and it seems to show that even a country with no foreign enemy, save on a few occasions, to repel, no invader aiming at the position of proud-footed conqueror to defeat, may yet, by the healthy play of its own internal passions or political activities, make shift to accumulate as goodly an array of historic battlefields as can be found in lands divided from their neighbours by frontiers of field and hedgerow instead of being "compassed by the inviolate sea."

The "silver streak," however, did not of course encircle one united island until the conjunction of the two Crowns, and thus on five at least of these foughten fields our English forefathers were actually paying the penalties of the field-and-hedgerow frontier, or at any rate of the hill-and-river boundary which divided them from what was then a separate kingdom. Northallerton (the Battle of the Standard), Neville's Cross, Otterburn, immortal in the ballad of Chevy Chase, Homildon Hill and Flodden, most famous of them all, were fought to beat back incursions of the Scots. At Fulford and Stamford Bridge the Saxon was at hand-grips with a Danish or Norwegian invader, and at Hastings he was vainly struggling to save his country from the grasp of a yet more formidable foreign foe. This however leaves, from Lewes in the thirteenth century to Sedgemoor in the seventeenth, a balance of twenty-nine battles of a strictly "civil" description; and, considering that for the whole of one of these four centuries the English were strewing French battlefields with their dead, and for the best part of another hundred years were buccaneering and filibustering their lives away in the New World, their military record seems a pretty full one for a nation of shopkeepers.

Had fate distributed our historic battles equally over England there would have been almost enough to "go round," and nearly every English county would have had its battlefield to show. But they have not been allocated on so equitable a principle. The north of England has had to pay the penalty of its proximity to the perfervid Scot; and it is partly in consequence of this that Northumberland, Durham, and Yorkshire account among them for more than one-third of the total. Three times in the first named of these counties, once in the second and once in the last, have Scotch and English closed in deadly conflict. Twice in Northumberland and twice in Yorkshire did the Red and White Roses set the battle in array against each other, and on the last occasion at Towton, for one of the fiercest and bloodiest of all the fights that ever were fought on English soil. But next to keeping the northern marches of the kingdom, or lying adjacent to one of the warden shires, contiguity to and command of the capital was the surest claim on the attentions of contending armies; and Hertfordshire, that cockpit of Yorkists and Lancastrians, comes next with its two battles of St. Albans and its epoch-making field of Barnet. No other county has attained to the honours of more than two, and out of the whole forty as many as two-and-twenty contain no historic battlefield at all. Fate and the fortune of war, the accident of geographical position, or of the territorial distribution of the power of the great feudal lords,

INTRODUCTION.

have combined to hold them scathless. The long, confused, and desolating struggle of the rival Plantagenets swept over the fair face of England from south to north and back again, from within a few score miles of the English Channel to the near neighbourhood of the Scottish border. The Northumberland dalesmen watched their charging hosts at Hexham; the thunder of their rude artillery was heard in the capital on the eve of Barnet. Between these two latitudes, along a comparatively narrow north and southward-stretching zone, the country is dotted with their battlefields. But east and south-west and furthest west escaped. Margaret of Anjou landed at Weymouth for her last struggle with the Yorkists. Devon and Cornwall were raised by her followers, Somerset, Dorset, and Wilts were traversed by her forces, but it was in Gloucestershire that the decisive battle was fought. Wessex, however, had its share of fighting in the Civil War, when East Anglia again escaped. From Stratton in Cornwall to Lansdown, that airy plateau overlooking Bath, whereon a monument still records the scene of stout old Sir Bevil Grenvil's death, Roundhead and Cavalier gave and took many a hard knock. The whole west country, indeed, from Bristol to Launceston, had lively times throughout the greater part of the war, as also had the midland and northern shires. Thanks to the "Association," the eastern counties once more succeeded in damming back the tide of battle from their fields and homesteads. There is perhaps no other district of England which has been held so scathless from the hand of war throughout the eight hundred years of our history since the Conquest as that tract of country within which is included the counties of Norfolk, Suffolk, Huntingdon, Cambridge, and Essex. This area excepted, it may be safely said that, taking one period with another, there is hardly any part of the country which has not seen its share of fighting. Mr. Barrett, of course, gives only the greater battles; indeed it is only these which ever attain to the dignity of a name. The countless skirmishes of the Civil War, and, more important still, the captures of towns—even great and important military centres—enter only by way of reference into his pages. Could we recover and record all the nameless conflicts between Parliament's men and King's men; could we represent all the casual bloodshed on one side or the other in an appropriate colour on the map of England, we should probably find, with the exception above referred to, no county without its spots of red. Only it would then appear that for some reason or other the majority of the larger stains were to be found in the midland and northern shires. Hastings only excepted—for the work of Barnet was not complete till after Tewkesbury — there has been

INTRODUCTION.

no decisive battle fought in this country anywhere within a hundred miles of the capital. Evesham, Towton, Bosworth, Flodden, Marston Moor, Naseby, and—to end with the county we began with—the scene of the "crowning mercy," Worcester itself, are all either in the Midlands or in the North.

Not that the decisive are necessarily the romantic battles of our history. Flodden is so, but that is due to peculiar circumstances—to the personal chivalry of the skilless and dauntless King of Scots, to the splendid devotion of the Scottish chiefs who fell in such numbers round their sovereign, and indeed to the unconquerable courage and fidelity of the whole of that ill-fated host, in whose ranks

> "Groom fought like noble, squire like knight,
>   As fearlessly and well."

Flodden could not but be romantic even if it had not inspired the finest poetic battle-piece in the English language. It was not often, even in times nearer the heroic age than ours, that a king fell fighting at the head of his army, and never before, perhaps, after staking the whole fortunes of his kingdom, like the luckless James IV., upon one desperate hazard.

But, after all, it is in most cases the bard who makes the battle. It is not its heaps of slain, nor its master-strokes of strategy, nor even the mighty political issues that hang upon its fortunes—not these is it, but its *vates sacer*, that keeps its story fresh in the memory of men, and the figures of its fighters vivid in the imagination of future ages. The nameless Scottish balladist who sang—

> "It fell about the Lammas tide,
>   When the muir-men win their hay,
> The doughty Earl of Douglas rode
>   Into England to catch a prey,"

—he and his equally unknown English rival, who flung across the Border that exulting answer,

> "The child that is unborn shall rue
>   The hunting of that day,"

have made the Battle of Otterburn and the name of Chevy Chase mean more to the lover of romance than many a field which has decided the fate of a dynasty. It is interesting to trace in Mr. Barrett's careful and strictly sifted account of this battle the clear historic outlines of the chivalrous story—a perfect mediæval epic—which chronicler and ballad-singer have left us, and of which Douglas and Percy are respectively the Hector and Achilles.

The Scottish earl, crossing the Border at the head of 3,000 men, has raided the "English side" right up to the Tyne, when the first "fytte" of the Homeric tale begins. In a skirmish under the walls of Newcastle the two leaders came into actual hand-to-hand conflict, and Percy, the renowned Hotspur, was borne to earth by his adversary, who seized the lance and pennon of his unhorsed foe, and vowed, shaking it aloft, that he would plant it on his castle of Dalkeith. "That," answered Percy, "shalt thou never"; and having raised a levy of the Marches to a strength equal, or (according to the Scottish chroniclers) much superior to Douglas's force, he followed in their retreating footsteps, and overtaking them at Otterburn, after an extraordinary march, gave battle by moonlight, as related in the text. The prose chronicler does not vouch, it is true, for the balladist's duel between Percy and Douglas, wherein the Scottish earl, entering unhelmeted into the encounter, was struck on the brow by the "good broad sword" of the English knight, and so slain. More authentic history relates that Douglas, plunging into the thickest of the English battalions attended only by his chaplain, Richard Lundie, "afterwards Archdean of Aberdeen" (how quaint a touch is that!), and by two squires of his body, Robert Hart and Simon Glendenning, was surrounded by the enemy before his followers could come up, and was found by them stretched on the ground with three mortal wounds, his two squires dead beside him, and the future Archdean standing over his prostrate patron and defending him with a lance. "I die like my forefathers," said the earl, according to Godscroft, "on a field of battle, and not on a bed of sickness. Conceal my death, defend my standard, and avenge my fall! It is an old prophesy that a dead man shall gain a field, and I hope it will be accomplished this night." It was the "dreary dream" of Douglas in the Scottish ballad—

"I saw a dead man win a fight, and I think that man was I."

It would have been dramatically fitter that he should have fallen by the hand of Percy, but considering that the artless old ballad-weaver represents Percy a few stanzas later as unaware that Douglas has been killed, we must reluctantly conclude that Godscroft's version of the affair is the correct one.

It is with still greater unwillingness that we give up the legendary burial-place of the Scottish earl. He was not "buried at the bracken bush" that he chooses in the ballad as his last resting-place. A spot near which he is supposed to have fallen is still marked by a cross; but the hero himself was carried home over the Border and buried at Melrose Abbey, where his tomb is still shown. The dead man, however, won his fight, for the English were soundly beaten, and "the Percy," as the balladist avers, redeeming his reputation for veracity in the last line, was, in fact, "led captive away." He surrendered to Sir Robert Montgomery, ancestor of the present Earl of Eglinton, on whose barony of Eaglesham stands (or stood) the castle of Penoon, built by the captive as his ransom.

Hotspur, thanks to Shakspeare, carries romance with him wherever he goes, and it accompanies him when, fifteen years after Otterburn, he crossed into Cheshire with the 4th Earl of Douglas (the same whom he had taken prisoner but a few months before at Homildon Hill), and began that spirited race with Prince Hal for Shrewsbury, which the latter only won by a few hours. Falstaff, it will be remembered, was at the same time advancing northward from his base at the Boar's Head in Eastcheap, though by more leisurely stages, and rendered more deliberate in his movements by a certain disinclination to march through Coventry. We get a glimpse of the breathless haste of the Royalists in the dialogue between Sir John and Westmoreland. "My Lord of Westmoreland, I cry you mercy. I thought your honour had already been at Shrewsbury." To which the answer is, "Faith, Sir John, 'tis more than time that I were there and you too. . . . The King, I can tell you, looks for us all; we must away all night." Falstaff's reply was slightly evasive; but, as we all know, he arrived in time to take part in the engagement, and even to cross swords with no less doughty a warrior than the Douglas.

One may speak of this famous passage of arms, terminated by a stratagem on the part of the English champion, as though it were historical, for in truth it is not more mythical than the Homeric duel between Prince Hal and Hotspur, in which the youth of fifteen fighting his maiden battle is represented as slaying a seasoned soldier of exactly twice his age. Shakspeare, however, like the ballad-maker who sang of Otterburn, gives the poetic truth of a battle in which the stripling Prince stood, far more than his gloomy and conscience-stricken father, for the strength and hopes of the new dynasty, while the warlike Percy was the life and soul of the rebellion. It is these two who dominate the scene, and the attention is not distracted from them even by the spirited Shakspearean sketch of the reckless and luckless Douglas—the "tyneman," or "lose-man," as his countrymen called him —whose life was a succession of failures, who was defeated, lost an eye, and was taken prisoner at Homildon Hill, was beaten again at Shrewsbury, where he fell over a precipice, and was once more taken a prisoner, in attempting to escape, and finally perished on a French battlefield.

After Shrewsbury the land had rest for over fifty years—its longest interval of repose since that which Prince Edward won for it on the field of Evesham. English blood flowed freely enough during the half-century that elapsed between the suppression of the Glyndwr rebellion and the outbreak of the Wars of the Roses, but it sank into a foreign soil. France took toll of our dead in many a battle of those three-and-fifty years, from Agincourt to Formigny; and when at last the weary struggle of the French wars was brought to an end, and the nation was able, for the first time in the course of a century, to draw back its outstretched hand, to stanch the exhausting flux which had been steadily draining its life-blood since the days of Edward III., and to concentrate its strength within its own four seas, it was only to find itself called upon to submit for another sixteen years to the ordeal of the most cruel and desolating struggle by which our island has ever been laid waste.

Yet it is strange how faint an impression this terrible if tedious dynastic duel of the Two Roses has left upon the imagination of the English of later days. One may almost fancy that the weariness of the distracted and impoverished nation had descended as a legacy of indifference and almost of disgust to its posterity, and that it is the unhappiness of these "old unhappy far-off things, and battles long ago," which leaves even a remote generation insensible to such romantic appeal as they make. Yet savage and selfish as was this struggle between York and Lancaster, it was undoubtedly signalised by notable feats of arms, and produced or brought to maturity more than one illustrious man. The heroic figure of the king-maker looms large in our history; and though it is difficult to recognise the statesman and warrior in the silken voluptuary who ruled England for the twelve years which followed Barnet and Tewkesbury—a Byronic Sardanapalus, alike in his courtly vices and his soldierly virtues, though without the atonement of the Assyrian's heroic death—yet it is beyond dispute that from the furnace of war and the icy waters of political adversity Edward IV. came out hardened and tempered into the astutest ruler and the greatest captain of his age. To have crushed the armies of Warwick and Queen Margaret within three weeks of each other, and the latter on the morrow of a forced march of forty odd miles, was a memorable exploit, and well worthy of a Prince who had never throughout the whole war lost a battle in which he personally commanded. The rush by which the Yorkists carried St. Albans in the opening fight of the war was a brilliant and dashing exploit. The desperate valour of both victors and vanquished during the ten hours' struggle on the dreadful Palm Sunday of Towton, won the unstinted praise of Froissart. But romance is somehow wanting to the long-drawn struggle—a want which not even the genius of Shakspeare has been able to supply. He who could so kindle our enthusiasm with his presentment of a warrior and stir our pulses with a warrior's voice, imprints on our minds no vivid image of a martial presence throughout the three Histories of Henry VI., save that of Talbot; and Talbot himself seems tame beside the splendid figure of Hotspur, the true hero of "Henry IV.," or of that of Henry's gallant gasconading son in the History that bears his name. There is no soldier-hero in the Second and Third Parts of Henry VI. The eye glances indifferently over the fierce Princes of the House of York, and even the mighty baron who by turns exalted and abased them, to rest upon the pathetic shadow of the meek and nerveless king as he muses yearningly on the shepherd's lot within earshot of the most famous fight and deadly battle of the war. Even the great historic issues which hung upon the fate of individual combatants seem unable to hold our interest, and the death of Warwick and of the baronial power that perished with him hardly affect us like the fate of Douglas in the mere border foray of Otterburn, or like that of Hotspur at Shrewsbury, of Falkland at Newbury, of John Hampden at Chalgrove Field. The whole period of the Wars of the Roses seems less like a stage of real, if violent, national development, than a mere confused, bloody and irrelevant interlude in the national life. England—the true England of our filial devotion, the England great in arms and jurisprudence, as we knew her under Edward I., the England illustrious in poesy and adventure as we are again to know her under Elizabeth, seems, as it were, to be standing sullenly at gaze amid her crippled commerce and her ruined fields, and waiting until a fratricidal conflict in which she has no part or lot, shall wear itself to an end. No wonder she was ripe for the New Monarchy, that wholesome despotism of the Tudors which rescued the nation from the alternating grasp of savagely warring factions, to place it under the firm and steadying pressure of a single masterful hand.

Very different, however, is the feeling with which we look back on the struggle of the great Civil War. If Red Rose and White Rose knights and men-at-arms have become shadows for us, Cavalier and Roundhead are flesh and blood enough. Their spiritual heirs indeed are with us to this day, with unmistakable ancestral lineaments to keep the faces of their forefathers fresh in our minds; and as has been well said, it is one of the few historical instances of a civil combat in which the combatants possess almost equally balanced claims on the sympathy and admiration of posterity. If, moreover, they are not both equally picturesque in point of externals, the very contrast between them is of that dramatically striking type which enhances the picturesqueness of the general effect. For never, perhaps, was a more pregnant and a more stimulating contrast ever arrayed by Fate between two such conspicuous groups of actors on so admirably suitable a stage. On the one side chivalry, brilliancy, gallantry, gaiety, recklessness—all the qualities that appeal to the eye and inspirit the imagination; on the other side fortitude, tenacity, enthusiasm, stern devotion to duty, unshakable religious faith, inextinguishable religious ardour—all the qualities that impress the mind and touch the deeper emotions. The glow of romance illumines both; for though the Puritan in times of peace as we see him to-day is not outwardly a romantic figure, we are or should be conscious of that inner and ideal side of him which great cases of action have never failed to bring out—as in our Havelocks, and Lawrences, and Gordons, and all those other "fighting and praying soldiers" who are in fact our Ironsides of to-day.

It is indeed characteristic of these great but latent qualities that they were developed among the mass of the Roundhead army in the seventeenth century under stress of the same forces as are required in our day to evoke them in the individual; and it is their gradual growth into overwhelming potency which makes the history of the Civil War as interesting as a great romance. It had its opening chapter in that memorable conversation between Cromwell and Hampden which took place on the morrow of the wild and indecisive struggle of Edgehill, and which he afterwards related as Lord Protector in a speech to his second Parliament. Even at that early date and from his observation of the very first encounter of the war, his instinct told him that, military capacity apart, the moral impulse which carries men to victory was on the Royalist side. "Your troops," said he to Hampden, "are most of them old decayed serving-men and tapsters, and such kind of fellows, and their troops are gentlemen's sons, younger sons, and persons of quality. Do you think that the spirits of such base mean fellows will ever be able to encounter gentlemen that have honour and courage and resolution in them?" Men of a spirit as potent as that which animated the Royalists must be raised to combat them, and Cromwell knew of but one such animating and sustaining impulse. Piety must be matched against chivalry. To cope with men of honour they must have men of religion. To this Mr. Hampden made cautious answer that, "it was a good notion if it could be executed"; and executed it could be and was. "I raised such men as had the fear of God before them, as made some conscience of what they did; and

INTRODUCTION.

from that day forward I must say to you they were never beaten, and whenever they were engaged against the enemy they beat continually."

But this "little leaven" was slow in leavening the whole lump. The great soldier who spoke these words had yet to rise from command to command, to create first a troop then a regiment, to organise the Eastern Association and its forces, to develop these forces into the New Model army, and upon that model to reconstruct the entire military array of the Parliament before the crushing blow of Naseby could be delivered. And in the meantime, as though to sustain the interest of this great romance of history, the Parliamentary cause throughout this entire period of two years was almost uninterruptedly losing ground. The Royal cause was triumphant in the north; Waller was annihilated in the west; the Fairfaxes were driven into Hull; Bristol surrendered to Prince Rupert. The only Parliamentary successes of the year 1643—the relief of Gainsborough and later on of Hull, the clearance of the Royalists out of Lincolnshire, and the addition of that county to the Eastern Association—were all of Cromwell's winning. Elsewhere the King was carrying all before him; and in the autumn of 1643 it looked as if the game of Parliament was up.

It was at Marston Moor that the tide of warfare turned at last against the Royalists, and at Naseby a twelvemonth later that it reached its flood and swept the armies of the ill-fated King resistlessly before it. This is not the place to rehearse in detail the stirring story of that last great battle, and of the southern and western march of the victorious army during the months that followed it, when town after town and fortress after fortress fell before Cromwell and Fairfax until stout old Sir Jacob Astley, the last Royalist in the field, surrendered with his little force at Stow-in-the-Wold, remarking drily to his conquerors, "You have now done your work and may go play—unless you will fall out among yourselves." Their falling out was to come promptly enough for Presbyterians and Independents; and some of their work was still to do in Scotland, Ireland, and (biggest job of all) within thirty miles of the spot whereon the old Cavalier was standing as he spoke.

But Worcester was really the finishing stroke of the war and—since one cannot dignify by such a name the butchery of peasants in a hopeless cause at Sedgemoor—the last of the battles in the last, as it was the greatest, of our civil quarrels to be fought out on English soil. More than two centuries and a half have passed since the first blood of that famous war was shed at Edgehill; it is two hundred and forty-five years since its final blow was delivered at Worcester. Its battlefields dot the island from the North Cornish coast to the moors of Yorkshire, their peace unbroken, their scars long healed. Here and there, of course, their very sites are with difficulty traceable. Road and hedgerow parcel out and transfigure what once was open plain; cornfield and garden, even sometimes street and suburb, cover the ground over which the waves of Rupert's horse dashed furiously on the breakwater of Roundhead pikes. Such a battlefield as that of Worcester, where the conflict raged at the very gates of the town itself, is naturally hard to decipher; yet it is surprising how many points of attack are still to be identified even here, while on the breezy height of Lansdown, or on the mounded moorland of Naseby, man, at any rate, has little interfered with Nature, and the countryside lies broad and open and in its main features unchanged from the day when the smoke of the Ironside matchlocks floated thick above it, and its sweet green turf was ploughed by the hoofs of charging horses, and soaked with the blood of dying men.

The contrast between peace and war is among the tritest commonplaces of human thought, and one of the most familiar topics of the sentimental rhapsodist. War with its cruel barbarities, its hideous and seemingly aimless waste, its outrage upon all the fair amenities of Nature, all the milder humanities of man, provokes so irresistibly, and is so constantly calling into articulate utterance, the indignant protest of the modern child of civilisation, that it needs exceptional originality and force of expression to denounce or to lament it otherwise than in the most threadbare platitudes. And when here and there a prose-poet like Carlyle gives voice of passionate eloquence to this essentially modern feeling he is apt to run into exaggerations which the modern historical sense must discountenance. Yet it is to History that he appeals. "History (ever, more or less, the written epitomised synopsis of Rumour) knows so little," he cries, "that were not as well unknown. Attila Invasions, Walter the Penniless Crusades, Sicilian Vespers, Thirty Years' War: mere sin and misery, not work, but hindrance of work! For the earth all the while was yearly green and yellow with her kind harvests; the hand of the craftsman, the mind of the thinker rested not; and so after all, and in spite of all, we have this so glorious high-domed blossoming World, concerning which poor History may well ask with wonder whence *it* came."

It is a noble passage, but how perverse! For why should History intrude upon the domain of Cosmology and Metaphysics, and ask questions which lie outside her own proper province? She is concerned not with the origin of the world, but with the fortunes of man—with his past, his present, his future—in this world of unknown origin. And to say that History, since that origin is unknown, might as well know nothing of the sin and misery of barbaric conquests, religious wars, religious massacres, for that they are "not work, but hindrance of work," is as though one should assert that a chain is broken because some of its links are concealed from view. The historian of Cromwell would assuredly not have spoken of his hero's victories as mere "hindrance of work," and we have as little right to say it of the turmoil and bloodshed of the continental wars of religion, merely because we can trace in them no forces of national evolution plainly working to a predestined end. We can, at any rate, clearly see in these days that the fierce convulsions by which our island has been shaken are as much a part of the great order of the world as that sweet procession of the seasons with which Carlyle so sadly contrasts the strife of man; and we know and feel, as we gaze fondly on the smiling face of England, unvexed for centuries by fratricidal conflict, that the scattering of the seeds of quarrel and the ingathering of the sheaves of death by our warring forefathers were as necessary and as beneficial to us who came after them as are the alternations of green corn and golden harvest to the fair and peaceful fields on which they fought.

H. D. TRAILL.

PREFACE.

I HAVE attempted in the present volume to describe and illustrate the battles and battlefields in England. In my survey I include all combats of importance. Sieges, whether of city, town, castle, or fortified house, except incidentally, do not come within the scope of my book. The illustrations consist of topographical views, buildings connected with battles, battle crosses and tombs, all reproductions of drawings taken during my journeys. Heraldic shields, badges, and a few relics are also introduced. Where illustration is lacking the reason is to be found either in the fact that the topography of a place has been so changed by the hand of man as to render sketching impossible, or that the state of the weather prevented the use of pencil and book. Sketch plans of some battles have been inserted, but merely as explanatory of the dispositions of troops or the movements described. For my authorities I have endeavoured to consult all available sources of information. To the chroniclers of old, to the statesmen or soldiers of the past whose documents and letters have supplied me with facts, it were vain to express my obligations; but I can and do most freely acknowledge the guidance and aid I have received from the perusal of the standard histories of Sir James Ramsay and Mr. S. R. Gardiner.

PREFACE.

My intention has been to include in one view a strictly historical account of the battles in England between 1066 and 1685. Discarding legend and touching but slightly on archæology, I have traced the movements of armies, the progress of campaigns, and the various phases and results of battles. In an appendix I have briefly referred to marching, arms, and armour, strategy and tactics, as explanatory of the conditions which obtained of old.

Lastly, I have endeavoured to treat the military exploits of those of whom I have written from a purely military standpoint. Too often has the popular estimate of a soldier been determined by the accident of his political or religious creed.

C. R. B. BARRETT.

TOWYN, WANDSWORTH, S.W.
    Sept. 1, 1896.

CONTENTS.

CHAPTER I.
FULFORD AND STAMFORD BRIDGE . . . 1

CHAPTER II.
HASTINGS . . . 11

CHAPTER III.
NORTHALLERTON (THE BATTLE OF THE STANDARD) . 26

CHAPTER IV.
LEWES 37

CHAPTER V.
EVESHAM 49

CHAPTER VI.
BOROUGHBRIDGE 58

CHAPTER VII.
NEVILLE'S CROSS 68

CONTENTS.

CHAPTER VIII.
OTTERBURN 81

CHAPTER IX.
HOMILDON HILL 97

CHAPTER X.
SHREWSBURY 101

CHAPTER XI.
ST. ALBANS 112

CHAPTER XII.
BLORE HEATH 118

CHAPTER XIII.
NORTHAMPTON . . . 124

CHAPTER XIV.
WAKEFIELD 131

CHAPTER XV.
ST. ALBANS . . . 141

CHAPTER XVI.
MORTIMER'S CROSS AND TOWTON 145

CHAPTER XVII.
HEDGELEY MOOR AND HEXHAM . 166

CONTENTS.

CHAPTER XVIII.

	PAGE
BARNET	182

CHAPTER XIX.

TEWKESBURY	198

CHAPTER XX.

BOSWORTH	212

CHAPTER XXI.

FLODDEN	222

CHAPTER XXII.

NEWBURN	239

CHAPTER XXIII.

EDGEHILL	248

CHAPTER XXIV.

STRATTON	261

CHAPTER XXV.

CHALGROVE FIELD	267

CHAPTER XXVI.

LANSDOWN	275

CHAPTER XXVII.

ROUNDWAY DOWN	286

CONTENTS.

CHAPTER XXVIII.

NEWBURY 296

CHAPTER XXIX.

CROPREDY BRIDGE 308

CHAPTER XXX.

MARSTON MOOR 320

CHAPTER XXXI.

NEWBURY 352

CHAPTER XXXII.

NASEBY 364

CHAPTER XXXIII.

WORCESTER 382

CHAPTER XXXIV.

SEDGEMOOR 395

APPENDICES.

I. MARCHING 419

II. ARMS AND ARMOUR 432

III. STRATEGY AND TACTICS 440

CHAPTER I.

FULFORD AND STAMFORD BRIDGE.

September 20 and 25, 1066.

THE coronation of Harold—Harold II. to give him his proper title—took place early in the year 1066. The old Chronicle gives the date of the ceremony as "soon after Twelfth-day." It will be remembered that Tostig, his tyrannical brother, after being exiled from the earldom of Northumberland, accompanied by his wife, family, and a few followers, had taken refuge with his brother-in-law, Baldwin, Count of Flanders. Morcar ruled the earldom in his place. Mercia was governed by Edwin. In exile Tostig prepared his plans for reconquest and revenge. But unable single-handed to even hope for victory, he naturally looked about for external aid. This he found after negotiation in Norway, where alliance was made with the King, Harald Hardrada. King Harald Hardrada prepared a mighty fleet—the largest that had ever sailed forth from Norway—to engage in hostilities with England.

During the time which was occupied in equipping this fleet

Tostig, with some sixty vessels, started on his expedition. His first point of attack was the Isle of Wight, where great barbarities were practised and a heavy fine in money was exacted. Sailing eastwards along the coast he ravaged all the maritime towns as far as Sandwich. Meanwhile Harold in London had heard of the invasion, and marching himself with troops to Sandwich also sent a fleet in pursuit of Tostig. Both his endeavours missed their aim. He arrived at Sandwich only to find that Tostig had sailed away northwards, and that he had slipped by the fleet. The invader kept out at sea till the coasts of Essex and Suffolk had been passed; but, descending on Norfolk and Lincolnshire, repeated the barbarities he had already practised in the south. He then entered the Humber and ravaged Yorkshire. Edwin, Earl of Mercia, and Morcar, Earl of Northumberland, apprised of the invasion, collected what forces they could, and marched prepared to combat the invaders. This they successfully did, and drove the rebel earl back in disorder to his ships. Sailing in haste from the Humber, Tostig found his passage blocked by the fleet of Harold and was forced to give battle. Here on the sea as previously on land he suffered defeat, so much so that with only a bare remnant of his fleet, some dozen ships, he managed to escape to Scotland.

These events took place in the early summer of 1066. Meanwhile the Norwegian preparations were completed, and a mighty fleet started forth from the rugged inlets of that much-indented coast. Accounts differ as to the number of vessels, some authorities placing it as low as two hundred, while others estimate it as high as one thousand. Probably three hundred is about the correct figure. Harald Hardrada sailed for the Tyne, and there awaited Tostig, who, having obtained more ships and men in Scotland and even from the far Orkneys, effected a junction in safety. The united fleets sailed for the Humber, and made their way up the Yorkshire Ouse to a spot near the village of Riccall and situated ten miles south of York. Here the ships were drawn up, and the invaders effected an unopposed landing. Proceeding rapidly to York, they designed to storm that city. Fugitives —for everywhere the country people fled panic-stricken before the advance of this terrible host—brought news to the Earls of Northumberland and Mercia. These again gathered their forces, enlisted all possible additional fighting men, and, together with the garrison of York, marched out to repel the invasion. With the city of York a mile and a half to the north and behind them, they met Tostig and Hardrada. The scene of the encounter was the village of Fulford, situated on the northern bank of the Ouse; the date Wednesday, September 20, 1066, the Eve of St. Matthew.

The battle was of short duration, though the fighting was hard and the loss of life severe. No specific details of importance have come down to us, and it may be safely assumed that the ordinary formation of locked shields was employed according as one side or the other found itself compelled to act on the defensive. At first victory is stated to have inclined towards the English, who doubtless in the commencement of the battle acted as assailants. Later in the day the invaders changed the fortune of the fight, and the English fell in heaps beneath the onslaught of the terrible two-handed swords of the Northmen. Rolled back westwards, numbers met their death by drowning in the river Ouse, many more never even reached its banks. The clergy of York who, with the view of encouraging their Christian countrymen, had accompanied the force into the field, died, it is stated, to the number of one hundred. The defeat became a rout, and the dispirited remnant fled headlong into the walled city, only to surrender at discretion without further resistance. On September 23rd the victorious invaders exacted a large supply of provisions and seized 500 hostages. Orders were given that the Norwegian dead should be respected and honourably buried. It is stated that 150 Norwegian hostages were left in the city by the invaders as a pledge of good faith. This is a curious fact if true, and it is more reasonable to suppose that this body of men was detailed to perform or ensure the performance of the pagan rites at the numerous funerals of their slain. Christian York would not have done this satisfactorily, even if the ritual in all its details had been familiar. Retracing their steps to Riccall the 500 hostages were left under the guard of Olaf, the son of the Norwegian king, and a compact to subdue the entire kingdom was solemnly entered into by the rebel earl and Hardrada.

Harold, after his unavailing march to Sandwich, had been employed in watching the southern coast of England, knowing that a Norman invasion in that quarter was imminent. His headquarters were in the Isle of Wight, which place he left on September 8th, provisions failing, and crossing to Hampshire returned to London, the fleet sailing round. In London the news of the combined attack of Hardrada and Tostig on his northern dominions reached him, and with forced marches he hastened to oppose them. On his way intelligence of the landing at Riccall, speedily followed by the tale of the disaster at Fulford, was reported, and without doubt still further urged him on. Too late to avert the surrender of York, he reached Tadcaster on Sunday, September 24th, the day after that event. Without turning aside to demolish the camp and the ships of the invaders at Riccall, he immediately marched to Stamford Bridge, where the invaders' army was drawn up to give him battle.

The village of Stamford Bridge now stands on both sides of the river Derwent, at a distance of eight miles to the east of York. At the time of the battle the river, which is between 35 to 40 feet in width, was spanned by a rough wooden bridge resting on stone piers. This bridge has now been destroyed. A second and later bridge, which stood nearer the present one, has also vanished. The bridge now standing occupies a site rather more than a quarter of a mile below the bridge existing in 1066. On either side of the river, which runs in a deep channel and with little current, there are two ridges of high ground, the steeper of which is on the east bank. The invaders posted troops on the western ridge, a strong party occupied the ground on the bank and held the bridge, while the main body was extended along the higher ground on the eastern bank. Harold, it will be remembered, was approaching from the west. The ground was well chosen, and according to the generalship of those days the disposition of the troops was excellent. The outposts on the west bank would act as scouts and obtain early notice of the advent of Harold. They would then fall back on the body guarding the bridge and would augment it to a strength assumed to be more than sufficient to successfully hold its narrow passage. At the worst, and if driven across, the bulk of the army would be prepared to deal with the

Stamford Bridge

English as they hurried in single file over the dead and dying on the bridge itself. These dispositions were apparently complete before nightfall on Sunday, September 24th, for by dawn on Monday morning, in a " cloud of dust," the avenging English rushed onwards to the attack. In a semi-circular formation, or at any rate not in a complete circle, the Norwegians, with locked shields and acting on the defensive, endeavoured to maintain command over the western bridge head, and for some hours did so successfully. After a while, however, the English were not to be denied, and the bulk of the foe retreated across the bridge. At this period it is stated that, single-handed, a gigantic Norwegian, armed with an axe, regardless of arrow, axe, sword, or spear, held the bridge against all comers, and for some time kept the entire English army at bay. The statement that he did so for a space of nine hours is of course ridiculous. This brave man met his death by a spear-thrust delivered through one of the cracks in the bridge, a house-carl in a flat-bottomed boat having managed by good luck to get beneath that probably rickety structure. Curiously enough Hereford lost his life at another battle in Yorkshire, viz., Boroughbridge, in precisely the same way. The story of the huge Norwegian is a grand one, and he deserved at least to have fallen in fair fight. Some writers have credited Harald Hardrada, a man of notoriously tall stature, with being the hero of this noteworthy exploit ; but of this there is no proof.

The bridge was won, for on the fall of the champion those who had supported him fell back on the main army. On pressed the English, slowly but surely, for the passage was not wide enough to admit of speedy crossing, even if the use of boats and possibly of bits of timber be admitted. Anything like a dam of dead bodies could not have taken place, for the river is too deep. Steadily the attack was pressed home, and inch by inch, foot by foot, the battle line mounted the rising ground on the east bank of the river, topped the crest, and driving their opponents down the opposite side finished the struggle in the " Battle Flats " beyond. The whole of the strife was noble even in its utter barbarity. Tostig himself died by the sword of Harold. Harald Hardrada fell pierced by an arrow. The Norse standard, "The Land Ravager," was overturned, never to be again raised in England.

Of the number of the slain, either in the battle or in the subsequent pursuit, there is no record. But it is significant to read that but twenty-four ships sufficed to convey back to

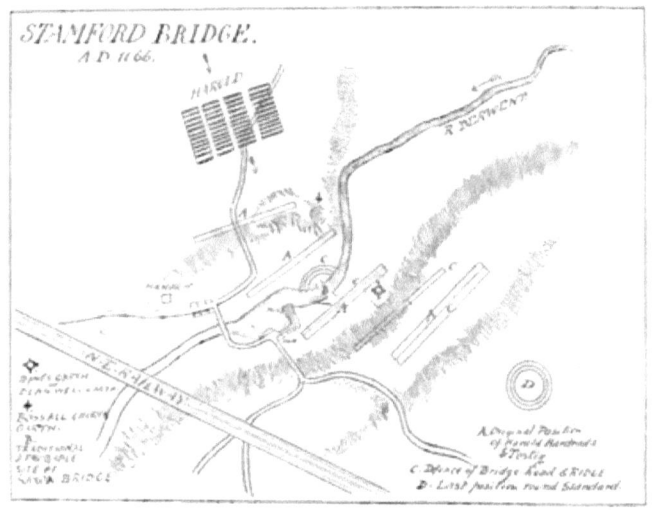

Norway the relics of a force which had filled three hundred when outward bound. But little mercy was shown by the victors, save in one notable instance. Fugitives were pursued and slain whenever met, both by the victors and the country folks. Driven into the Derwent many were drowned; even more, perhaps, lost their lives in the Ouse. The fleet at Riccall was burned, but with a wise moderation Harold saved the lives of Olaf the Prince, and Paul, the Earl of Orkney, who were taken prisoners. Politically it was a most sagacious act to set free and to send these two prisoners home bearing sorrowful news indeed. Pledges were of course extracted from them, and such was the lesson taught the Northmen by Harold the ill-fated, on the Battle Flats of Stamford Bridge by the Derwent, that those pledges have never yet been broken. The accumulation of English loot found in the Norwegian camp became the spoil of the victors—or rather of Harold, for he appears to have appropriated rather more than the lion's share. The slain, it seems, were in part honourably buried—probably those of higher rank; the commoner sort being left to rot where they lay. Tostig's body being recognised, was carried to a spot near Riccall, where, according to tradition, it was buried beneath a tumulus. There is an encampment and several tumuli at Skipwith Common, to this day locally known as Danes Hills. A place-name near—viz., Olaf's Lane—curiously recalls this long-gone fight. Round the actual battlefield itself traces of the slaughter have often been found. One field to the north-east of the village is still called Danes Garth or Dean-Well Garth. In a little close, surrounded by a small earthwork and belonging to Bossall Church, many bones of the slain were collected long after the battle from the fields by the river-bank and buried. A memory of the exploit of the man in the boat who slew the defender of the bridge yet survives in a curious custom, or did so till lately. It was called "Pear-Pie Feast," and was celebrated in September. Queer tub-shaped pies were made and consumed, it being a local tradition that a swine-tub, not a boat, was used by the house-carl beneath the bridge.

This is the unvarnished tale of the great victory of Stamford Bridge—a victory which for a month saved the kingdom. The night of the battle Harold, victorious, entered York, and there remained for a space of three days feasting. At the festive board, on the third day, came the news that the long-dreaded invasion from Normandy was an accomplished fact, as Duke William had landed at Pevensey.

CHAPTER II.

HASTINGS.

October 14, 1066

ON September 27th, when at length the wind was favourable, William Duke of Normandy set sail for England, landing on the following day at Pevensey. The disembarkation, contrary to expectation, was unopposed, thanks probably to the absence of the English fleet, which had been withdrawn during August to act against the invaders of the east coast. Harold, too, was in the north, and hence, to all intents and purposes, the south was perfectly defenceless. It was owing to the withdrawal of the fleet that William had been enabled to move his expedition from its first mustering-place at the mouth of the Dive to a second base of operations at the mouth of the Somme.

The disembarkation of the invaders was conducted with all care and military precaution, the ships being run ashore in line. Armour, horses, and stores were prepared for landing, the men armed, and finally in military array the expedition formed up on the beach, William himself being traditionally the first to set foot on land. That William was a leader who had due regard for details is evident, if old chroniclers and poets are to be credited even in part. The very orders issued to the fleet before starting point to this, so does the fact that the archers landed first and then spread in skirmishing order along the shore, to give time for the more heavily armed foot to form and the mailed knights to mount the horses as soon as they were hoisted out or forced over the low bulwarks of the vessels. No enemy, however,

BATTLE ABBEY.

appeared, and Pevensey was duly occupied. There the invaders remained for the space of one day—a day busily occupied in either forming an entrenched camp or adapting some of the existing Roman earthworks, to the end that a garrison left therein should protect their ships.

On the morrow an advance was made to Hastings, and if by

HASTINGS.

any road it must have been by a Roman road. Here, too, the invader met with no opposition, though a garrison (probably small) occupied the place. At Hastings William established his headquarters, and there sat down wisely to await events. Of its fortifications there are no records, and presumably the Norman camp was pitched on the hill where now the ruins of the castle stand. In the move from Pevensey to Hastings there was

THE INNER FACE OF GATEHOUSE

wisdom, since here roads run east, west, and north, the last named leading to London. At Hastings some kind of a fort was erected as a defence to the camp, and the balance of probability is that this took the form of a wooden castle similar in type to those known to have been at times constructed across the Channel, viz., a ditch within which was a mound and on the summit of the mound a wooden tower. William had not brought with him a large store of food—in fact, beyond wine his supply seems to have been scanty. Food to support an army was soon needed, and then foraging parties spread over the neighbouring country. Ravaging became the order of the day; but this was a deliberate policy.

William, leaving his ships under a slender or even a strong guard at Pevensey, dared not march into the interior. That a battle and a great one must be fought he, despite all the soothsayers in the world, knew full well. Defeated near his ships there would at least be a chance of retreat; defeated far inland a retreat through miles of hostile country would in all probability have meant extermination. The fall both of garrison and ships might be anticipated if once his main body marched inland for any distance. William the invader therefore awaited with patience the Saxon host he well knew would soon appear and fight. Harold to defend his kingdom must come to the south coast; William to obtain that kingdom would not budge without first forcing a battle on that coast.

This is noteworthy, for whether Yorkist, Lancastrian, Stuart, or common rebel in later times landed on the coast the custom almost always was to march instantly into some town or city. But in civil strife to raise the country was ever the first intention. William the invader had no friends in England either pledged to rise or whom he could reasonably hope to win over. But the manner of the fight to come was as yet uncertain. He was defended in his Norman camp — a camp fortified after Norman military fashion — a stronghold which he and his knew full well how to defend.

Would Harold attack this camp? Could he be induced to? Or would it be possible to bring about a battle in the open? In either of these cases the balance in favour of success lay with William. A third method of battle there was and this, as we know, was that adopted by Harold, who, with the utmost skill, selected and fortified his position, disposed his men according to the canons of Saxon defensive military art and fought as we all know how. But William, by giving over the country to fire and

ORATORY & CLOISTERS

sword, knew best how to bring Harold on to him with speed, and in the face of an army to feed, the speedy appearance of Harold was that for which he devoutly prayed. Established at Hastings, news of the victory at Stamford Bridge reached William, though it is not easy to assign a date. Stamford Bridge had been fought on September 25th; William landed on September 28th early in the morning. A Saxon thegn who witnessed the disembarkation, riding to York, announced the fact to Harold on October 1st. Assuming that the news of the fight had by that time reached London it would have taken more than a day for it to spread to Hastings. Hence the probability is that not before October 3rd or 4th was William acquainted with the defeat of those on whose success some part at least of his scheme depended. Harold at once started for London, taking with him his own trusty house-carls and such men from the south as had accompanied him to Stamford Bridge—an army victorious but, alas! sadly diminished. London was appointed as the place of muster, and thither Edwin and Morcar were enjoined to bring the levies raised from their earldoms. In the event, however, neither of these marched a step southwards or called out a man to assist their king. Men they did call out, but only to form a watching force—watching for the opportunity which never came, of turning Harold's troubles to their own advantage. But that Harold himself had no suspicion of their intention—call it lukewarmness or desertion or treachery—is shown from the fact that during their expected absence he committed the charge of the north to the Sheriff Merlswegen.

Marching rapidly southwards Harold was joined by men on all sides. From Wessex, from East Anglia and Eastern Mercia they flocked in to his standards. From North-west Mercia they came not, nor from Northumberland, as we have said, save unofficially perhaps. Huntingdon and Northampton sent their contingents as in duty bound. Practically at Hastings the whole of England save the earldoms of Edwin and Morcar was represented by contingents of fighting men.

HASTINGS.

Harold reached London on October 5th—a truly marvellous march, especially when the work of the few days preceding that march is taken into consideration. Here he halted to give time for the men of the distant parts of the kingdom to come up, and here he expected in vain the forces of Edwin and Morcar. Of the traditional visit to Waltham and the story of the alleged miracle there nothing need be said here. Far more to the purpose is it to note the messages and negotiations which took place between the king and the invader. While halting in London Harold received at least one message from William, the messenger being Hugh Margot, a monk of Fécamp. Harold received him in state, listened to his demands, and was then with some difficulty restrained from venting his wrath on the person of the ecclesiastic. Harold by him sent a reply in which William's claim was denied and the grounds thereof traversed, and which wound up with a challenge appointing the Saturday following as the day of battle. One account is that Harold offered William bribes to return to Normandy. Gurth, the brother of Harold, now in council proposed that he should lead the army, the king remaining in London, to save his oath. This proposal was negatived and similar rejection attended Gurth's scheme for wasting all the country between Hastings and London. Harold absolutely refused to accede to either; yet the advice was good, and shows Gurth to have been both a soldier and even more than a soldier. Gurth victorious, the ravaged land behind him would have been a cheap price to have paid for the crushing of the invader, and Harold would be both safe and unperjured. Gurth defeated and slain Harold would still be safe and unperjured, but the devastated land betwixt Hastings and the City would have effectually barred any forward movement of the invader. Nay more, starvation or retreat must have swiftly followed. To Harold's ships the task of discomfiture would then have fallen, or failing discomfiture at sea the duty of preventing a second attempt at invasion. Harold marched from London on October 12th at the head of whatever troops had by that time mustered, augmented by the Londoners. On his road through Kent more

LOWER TERRACE & GVEST HOVSE

men came to his standard, and the spot selected for battle was reached on October 13th. Spies had of course been at work, and the king knew to a nicety what the number of the enemy amounted to, where he was stationed, and how his camp was defended. That he ever had the design of attacking that camp is on the face of it absurd.

The site of the battle is one which was selected with the

greatest care, and in the selection the generalship of the Saxon king is most plainly manifest. Here his army was to be opposed by an invading force, armed with weapons and in a manner with which he personally was acquainted, but which to the majority of his men would be a revelation in the art of war, and led by a man who was both a brave soldier and skilled in arms, likewise experienced in and a master of his native method of war. For all military qualities without doubt Harold gave William credit to the utmost limit, and he set himself to marshal his battle array so as to place the invader at a disadvantage. On Senlac, therefore, he drew up his men and planted the Dragon Standard and the Fighting Man.

Senlac, the site of the battle, is a long hill facing south. In the centre of this ridge the standards were placed, and around them the pick of his troops, the English house-carls were posted, forming a compact body, and on either flank were light-armed troops. The ground from the ridge sloped away steeply in the centre, less so on the left and quite easily on the right. In the rear of both left and right the ground is hollowed, and in rear of the centre a ridge runs northward. A ditch and some swampy ground, known as Malfosse, was in the hollow in rear of the left. The extreme right rested on a brook, where the soil was also swampy; and rather east of this brook and in front of the right was a small detached hill. The balance of evidence is in favour of believing that a ditch protected the immediate front of the English line. Whether this was hastily dug on the night of October 13th, or whether it was an existing work, who can now say? That, however, there was a ditch on the day of the battle is certain, and that the earth cast out therefrom was surmounted by rudely fashioned wattle hurdling is a reasonable supposition. In this wattling it would seem that by design openings were left. William (seven miles distant, at Hastings) left his camp early on the morning of October 14th, and soon reached Telham, where from the high ground the English army

and its disposition was clearly visible. At Telham the heavy armour was assumed, and the force, drawn up in three columns, advanced over the intervening ground (some one and a half miles). William in person, accompanied by Odo, Bishop of Bayeux, and Robert of Mortain, commanded the native Normans in the centre. The right, composed of the men of Picardy and others, was led by William FitzOsborn and Roger de Montgomery; while the left, troops from Brittany and Maine, was the charge of Alan of Brittany. It is stated that in this left wing was the only Englishman, one Ralph of Norfolk, who fought on the Norman side. Each division consisted of archers, heavy-armed foot and mounted knights. William himself is stated to have been armed with an iron mace. Among the archers, those belonging to the centre, who came from Evreux, were noted for their skill in the use of the bow. On nearing the English entrenchment the Normans deployed, throwing out their archers, apparently in skirmishing order, to annoy, by flights of arrows, the defenders, and if possible to lure them out. The ground over which the Normans had been compelled to advance was not favourable to cavalry, neither did it become more so as they neared the English position. The steep ascent rendered the archery fire very ineffectual. Any of the heavily armed infantry who reached the stockade fell before the Saxon axes. Charging up a stiff hill, with a ditch and stockade at the top, is an awkward task for cavalry, whether lightly or heavily armed. Darts, stones, and javelins met the advancing Normans, and for those who escaped these missiles the ever-ready and terrible axe was present. Without wonder do we read that the first attack ended in a repulse, and that down the slope rolled the discomfited foot. William then tried a cavalry charge, with the same disastrous result, and this time the Norman left fled in confusion; panic spread to the centre, and defeat was imminent. Presence of mind—a quality eminently possessed by William—restored the battle and reassured his troops. The

Bretons fleeing on the left were handled somewhat severely by the light-armed English, who, contrary to orders, left the entrenchment in pursuit. When the battle was restored, the fugitives turned on their pursuers and inflicted great loss on them. But the demoralisation of the English right had very serious results, as will be seen. William's next charge was directed right on to the English standards, and therefore at the absolute centre of the English position. In this charge

he lost his Spanish war-horse, and one authority states he slew Gurth. One of the knights in his immediate neighbourhood slew Leofwine, the brother of Gurth and Harold, but the king himself was as yet unhurt. This was a sad loss to the English; still the injuries inflicted on the Normans had been so heavy that a few more similar attempts would have weakened them so as to preclude further attack. Hitherto their archers had been useless, thanks to the position taken up by Harold and the double defence of stockade and shield. William now ordered a renewed attack, and gave directions to the left to feint a retreat on nearing the stockade. If the English pursued, they were to turn again and rend them. The stratagem succeeded, the supposed fugitives lured out the light-armed troops on the English right, and having got them in the open, turned and slaughtered them, though the losses of the Bretons were also immense. But this had cleared the most available

CRYPT.

side of the English position of its defenders. Round swept the mailed Norman horsemen, and in column (they could not in line) charged the English centre on its right flank. Harold then resorted to the old formation of a ring of shields round the standard, and this kept even the Norman chivalry at bay. Then it was that the order to the archers was given by William to shoot at a very great elevation, so that the arrows fell perpendicularly into the devoted ring of Englishmen.

With what effect this order was carried out we know. Harold fell pierced through the right eye just as four knights had fought their way through the human rampart. How he was slain and mutilated we need not relate. The standard of the " Fighting Man " was overturned, that of the Dragon had already been captured. Yet resistance was by no means over. Doggedly the defeated English fought on, no longer in line or ring, but in scattered bodies, till the darkness put an end to the battle. Of Harold's personal followers not a man turned his back on the field. Did one survive it was because he was too sorely wounded to fight, and thus escaped. The light-armed troops were the first to leave the battle; nor is it to be wondered at, seeing that they were totally unprovided with armour of a defensive kind, and were utterly unfit to cope with either the heavily armed foot or the mounted knights of the Normans. In their flight, however, they left their mark on the enemy, and in rather a curious way. Retreating in the direction of the ditch and bog already mentioned, a ditch called Malfosse, in consequence of what then happened, they were hotly pursued. In the boggy ground, however, in which a light man could with difficulty trust himself, the heavily armed Normans, and especially the knights, instantly sank. How many perished at that ill-omened ditch will never be known. This, as far as can be ascertained, is in brief the story of the battle of Hastings, fought on Senlac, October 14, 1066. The changes in the battlefield, both from the building of the grand abbey, and also the position of the present town, have rendered it impossible to obtain anything like a satisfactory view of the actual scene of the fight. But the abbey ruins are in themselves so picturesque that the writer may be perhaps pardoned for interspersing sketches of some portions thereof through the pages occupied by the present chapter.

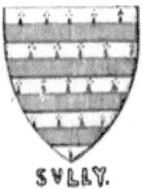
SULLY.

WARD.
BOROUGHBRIDGE.

ELINGTON.

CHAPTER III.

NORTHALLERTON (THE BATTLE OF THE STANDARD).

August 22, 1138.

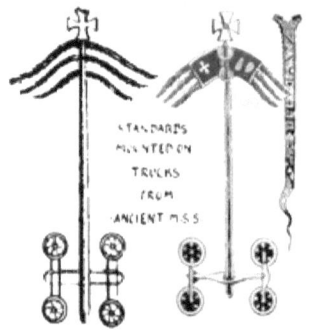

STANDARDS MOUNTED ON TRUCKS FROM ANCIENT MSS.

N the year 1138, taking advantage of the disturbed state of England, David, King of Scotland, invaded the kingdom. The hands of King Stephen were fully occupied in keeping order among the disaffected inhabitants of the south of England. The north of England for years had periodically suffered from Scottish incursions—in fact the condition of things there may be best described as a state of perpetual apprehension. For it must be remembered that the conditions of what is called civilised warfare—bad enough in these days—were in those totally absent. An invasion meant plunder, destruction of property, and outrage of every description—the excessive cruelty of the Scotch being a marked feature.

Thurstan, Archbishop of York, an aged ecclesiastic, had

been appointed by Stephen, the Lieutenant of the North. News came to him of the intended Scottish invasion, and that Yorkshire specially was the object of attack. There could, indeed, have been but little plunder to be obtained in either of the other more northerly counties. Assembling in all haste the forces available in the neighbourhood, and appealing to the dwellers further south, an army of defence was organised. In this campaign—a campaign which, on the English side, assumed almost the appearance of a holy war—the full power of the clergy was employed. Commanded by Thurstan's pastoral letter, the village priests preached resistance, and with unqualified success. Locally, the response was as it were a *levée en masse*. Of the names handed down as joining in the capacity of leaders, the following list will suffice: Walter l'Espec, William, Earl of Albemarle, Robert de Bruce, Bernard de Baliol, Adam de Bruce, Gilbert de Lacy, Walter de Gaut, Roger de Mowbray, William de Peverill, Robert de Ferrers, Robert de Stuteville, Richard de Courcy, William Fossard, and Galfrid Assaline. These were, of course, accompanied by their retainers, who were presumably well armed and equipped. Baliol brought a small contingent direct from Stephen. De Stuteville hailed from the county of Nottingham, while Ferrers, Peverill, and Assaline were Derbyshire men. The place of rendezvous was York, and there the army was augmented by the personal retainers of the archbishop. Into the custody of this army was committed the cross and banner of St. Peter of York and the banners of St. John of Beverly, St. Wilfred of Ripon, and St. Cuthbert of Durham. Numerous clergy accompanied the army when it set forth, at the head of these being the suffragan, the Bishop of Orkney, by name Ralph Nowell. The position of the Scotch king was somewhat peculiar. Son of Malcolm Canmore and Margaret, sister of Edgar Atheling, he had married Matilda, widow of Simon de St. Liz, the Norman Earl of Northampton, and daughter of Waltheof, Earl of Northumbria. He received the honour of Huntingdon on his marriage, and thus became an English baron. As an English baron, though for three years King of Scotland, he swore fealty to Matilda in 1127. By the will of his brother Edgar, who died in 1107, David became Earl or Prince of Cumbria; and over this district, a wide and important one, he reigned almost as a king. Objections were raised by Alexander I. to this dismemberment of the Scottish kingdom; but David, supported by the Norman barons, managed to retain his possession. It is curious to note that during the negotiations prior to the battle of the Standard, both Bernard de Baliol and Robert de Bruce did not hesitate to remind him of the fact while urging his withdrawal.

On the pretext of acting in the interests of Matilda, David invaded England in 1135, but, Stephen proving too powerful, a treaty was entered into at Durham which involved the cession of certain territory by David. As a recompense his son Henry was confirmed in the honour of Huntingdon, with the addition of Doncaster and Carlisle. Stephen also pledged his word that he would make no grant of the earldom of Northumbria until the claims of Henry were fully considered and legally argued. This peace was, however, broken, and for three years a barbarous war was carried on. Then, in 1138, came the invasion of Yorkshire—an event finally precipitated by the point-blank refusal of Stephen, in 1137, to adjudicate without further delay on the disputed claim to the earldom of Northumbria.

On January 10th a night attack, under the command of FitzDuncan, was made on Walter l'Espec's Castle of Wark, and failed. Reinforced by the army under David and Prince Henry, the Scotch laid siege to the place in regular form, and beset it for a space of three weeks. David and Henry then passed into Northumbria, bent on plunder. The siege was raised.

On May 8th the garrison, still under the command of John de Bussey, the nephew of l'Espec, sallied forth and intercepted a convoy of Scottish provisions. This brought their foes back, and the siege was recommenced. Wark surrendered on November 11th.

To return now to the battle of the Standard. The English army marched from York to Thirsk, where it encamped, while Bruce and Baliol set forth to visit the Scottish camp in an endeavour to procure the withdrawal of the invaders. As a bribe the coveted earldom was plainly promised. David, however, would not give way; nay, he is even stated to have laughed scornfully at the envoys. Formally renouncing their homage due to the king—Bruce held in fief the lordship of Annandale, and Baliol the manor of Woodhorn—the two returned to Thirsk. Both men were old companions of the Scotch king; both had been on most friendly terms with him at the court of Henry I., and Baliol had certainly been present on the occasion of the homage to Matilda—nay more, had himself done homage at the same time. A curious tradition states that the fief of Annandale was saved to the Bruce family through the second son of Robert Bruce, who, it is averred, fought in the Scottish ranks at Northallerton, and, it is added, was actually taken prisoner by his own father.

From Thirsk the English army marched towards Northallerton, and took up a position on Cowton Moor, distant three

STANDARD HILL, NORTHALLERTON.

miles north-west of the town. Here, on a small rising ground, was raised the historic standard from which the battle takes its name. This standard was thus composed: A mast was affixed to a small, low waggon; on the top of the mast, in a pix, a consecrated wafer was enclosed, while from cross-pieces nailed to the mast lower down were hanging the four sacred banners previously mentioned. A discrepancy exists in the accounts of these banners; some authorities name four, others only mention two, but of these that of St. Peter of York is always named as one. On a scroll nailed to the pole, and within reading distance for those who could read, was the legend—

> "Dicitur a stando standardum, quod stetit illic
> Militiæ probitas vincere sive mori";

the author of these quaint lines being Hugh Sotevagina, the precentor and archdeacon of York.

This remarkable and conspicuous standard, posted as it was upon the crest of the little hill, formed, as it was intended to form, a rallying-point for the English. Of the site of the battle little description is needful. The Standard Hill is the highest point, and from it down to the town the ground gently slopes. The English were drawn up in three lines half way down the hill. The front rank was composed of archers, the second professedly of spearmen, but doubtless considerably leavened with men armed with all kinds of weapons, such as scythes, bills, axes, and the like. Behind these were drawn up the knights, squires, pages, and men-at-arms, all being dismounted. On the top of the hill the standard was guarded, and the ecclesiastical division offered prayers. In the rear again the horses were collected and picketed. David, who knew well both the value of mailed knights and the value of archers, at first disposed his army in a rational manner, *i.e.*, with the mail-clad troops and the archers in the front line. National jealousy, however, caused a most angry altercation and a fatal alteration in the dispositions. It appears that the Galwegians, *i.e.*, men of Galloway, who fought almost naked with the utmost ferocity and disregard of their lives, had been wont ever to fight in the front line. They, in common with their chiefs, utterly despised mail-clad troops, and, headed by Malise, Earl of Strathearn, they angrily complained of the slight. Earl Alan de Percy rejoined, and words nearly led to blows. The king was compelled to give way, if only to prevent disaster. The men of Galloway were placed in the front rank, supported by his bodyguard of French and English knights and the Scotch troops. This was the composition of the centre. One wing (the right), chiefly derived from Cumberland and Teviotdale, consisting of archers, spearmen, and knights, was commanded by Prince Henry; the leader of the other, furnished from the west of Scotland, the Isles, and the Lowlands, is unknown, though it may have been Earl Alan.

The battle commenced by a savage charge on the part of the centre, the Galwegians rushing up the gentle slope with loud war-cries and nearly into the English line of spears which were levelled between the archers. Then the archers who had reserved their fire poured out volleys in quick succession and at short range. The execution done was terrible, and it was a method of warfare to which the savage men of Galloway were entirely unaccustomed. They recoiled and fell into confusion— in the hail of shafts blindly striking at friend or foe alike. At this point, when his presence was most needed, the Earl of Lothian was fatally wounded by an arrow, and this loss completed the discomfiture of the Galwegians. Wounded and without a leader, they gave way; next some fled, and soon the relics of the tribe were in full retreat. The flight of the centre had by this time become general. Still in the circumscribed space, for the battle-ground is of small dimensions, it was impossible that the wings should not have known the fate of the centre. A sort of panic occurred which was only checked by the personal intrepidity and influence of Henry, who rallied his men, and, more than that, led them in a charge which went far to redeem the fortunes of the day. Henry, with a few followers, cut his way through the English lines, and had some difficulty in disengaging himself therefrom. It

THE BATTLEFIELD.

is stated that he was compelled to cover his armour with a cloak in order to pass as a friend among the enemy, with whom he mixed, and that thus he escaped.

By the time Prince Henry had succeeded in returning to his own side of the field his wing was in full flight, and similar defeat had been sustained by the other wing. The Galwegians had vanished from the battle, leaving their two chiefs, Ulgeric and Dunewald, dead. Only the royal bodyguard, a picked corps of English and French knights, stood firm. It is said that Prince Henry, placing himself at the head of this forlorn hope, endeavoured in a fruitless charge to avert complete disaster.

This gallant effort, fruitless in one way as it was, yet served the purpose of covering the flight of the king. All was lost. The entire army, in utter rout, throwing away baggage and heavy arms, made off in the direction of Carlisle. David reached the place in safety, but was not rejoined by his son for two days. Considering the amount of slaughter and the hard

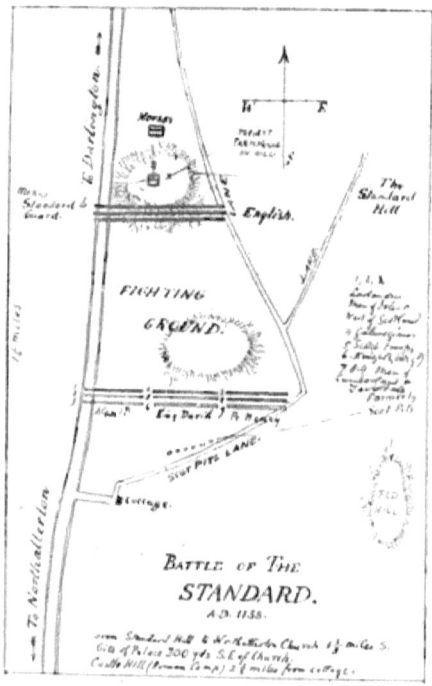

fighting while it lasted, it is wonderful to think that the battle occupied a space of little more than two short hours. The retreat of the Scotch was, in the main, unmolested, but stragglers and wounded men, especially Galwegians and tribesmen, were ruthlessly slain when met with or discovered in hiding. Some fifty of the Scottish knights were taken prisoners and held to ransom, while of those who escaped it is reported that only nineteen out of two hundred saved their armour. The total loss on the Scotch side may be computed as having approached eleven thousand. Chroniclers vary from ten to twelve thousand in their estimate. On the English side the casualties were few, and the only man of rank recorded as killed was De Lacy.

The battlefield in the present day has been cut up into fields; one of these, the burial-place of the slain, is known still by the

SCOT PITS LANE.

name of Scot Pits, and the lane along it is called Scot Pits Lane. Hedgers and ditchers have frequently found fragments of weapons and bones there. The graves in the field, thanks to the plough and other causes, are no longer visible. The name Red Hill suggests connection with memories of the fight, and local tradition upholds this view. Recently, *i.e.*, within the last two years, on the Standard Hill itself a beautiful little bronze cross, about four inches in length and ornamented on its face with a knot decoration, was discovered. This cross is now believed to be in Edinburgh, whither, having been borrowed, it was sent professedly to be examined. The results of this battle may thus be summed up: Northumbria was henceforth English, yet so weak and powerless was Stephen that, after the Peace of Carlisle, Prince Henry was granted the previously refused earldom. David died in 1153, having lost his gallant son within the year.

THOMAS OF LANCASTER.

DE BOHUN.

BOROUGHBRIDGE.

CHAPTER IV.

LEWES.

May 14, 1264.

ON December 13, 1263, a deed was signed and sealed in London by which the King of France was appointed arbitrator between Henry III. and the Barons. Representatives of both sides repaired to Amiens to state their case. Henry in person arrived there on January 12, 1264, and remained until January 25th. Simon de Montfort started from Kenilworth in order to be present as leader of the Baronial party, but, owing to a fall from his horse, was so injured as to be compelled to return before he had proceeded more than twenty miles.

The decision of Louis of France, delivered with much ceremony on January 23rd at Amiens, was practically hostile to the Barons. Both sides, however, seem to have construed the decision as suited to their particular views, and it was clear that peace would not be maintained. In the resumption of actual hostilities probably the Barons were the aggressors, evidence pointing in that direction.

Henry, on his part, began to prepare for war at Windsor, then marched to Woodstock, whence he summoned the leaders of his party to meet him at Oxford. On March 12, 1264, he ordered Oxford to be cleared of all the students, probably because he mistrusted them, and not without reason. On the following day the Bishop of Lichfield and the Archdeacon of Norwich were named to go to Brackley in Northamptonshire to meet certain delegates from the Barons, the meeting to be presided over by John de Valencia, envoy from France. Immediately Henry was calling on all his adherents to arm and collect by March 30th. Still attempts at negotiation went on, but all came to nothing. London disregarded the award of the French king; so also did the Barons of the Cinque Ports, and by the majority of the general public the same course was taken. The city rose on March 31st under the leadership of two citizens, by name Thomas de Puvelesdon and Stephen Buckerell. The bell of St. Paul's was rung to muster the malcontents, who armed, and then proceeded to destroy the houses and property of those known to be loyal, the king's own houses, and those of his brother Richard (titular king of the Romans), being included in the general destruction.

Simon de Montfort summoned the Barons to meet at Northampton, where he raised the banner of Peterborough Abbey. Before, however, the assembly took place, Prince Edward, with a hastily raised force, assaulted the town. The assault took place on April 5th. Through the treachery of Guy, Prior of the Cluniac Priory of St. Andrew, a band of forty Royalist knights, under Philip Basset, was admitted through a secretly contrived and cleverly concealed breach in the convent wall. The garrison of the castle had been occupied meanwhile by a sham parley.

Basset took possession of the town with ease, and the castle surrendered two days later, Simon de Montfort, junior, being among the prisoners. Northampton was sacked, and many barbarities committed by the victors. The loss of so many important partisans was a serious blow to De Montfort. According to chronicles, the Oxford men ejected from their colleges were in arms, and did much execution during the fight at Northampton with slings, bows, and crossbows, becoming prisoners and narrowly escaping death after the fall of the castle. Simon de Montfort had already advanced as far as St. Albans to the relief of the besieged, when the news of the fall of Northampton reached him. He returned to London and retaliated by plundering the property of De Valena and other foreigners. The deposits of money in the Temple were seized, and a general massacre of Jews took place on the plea of treachery intended by that ever unpopular and wealthy race. Montfort now besieged Rochester, using for the purpose of breaching the walls many curious engines of war of a kind till then unknown in England. Warenne, Hugh de Percy, Roger de Leyburne, and John Fitzalan defended the town and castle. By the means of a fireship Montfort destroyed the bridge and seized one of the city gates during the confusion, the garrison retreating into the castle. Rochester was then pillaged, the ecclesiastical buildings suffering severely. For several days the siege was pressed, but on news of the approach of the royal army Montfort withdrew, returning to London on April 23rd. Prince Edward had in the meantime captured in succession Leicester and Nottingham, the latter, like Northampton, being betrayed. Both towns were plundered, and he then determined to perform the same kindly office for London. Montfort had, however, forestalled him there by his return from Rochester. Edward therefore crossed the Thames at Kingston and marched straight for Rochester, reaching it on the fifth day after leaving Nottingham. It is said that the *horses*, not men, suffered heavily on this rapid march. A small body of Montfort's men, who had been left to blockade Rochester Castle, were captured, and as a punishment deprived of hands and feet.

Edward, on May 1st, captured Tunbridge Castle, the stronghold of the Earl of Gloucester. This was garrisoned by royal

troops under the command of twenty knights banneret. The army, with the king accompanying it, then turned to the Cinque Ports. Battle, near Hastings, was plundered, despite the fact that the monks, issuing in procession, met him *en route* thither. At Winchelsea the army halted and summoned various of the Cinque Ports to send a fleet up the Thames to attack London. The Wardens of the Cinque Ports, whose sympathies were enlisted on the side of the Barons, refused. After a delay at Winchelsea which lasted three days, the king and his army left for Lewes, with the intention of concentrating the forces at that strong place. Lewes was reached on May 11th, but provisions were scarce, and much privation therefore was undergone by the rank and file both on the march and after arrival.

Montfort in London was now receiving most hearty support.

The royal cause was unpopular there, not only because the king was unpopular but because the traders needed peace and thought that by supporting the Barons' party they were more likely to obtain it. Henry had touched their pockets frequently and deeply by fines and other illegal means of raising cash. Various cherished privileges had been set at naught, &c., and undoubtedly the king personally was hated in consequence. Hence to Montfort's standard flocked the London citizens, prepared to fight to the best of their abilities; they did fight, but it cannot be said that their military achievements at Lewes were by any means a subject for either pride or congratulation. Montfort, at the head of an army variously estimated as numbering from 40,000 to 60,000 men, left London on May 6th. This estimate, like nearly all other estimates of numbers engaged in mediæval battles, is probably much exaggerated. Forty thousand men might have fought on the side of the Barons at Lewes, but it is very improbable. Previous to a final battle, Montfort, after consultation with the confederated Barons and clergy, made one more effort to avert further bloodshed, and for this purpose despatched Richard de Sandwich, Bishop of London, and Walter de Cantelupe, Bishop of Worcester, to treat with the king. They were empowered to even purchase peace by the offer of 50,000 marks as compensation for injuries done by the Baronial party at London, Northampton, Leicester, Nottingham, and elsewhere, with the sole stipulation that the provisions of a former arrangement at Oxford should be observed. The two bishops carried a letter, sealed by Montfort and Gloucester, dated May 13, 1264

LEWES CASTLE, NORMAN ARCH IN THE REAR THRU GATE.

which was issued from the Baronial camp at Fletching, nine miles north of Lewes. Henry, with his army, had established himself at Lewes on May 11th. The king occupied the Cluniac Priory of St. Pancras, south of the town. Prince Edward stayed in Lewes Castle with Warenne, whose stronghold it was. The negotiation, which occupied May 12th and 13th, came to nothing, and the two bishops returned to Fletching, bearing an answer from the king, couched in the plainest terms, to which was added a letter of mortal defiance, signed by Prince Edward and Richard, king of the Romans.

Montfort then prepared for immediate action, and wisely. His army numbered less than that of the king. In the midst of a huge wood, for such was the place where it was encamped, it was impossible to remain long, and the country around, being thinly populated and destitute of supplies, could not maintain an army. Early in the morning of May 14th the Barons marched out from their camping ground—barons, knights, squires, and rank and file alike having assumed the badge of a white cross, which was worn both on the breast and on the back. It is stated that a strong religious sentiment pervaded the army, and that all at the hands of the Bishop of Worcester were shriven on the preceding night. Montfort knew that he was outnumbered, and consequently cast about to take up such a strategical position as would place him in a position of advantage. Clearly to draw up in regular battle array, according to the method of the times, and to await the onslaught of the superior force under the king, an onslaught delayed till they too had drawn up in battle order, would have been unwise, to use a mild term. Montfort's exact position was known to his enemies ; if he did not attack them it was quite possible for a system of blockade to be established, and his already poorly supplied men would then inevitably starve. Much turned on whether the Royalists had scouts or had not, and, if they had, whether the duties of those scouts were efficiently performed. Advancing, therefore, southwards, as if marching directly on Lewes, Montfort's men, in the dim of early morn, slanted slightly westward before their march was visible from Lewes Castle, at a point probably near Offham. Thence, hidden behind the crest of the ridge, they made their way along to Lewes Beacon, ascending the ridge *viâ* the Combe.

The site, at least the probable site, of the battle may be thus described. Old Lewes the town, which was walled, lay between the castle on the north and the priory at Southover on the south. The river Ouse runs to the sea, intersecting two high ridges and half encircling the town. North of the town it bends south-east on its way to the sea, and on the eastern side Lewes Bridge stands. It is a tidal river, and at the time of the battle the incoming tide was wont to flood all the low ground south of the town. On the north of the town, and stretching westwards, is a high ridge from which jut out several spurs nearly parallel to one another. Lewes Beacon is at the junction of the second and third spur, while beyond it westward is Mount Harry. On the east side of the river the ground rises very steeply, the highest elevation there being known as Mount Caeburn. At the Beacon Montfort surprised a solitary Royalist scout, who alone remained at his distant post, his fellows having without orders returned to the town the night before. From the scout much valuable information was obtained.

The Barons' line of battle was now drawn up, the dispositions being as follows: On the left were the Londoners,

under Nicholas de Segrave and Henry de Hastings; on the right Henry de Montfort, and Guy, his brother, were in command, while the centre was led by Gilbert de Clare, Earl of Gloucester. Simon in person held a body of picked troops in reserve (a most unusual thing in battles of those days). Behind, on the ridge of the down, the baggage was left, and a kind of waggon, on which De Montfort's standard was mounted. This waggon is said to have contained certain prisoners, Londoners who had been seized as disaffected and taken away by the army on its march for safety. Over the baggage, the prisoners, and the standard, a sufficient guard was placed. In the royal army the disposition was this: Prince

Edward commanded the right wing, Henry the centre, and Richard (king of the Romans) the left wing. Montfort's army advanced down the slopes and were unperceived till they came into contact with a foraging party. Some of the foragers were slain, but the rest escaping, took into the town the news, and the royal troops were soon alarmed. Montfort was then hardly more than a mile from the castle, and not more than a mile and a half from the priory. Prince Edward armed himself hastily, and appears to have been the first in the field with his wing. To him were opposed the Londoners— that is, if they were seriously intended to enter into the fight. There seems good ground, however, for supposing that the men under Segrave and Hastings were not intended to stand in the line with the rest. They were in advance of the other two bodies, and it seems reasonable to accept a suggestion which has been made with regard to their intention, viz., that to them the duty of firing the town and delivering an attack in the rear flank had been committed. Edward, however, spied the Londoners, and with his wing charged them impetuously. Raw troops, unused to arms and unskilled, the Londoners fled incontinently, and were pursued with great slaughter for some miles. The waggon with the standard, the baggage and its guard, were descried, and supposing Montfort in person to be there, this was next the object of the prince's attack. The wretched Londoners, imprisoned in the waggon, were slain, despite their protestations of friendship. On sped Edward again in pursuit, heedless of the battle in his rear, which had by this time developed. Gloucester had now come to close quarters with the centre, led by Henry in person, and after a stubborn fight had succeeded in driving it back again into the priory. Montfort's right, under Henry and Guy, his sons, taking the easiest line down the slope, and consequently near, or quite near, to the centre, then fell on the left wing of the Royalists, under the king of the Romans. Success, however, was not immediate in this part of the field. Richard's men fought well and stubbornly, so

much so that it was not until Montfort in person brought up his reserve that the fate of the Royalist left was decided. Then disaster overtook them, Richard himself being compelled to take refuge in a mill (? King's Mill) the door of which he barricaded. After a parley, in which many opprobrious epithets were bestowed on his Sacred Majesty, he duly surrendered. During all this time the prince had been absent from the field, and now returned too late, only in fact to find the remainder of the royal army a wreck. Most of the leaders had fled, including Warenne, and the victorious army

of the Barons were pursuing the fugitives through the town
and into the marshy land to the south. Hundreds perished
at the bridge (as usual), and in the river, into which they
cast themselves in their eagerness to escape. In the marshes
many men sank seated on their horses, perishing through the
weight of their armour. Prince Edward made an unavailing
attempt to throw himself into the castle, and then succeeded
in gaining admittance to the priory, where he found the king.
Late that night a truce was made, the prince surrendering
himself as hostage for his father, and the Prince Henry of
Almaine acting similarly for Richard, king of the Romans.

LEWES. THE MARSH., NOW DRAINED, FROM NEAR FIRLE HILL.

The causes which led to this defeat are not far to seek.
Skill in handling made up for inferiority in numbers. Wisely
did Montfort, who knew the disposition of the royal army,
pit the comparatively useless Londoners against the pick of
the royal troops. His alternative, to fire the town and attack
in the rear, would have been equally efficacious. But Montfort calculated on the youth of the prince, and made allowance
for his impetuosity; nor was he wrong in his calculations.
Moreover, the grudge borne by Edward to the citizens was
a strong one, and dated back to certain slights passed on his
mother. Whether Gloucester defeated the royal left before

or after the defeat of the royal centre seems hard to settle in the absence of direct evidence. One thing is clear, however, and that is that the royal centre was cleft in twain, part escaping into the priory and part into the castle. It seems more probable that the defeated royal left suffered most heavily near to the town, while relics of the centre and stray fugitives were slaughtered on the bridge or drowned in the river. If 60,000 men fought on the king's side, as stated, the rout of centre and left wing would mean at least 35,000 fugitives. Pits containing several hundred skeletons have been found in what was then open down, just outside the town, while on the high ground, where Prince Edward pursued the fugitive Londoners, smaller pits, containing from six to nine skeletons, have at times been discovered. The long lists of names extant show how universally, or almost universally, the barons of those days took one side or the other. Even assuming that the number of men engaged in these armies is greatly exaggerated, without doubt till Towton, in 1461, so many Englishmen were never again gathered together in strife.

CHAPTER V.

EVESHAM.

August 4, 1265.

THE victory of the Barons at Lewes was not followed by any permanent peace. Discordant elements were everywhere in the State. Montfort, distrusted by some of his own party and of course obnoxious to the Royalists, found the difficulties with which he had to contend too great to be overcome. The experimental Parliament met, but did not appear disposed to strengthen the hands of the leader of the Barons. Prince Edward, hitherto in captivity, was released, and was only retained under a species of surveillance. The first serious defection was that of Gilbert Clare, Earl of Gloucester—a defection probably due to jealousy. In the earlier months of 1265 the state of things in the country began to wear a very ominous look. There was trouble as usual on the Welsh marches, and Montfort had journeyed to Hereford, taking with him both the king and the prince and intent on restoring order in those parts. While there,

news arrived, that with a view to augmenting the Welsh trouble and profiting thereby, Warenne, Earl of Surrey, and others of the royal faction had landed in South Wales in considerable force.

Finding an opportunity, Prince Edward escaped on May 28th and joined his partisans, becoming at once the leader of the campaign. Rapidly possessing themselves of Bristol, Gloucester, and Worcester, the main passages over the Severn were commanded by the Royalists. By a clever stroke they attacked and captured the galleys and boats then lying at Bristol and Gloucester, thus destroying any chance of succour to Montfort by water. Montfort, out-generalled as well as outnumbered, could not embark on active hostilities until he had obtained an accession of strength. His main source of supply was Kenilworth Castle, and thither he directed his son Simon to proceed for the purpose of equipping a force, collecting stores, and convoying them to Hereford. Simon, who at the time was besieging Pevensey, consumed a far longer period in reaching Kenilworth than the serious state of affairs warranted. He, in fact, does not seem to have grasped the exigencies of the case. On arrival at Kenilworth—an event which did not take place till about the last week in July—Simon found the space within the castle walls insufficient to contain the force which accompanied him, and in consequence encamped his men outside. To this there would have been no objection had proper precautions been taken. But unfortunately neither guards nor sentries were posted, and anything like outposts were conspicuous by their absence. Prince Edward, probably by means of spies, ascertained the condition of things at Kenilworth and planned a raid from Worcester where his army then lay. The distance between the two places is thirty miles. To strike an effective blow at Simon at Kenilworth would be important in that it would cripple the army of Montfort the elder, sufficiently to preclude it from assuming the offensive. By a night march on July 31st Prince Edward succeeded in completely surprising the troops at Kenilworth, capturing stores, baggage, many prisoners, and arms. Simon, with the relics of the force, was compelled to take refuge within the castle.

Montfort's plan of campaign was apparently as follows: Acting in concert with his son, he had intended to make a simultaneous attack on the Royalists in front and rear. Had this plan been carried out, without doubt Prince Edward's force would have been in a sorry plight. But it was frustrated by the destruction of Simon's army at Kenilworth. It is reasonable to suppose that news of the arrival of Simon at Kenilworth reached Montfort, for, on the very day that the prince defeated the contingent at Kenilworth Montfort, by means of a few boats which he seized, effected a crossing of the Severn, and marching due east encamped at Kempsey, a place about three miles south of Worcester. This looks like the first move in some scheme of combined action. Rumours of battles generally spread with considerable rapidity, but in this case it is alleged that no report of the disaster at Kenilworth reached Montfort. Indeed, in life he never knew the exact fate either of his son, his castle, or his troops.

The immediate proceedings of Prince Edward after his

success are now somewhat puzzling, and to reconcile the various statements is by no means easy. How was it that no report reached Montfort? Edward is alleged to have prevented the escape of prisoners. Assuming this to be correct, that would not enjoin silence on the whole countryside. One account states that the prince returned at once to Worcester. If so, what happened at Kenilworth after he left it? Did he leave a detachment to keep Simon shut up within the castle? The reasons for propounding these questions will be seen later. One fact has been established, and that is, that on the captured horses the prince was enabled to mount a large number of his men, and that he armed them with the captured arms. By means of his spies (both mounted and on foot) the prince was made aware of the departure of Montfort from Hereford, learnt later of his arrival at Kempsey, and received due information when the camp there was broken up on August 3rd. Here his intelligence as to Montfort's movements ceased, and he marched on Evesham, guided merely by conjecture. Whether Montfort intended to make that town a halting-place or not the prince was quite ignorant. That he considered it probable subsequent events show, but of evidence of actual knowledge there is none.

Simon's force having been destroyed, it remained to repeat the operation, if possible, with Montfort; and to effect this the prince had the advantage of possessing a superior army. Assuming that the earl remained in Evesham for a night Edward's clear course was to force a battle on the morrow, so disposing his troops that the enemy should fight at the greatest disadvantage. Now Evesham, by its position, rendered an occupying force liable to be caught in a net, provided the old bridge was seized by the enemy. The town in its topography is somewhat peculiar. The river Avon running south-west from Stratford makes at Evesham a very sharp bend, then runs north-east by north and finally turns north-west. Evesham, joined by a bridge to Bengeworth, stands on the north bank about a quarter of a mile from the point of the bend. North of the town is a hill called Green Hill. South of the town and nearer the river stood the abbey. North of Green Hill is the village of Twyford, and beyond this more high ground. West of Green Hill and immediately above the road is the site of the battle. A well there is called to this day Battle Well, and a modern obelisk marks the spot where by tradition Montfort fell.

To return to the march of Montfort. Leaving Kempsey on August 3rd he proceeded through Pershore to Bengeworth, then crossing the bridge took up his quarters in the town of Evesham. The king is known to have heard mass in the abbey on the following morning.

Prince Edward had conquered Simon at Kenilworth on the morning of August 1st, and according to all accounts, returned to Worcester August 1st or 2nd and left that city for Evesham on August 3rd during the night. His course has been given as follows: Starting along the left bank of the Severn in a northerly direction, as if going to Shrewsbury or Bridgenorth, he proceeded for three miles to Claines and then turned directly east, passing quickly through Alcester and crossing the Avon at

Prior's Cleeve, a village about four miles north-east of Evesham. Here, finding that Montfort had not passed, he again crossed the river, this time near Offenham, and there took up a position on Green Hill overlooking Evesham. At Offenham it is alleged that he detached a force of cavalry under Roger Mortimer to march down the left bank of the river and seize Bengeworth Bridge. Clare, Earl of Gloucester, commanded the Royalist left wing and was with his troops stationed out of view from the town, Prince Edward with the main body alone being visible and displaying the captured banners and shields of Simon's force. The disposition of the Royalist troops seems reasonable, but the itinerary of the march is assuredly open to question. All agree that Montfort was hemmed in, and the only way in which he could be hemmed in at Evesham would be by the enemy crowning the Green Hill on one side of the town and seizing the bridge on the other. Let us now consider the march of Prince Edward in all its details. According to the above account the distance covered on the night of August 3rd was twenty-five miles or thereabouts—no great feat of marching; but the point is, Did Prince Edward start from Worcester? In other words, Was he ever at Worcester after the affair at Kenilworth? Kenilworth and Worcester are almost equidistant from Evesham. According to the story, a diary of the days between July 31st and August 4th works out as follows:

July 31st. Night march from Worcester to Kenilworth, thirty-five miles.

August 1st. Surprise of Simon, fight, capture of prisoners, stores, horses, &c. Simon shut up in castle.

August 2nd, or night of August 1st. Return march to Worcester encumbered with prisoners and spoil, thirty-five miles.

August 3rd (night). From Worcester to Evesham, bearing captured arms and banners.

August 4th. Battle of Evesham.

This gives a total mileage of ninety-five miles between the night of July 31st and the early morning of August 4th, during which period the Royalists had fought one successful fight, and were prepared immediately for another. Moreover, Montfort at Kempsey on August 1st, 2nd, and 3rd, was almost within sight of Worcester. Yet we are asked to believe that in addition to having no news of Edward's expedition on July 31st, and no intelligence of the disaster at Kenilworth, the luckless earl heard nothing of Edward's victorious return even from some place unknown, or at any rate unnamed. It seems far more reasonable to suppose that Prince Edward remained at Kenilworth during the days which intervened, and marched directly thence on Evesham.

Of the battle there is but little to tell. Montfort's troops, it is said, first discovered an armed force approaching as they themselves were marching out of the town.

At first, the display of Simon's banners deceived them into the belief that the looked-for reinforcements had arrived. It was not for long, however. According to a well-worn tradition, the earl's barber, who knew something of heraldry and was possessed of good eyes, ascended a tower and gazed to make sure. On his report that with the friendly banners those of foes were mixed, Montfort knew that his force was in jeopardy. In a brief space it was ascertained that hostile cavalry held the passage of the river at the Bengeworth bridge. Montfort was completely hemmed in. Nor did he fail to appreciate his probable fate. Without attempting to take to flight himself, he, however, appears to have vainly urged some of his oldest partisans to save themselves by cutting their way through the men at the bridge. Montfort then, having donned the old White Cross badge, marched out to meet the enemy, taking with him the semi-captive king. As Montfort advanced Edward's troops marched down to meet him. The old earl himself is reported even at this juncture to have admired the soldierly way in which his foes came on, and truly remarked that they learnt their art from him. It will be remembered that the men under Gloucester had been posted on the left of the troops commanded by the prince, and that their position was invisible from the town. Shortly after the first onset—*i.e.*, when Montfort and Edward came to close quarters—Gloucester's troops wheeling round or drawing up on Montfort's right flank delivered an unexpected oblique attack, which had the effect of driving Montfort's men into a hollow near the present Abbey Manor House. Here the main fight and the chief massacre took place. Montfort, almost deserted by his men, had his horse shot. His son Henry was killed at the beginning of the fight. On foot he made a desperate charge when he heard the news, and forced his way by the use of his sword nearly to the ridge of the hill. Supported, he might even then have cut his way through, but no aid was at hand. A common soldier, it is said, running in behind the earl, raised up his coat of mail and stabbed him in the back. Before the sun was well up all fight was over, and mere butchery supervened. One hundred and sixty knights and many of noble blood fell on that day. One spot by the river even now bears the name of Dead Man's Eyot a green meadow now and bridgeless, but in those times a ford over the river and possibly then, though certainly later, possessed of a bridge. Hither fled many of the earl's men, only to be cut down without remorse. Henry de Montfort, the eldest son of the earl, Hugh le Despenser, Justiciar', and Ralph Basset of Drayton were the most distinguished among the slain, while among the captives

LE DESPENCER

Guy de Montfort, John FitzJohn, Humphrey de Bohun the younger, John de Vesci, Peter de Montfort, and Nicholas de Segrave can be named. The shamefully mutilated body of Simon de Montfort, Earl of Leicester, was buried in the abbey of Evesham, a grand ecclesiastical fabric of which, alas, but few fragments now remain. A shrine covered the grave, and it would appear that the Franciscans, in whose schemes of religious revival De Montfort had heartily joined, drew up after his death an office in which he was invoked as guardian of the English people.

DE SEGRAVE (KENT)

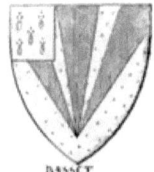

BASSET

CHAPTER VI.

BOROUGHBRIDGE.

March 16, 1322.

EARLY in February, 1322, the Barons were in arms, but being divided in council, as usually the case, their campaign was not being conducted with success. In the previous year not a few castles had fallen into the hands of the king either by capture or surrender. Hereford the city had been taken, and with it Hugh Audley the elder. Gloucester was occupied, and Lord Maurice de Berkeley surrendered. The Baronial faction assembled at Doncaster, the king being at Cirencester. Here, on the receipt of intelligence of the gathering, the king at once took energetic measures to quell the revolt and issued writs commanding a muster of royal troops at Coventry.

Thomas, Earl of Lancaster, marching with an army southward, was unfortunate almost at the outset of his campaign. Firstly, he lost stores to a large amount while crossing a flooded stream. At Burton-on-Trent he seized and held the bridge for three days, despite the attempts of the royal troops to force a passage. The king, however, finding a ford some four miles higher up the stream, effected a crossing, though not without much difficulty, the ground being thickly covered with snow. Lancaster, furious for no ostensible reason, fired Burton-on-Trent and advanced to meet the royal army. Finding, however, that his opponents considerably outnumbered him, he withdrew from the field and hurriedly retreated northwards. This act was immediately followed by the surrender of the castles of Kenilworth and Tutbury to the royal troops. Pursuit of Lancaster and his army was vigorously pressed by the royal forces under command of the Earls of Kent and Surrey. Lancaster, an incapable commander, has been much blamed for this retreat; yet, looked at from one point of view, there were good grounds for the movement. Aid had been promised to the insurgent Barons by the King of Scotland, and a reinforcement had been collected by a certain Robert de Holland in addition. To effect a junction with these, time was needed, and it was to gain this time that Lancaster retreated. Robert de Holland, though bound to Lancaster by many obligations, turned traitor. Hearing of his friend's retreat he robbed a few fugitives who had magnified the tale of reverse into a rout, and then betook himself to the king at Derby, where he surrendered. It was a bitter blow to Lancaster, though the promised reinforcement had not numbered more than five hundred men. Passing through Tutbury just prior to its surrender he was compelled to leave a valuable supporter, Sir Roger D'Amory, at the abbey there, dangerously ill. By hasty marches Lancaster reached his castle at Pontefract, where a council was held, at which, mutual distrust and unseemly bickerings were the chief features. The majority advocated a farther retreat northwards to the almost impregnable seaside stronghold of Lancaster, viz., Dunstanburgh Castle in Northumberland. Lancaster alone seems to have opposed the notion. His view was that a march so far to the north would have the appearance of a too overt alliance with Scotland, and would have the effect of alienating English supporters. He also urged that, Robert Bruce and Edward being at enmity, if they, the Barons, joined the Scotch king, or seemed to, they would at once be classed as traitors. It may be remembered that though in arms against the king the Barons throughout the struggles of this discordant time disclaimed personal animosity to him, professing only a desire to rid him of discreditable and obnoxious surroundings. Lancaster knew the larger resources of the king in the way of troops, and knew also that the Baronial force was but small and, moreover, was daily diminishing. Pontefract was a strong place, and was capable of standing a very protracted siege. Why not fight the matter out there? The council broke up in disorder after an altercation, in which it is recorded that Roger de Clifford even went so far as to draw his dagger on Lancaster and to taunt him with cowardice. Reluctantly the earl gave way, and the northward march was commenced. Meanwhile, in obedience to the king's writ, Sir Andrew de Harela (Harclay or Hartela), Warden of Carlisle and the Western Marches, had gathered men of the northern counties. On hearing news of the retreat from Burton-on-Trent Harela marched southwards to effect a junction with the royal forces that were pursuing

BOROUGHBRIDGE.

Lancaster. Harcla reached Ripon on March 15th, and had intended to halt there for a few hours. Through a spy, however, he learnt that the Barons were marching in the direction of Boroughbridge, and would probably reach that small town the next day. Immediately ordering his force again under arms, by a night march he forestalled his opponents in the possession of the bridge there, and also of a ford below it. Boroughbridge stands on the south bank of the river Ure, at a distance of six miles to the south-east of the city of Ripon. Pontefract is south, bearing a little east of Boroughbridge, and distant by road about thirty miles. The retreating army, in all probability, on leaving Pontefract, crossed the river Aire at Castleford (that usual place of passage in times of war) and the river Wharfe at Wetherby, thus reaching Boroughbridge by the direct road. Harcla, on his arrival, made an admirable disposition of his troops and patiently awaited the Baronial army. At Boroughbridge the Ure was nearly sixty yards wide in those days; in these its appearance has been greatly altered. The old bridge, a narrow timber structure on stone supports, has been removed long since. As far back as 1582 a stone bridge had superseded it. This second bridge, though widened on one side, still remains. A canal cutting and a small subsidiary crossing thereto does not aid the investigator in identifying the ground. The ford lower down in all probability was part of the Roman road which formerly crossed the river—a road which passed through Aldborough, the Isurium of ancient times. Aldborough is a little village about a mile to the south-east of Boroughbridge market-place.

The disposition of the troops under Harcla was as follows: Dismounting all cavalry he sent the horses to the rear. He occupied the north bridge-head with knights in armour and spearmen. At the ford he stationed the residue of his spearmen, drawn up according to the formation then employed among the Scots, viz., in the form of a shield. On the northern bank of the Ure the ground rises slightly, while on the side of the town it is flat. Harcla posted his bowmen along this ridge, so that some could completely command the town approach to the bridge and the rest the lane which led from Aldborough to the ford. Lancaster's troops reached Boroughbridge and halted in the town without apparently troubling to ascertain whether the crossing either by the bridge or the ford was clear or not. Suddenly they became aware of the fact that an unexpected force was prepared to dispute their passage. Practically they were hemmed in, and must either fight Harcla in front or the Earls of Kent and Surrey who were speeding after them in their rear. In all probability if they delayed battle, both forces would have to be dealt with simultaneously. All accounts agree that the troops of Lancaster were settling themselves into quarters in the town before this unwelcome discovery was made. How this could have happened is somewhat of a puzzle, seeing that the distance between the bridge and the market-place is certainly less than half a mile. It was on that market-place, the chapel in which Lancaster subsequently took refuge then stood. Harcla must have made his dispositions very silently, and with all the wariness of a man accustomed to Border warfare. Of their two alternatives, the Barons chose fighting in front; but prior to the commencement of active hostilities, diplomacy was resorted to. Lancaster (in these days the story sounds strange) sent for Harcla, and had a long interview with him. It appears that Harcla had received knighthood at the hands of the earl, and was appealed to, almost pathetically, to throw in his lot with the Barons and assist in destroying the Despensers and certain other persons, to wit the Earl of Arundel and Master Robert Baldock, "a false clerk." As a bribe one of Lancaster's five "countships" was offered to Harcla, but in vain. The fact is Lancaster's manifest inferiority in troops was well known to Harcla, and it would have been too risky to have turned traitor. That he was capable of changing his allegiance, or at least of criminal negligence, we know—witness his end. Harcla then remained obdurate. Lancaster cursed him as he had cursed his other former *protégé*, Holland, and foretold for Harcla "a shameful death within the year"; and that he would suffer all the barbarous pains and penalties then attaching to one who was proclaimed a traitor. Meanwhile, Lancaster's men had proceeded to the bridge and were awaiting the upshot of the conference. All fought on foot, and indeed the narrow bridge was totally unfitted for a mounted man to attempt a crossing —a rickety structure floored with planks with many a crack and crevice. When the negotiation ended and Harcla had recrossed the bridge, the royal archers, without waiting for attack, commenced the battle. Their shafts were directed against the men who were preparing to force the passage of the bridge. It was for some time an archery duel, in which the royal troops, through their superiority in numbers and, it is to be concluded, discipline, had by far the best of it. Obviously it lay with the Baronial party to make the next move; their opponents could afford to merely keep them at bay till by the arrival of Kent and Surrey in the rear they would be enclosed in a net.

Humphrey de Bohun, the 4th Earl of Hereford and 3rd Earl of Essex, then made a desperate charge at the head of knights and men in armour in the hope of cutting a passage through by sheer hard fighting. It was a splendid example of bravery, and deserved success. Hereford, fighting on foot as they all did, fell pierced by the spear of a Welsh soldier (so tradition holds). The man had managed to get beneath the bridge on to the bank and awaited an opportunity to thrust upwards beneath the timbers. As Harcla's party were at the north side it is obvious that Hereford must have reached at least to the opposite bank of the river. The next to fall was Sir Roger de Clifford, who was severely wounded in the head by an arrow. The death of Hereford had caused much dismay; the fall of Clifford completed the discomfiture of the attacking party on the bridge, and they withdrew again across the river, having been most severely handled. Meanwhile Lancaster, with a mounted force, endeavoured to effect a crossing at the ford. Down the lane they dashed and charged headlong towards the shallow water. But the archers, so carefully posted to prevent this very thing, were quite equal to their task. Volley after volley of arrows met the gallant band during their passage down the lane, and it is chronicled that so deadly was the hail of missiles that not one horse reached the water's edge. In this charge fell Sir Hugh Lovel, Sir William de Sully, Sir Ralph de Elington, and Sir Roger de Bernefield, together with three esquires and many others whose names are unrecorded. Here, as at the bridge, the attacking force was compelled to retreat, and soon the retreat became a flight. Lancaster indeed succeeded once in rallying his men, and led them in a second charge to the ford, but with the same result— horses and men went down before the terrible arrows. After this the battle was at an end. In every direction Lancaster's forces were melting away, while he himself had withdrawn into the town. How it was managed has never been explained, but a truce for the night was concluded with Harcla, the stipulation being that surrender, or a renewal of the conflict to the death, should take place on the following morning. How Harcla, seeing that he was in the position then to seize the earl and all his remaining followers, could have assented to this is inexplicable. That he did so is, however, a fact; and we have the curious spectacle of the victor, whose loss had been trifling, obliged to remain watchfully on guard at both bridge and ford during the night, while the vanquished ran away on the other side or reposed more or less comfortably in the houses of the town. During the night Sir Simon de Ward, the High Sheriff of Yorkshire, marched to the aid of Harcla with a force amounting, it is said, to four hundred yeomen. On the following morning Ward and Harcla crossed the bridge and called on those of their opponents who were left, to surrender. Lancaster, though he had been deserted by many of his following, refused. Clifford, wounded, had likewise been abandoned to his fate, and could offer no resistance, while the followers of the Earl of Hereford were not to be found. Throughout the hours of the night, stripped of their armour and disguised in whatever clothing they could lay their hands on, the bulk of the Baronial force had betaken themselves to flight. Harcla and Ward seem to have gone about the business of arresting those who did remain with little or no moderation either of speech or action. Lancaster managed for a brief time to elude his foes and took refuge in the chapel of Boroughbridge. It was not a sanctuary proper, but he thought that at the altar he would be safe. Not so, however, did it turn out, as he was straightway haled thence, stripped, clad in an old "ray coat or gown" belonging to one of his servants, and sent by water the same day to York. The rank and file who had not fled were hunted down promiscuously in the houses, lanes, and fields, and slain. Thus ended this rather remarkable battle of Boroughbridge.

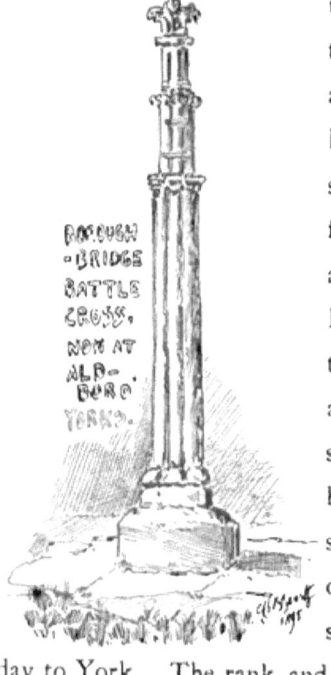

BOROUGHBRIDGE BATTLE CROSS, NOW AT ALDBOROUGH, YORKS.

Fragments of carved stone belonging to the chapel of Boroughbridge have been built into the wall of the present modern church. A curious freestone cross, erected in commemoration of the fight, which stood for more than five centuries in the market-place of Boroughbridge, was for some extraordinary reason removed in 1852 and re-erected at Aldborough. It would be beyond the purpose of this book to give the lengthy list of the names of the Barons, Knights Banneret, and Knights Bachelor who were either killed at, captured at, or who voluntarily surrendered after the battle of Boroughbridge. They are to be found in the Parliamentary Writs, vol. ii., part ii., pp. 194 201; Nos. 171 91 in Appendix, and in vol. ii., part i., p. 312. Similarly this is not the place to enter into the terrible vengeance which was taken on the vanquished. The alleged miracles worked at the tomb of the Earl of Lancaster, who was duly executed as a traitor, need not here be touched upon, seeing that they belong more to ecclesiology than to the subject of this book. Still it may be mentioned that a curious Latin "office" exists, which was used by pilgrims who visited the tomb of Thomas of Lancaster. The cult, which was very popular, had its counterparts in the veneration shown to the remains of two other popular leaders, viz., Waltheof and Simon de Montfort. With regard to Harcla it is recorded that the prophecy or curse of Lancaster came true. Though rewarded immediately after the battle by being raised to the earldom of Carlisle, within a year degradation and the scaffold had been his portion.

As has previously been said with regard to the battlefield of Boroughbridge, its absolute site cannot exactly be determined, thanks to the alterations in the ground. The town itself has suffered so much from the removal of its ancient buildings that beyond one or two quaint inn signs there is nothing left of interest. For these reasons, beyond the "Aldborough" Cross this chapter is devoid of illustration.

CHAPTER VII.

NEVILLE'S CROSS.

October 17, 1346.

THE story of the Scotch invasion of England in the year 1346, which terminated in the crushing defeat of the invaders at Neville's Cross, otherwise Red Hills, close to Durham, is as follows. With a very powerful army, composed of seasoned Scots and augmented by French auxiliaries, David (Bruce) II. crossed the border by the Western Marches, entering Cumberland not far from Kirk Andrews. Proceeding but a short distance the invaders attacked a pele, known as Lyddal's Strength.

Lyddal's Strength was in those days a fortress, of importance as a place of arms, not so much from its size as from its position. Standing on a lofty and fortified cliff (the earthworks are yet to be seen) the pele, a square tower, was a typical northern fortalice. Under Sir Walter Selby and his two sons, a brief but gallant defence was made. Accounts differ as to whether Lyddal's Strength was taken by storm or surrendered. There is a sad story, however, that with great inhumanity David ordered Selby to be beheaded, having previously strangled his two sons before the luckless chieftain's eyes.

The pele destroyed, the invaders resumed their march, Lanercost Priory being the next object of attack. Lanercost is distant about eleven miles from Lyddal's Strength, and lies in a fair valley on the banks of the river Irthing, eleven miles south-east of Netherby. The priory was pillaged and burnt, and with daily accumulating spoils the plundering Scots made their way by their accustomed road through Tynedale. They marched through Gilsland and Haltwhistle till they came to Hexham. Here the priory was also sacked, but the town itself was spared. Perhaps it was hardly worth pillaging; possibly, too, it was likely to prove useful either as a place of storage for their ill-gotten gains or as a base of operations. From Hexham David passed on to Corbridge, a place of note in Roman times, and situated on Watling Street, the great highway. Watling Street here runs due south-east, and the army advanced by it into the county of Durham, halting just within its border, at Ebchester (also a Roman station). On the following day the army pressed on, still keeping to the Roman road, and finally, without let or hindrance, encamped at Beaurepaire, or Bear Park. Beaurepaire lies to the west of the road, and is situated about two miles north-west of the city of Durham. Originally belonging to the see of Durham, these lands had been exchanged for others, about the middle of the thirteenth century, with Bertram, the Prior of the Durham Monastery, who built there a grange and chapel. Later on the grange was enlarged and the lands parked. In the previous reign the place had been destroyed by the Scotch, but the house had been rebuilt. Here King David took up his quarters, and encamped his men in the park. Durham, where the utmost consternation prevailed, appeared to be at the mercy of the invaders. Why it was that David did not at once attack it is not now to be learnt —an error certainly, for established in Durham it would have been hard for the English to have cleared him out. But David rested at Beaurepaire, sending out plundering parties into the country round about, and planning a raid on Darlington, twenty miles due south by the Roman road, on

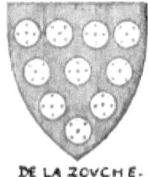
DE LA ZOVCHE.

MOWBRAY

ROKEBY

which it was situated. Meanwhile a force to oppose the Scotch was being collected with speed and zeal. William de la Zouche, and the Bishops of Durham, Carlisle, and Lincoln exerted to the utmost the authority of the Church to raise the men. Ralph 4th Baron Neville of Raby, Henry 2nd Baron Percy of Alnwick, John 9th Baron Mowbray, Edward de Baliol (ex-king of Scotland), Ralph de Hastings, and Thomas de Rokeby, the Sheriff of Yorkshire, gathered forces which numbered some 16,000 well-armed men. On October 14th Ralph Lord Neville, and his son John, joined William de la Zouche at Richmond in Yorkshire. They marched to the north-west through Rokeby to Barnard Castle, a distance of fifteen miles; then turning north-east, set forth to the place of rendezvous, the park of Auckland (Bishop Auckland), and reached it on October 16th. By taking this rather circuitous route the archbishop and Neville had the advantage of good roads, and moreover passed through Rokeby, Barnard Castle, and Raby, at each of which places it is probable that they received an augmentation of strength.

On October 17th the army advanced to Merrington, about three miles to the east, and took up a position on some high ground. Here it became a question as to future proceedings. The Scotch army, distant about eight miles due north, numbered nearly double the defending force. The intended raid on Darlington would appear to have been known to Neville, and two courses lay open to him: one, to advance and fight in the endeavour to save Durham, though possibly on disadvantageous ground; the other, to remain in the strong position at Merrington, barring the way on the great road southwards, thus abandoning Durham to its fate. But after looting so rich a city as Durham the Scots might retire, nay probably would, to secure their booty, especially as it would be known to them that a defending army was somewhere being raised. That David did not know the exact position, or indeed the comparative proximity of the English force, is shown by what occurred. It is more than probable that Neville never seriously contemplated adopting the second course of action; to have even advised it would have drawn down on his head the thunders of the Church. Abandon Durham, the most sacred spot in the north!—a sin not to be even mentioned.

It was, however, with the utmost precaution that the army advanced eastwards, and at a very slow rate of speed. The story of the accidental advance of the marshals and standards, and the consequent advance of the entire army, may be rejected as absurd. Neville and Percy were both too good soldiers and too practised in war to have permitted any such state of laxity in an army under their command. Slowly then the force advanced eastwards, till the village of Ferry Hill, situated on the Roman road, was reached. Here a body of Scots, numbering about 500, and under the command of Sir William Douglas, who had been detached and sent on a plundering raid, unwittingly marched into the advancing army. The Scots at once fled, and in the pursuit it is stated 200 perished. Douglas, who escaped, on arrival at Beaurepaire, brought the first definite information of the advance of an English force. David, hitherto secure in a belief that Durham could not be saved, had, it is stated, on the previous day drawn up his army in fighting order on Durham Moor. The force remained under arms the whole night, while the king unattended, or at any rate unguarded, slept quietly at Beaurepaire. The reason of this curious proceeding is not clear, unless it was intended as an act of defiance or of menace towards the good folks of Durham. Douglas on his arrival appears to have counselled the king to withdraw to the hills and avoid a battle until it could be fought on very advantageous terms. The advice, probably prompted by an exaggerated idea as to the numbers and composition of the English army, was good. By David it was, however, most scornfully and disdainfully rejected. The English pursued the retreating Scots in the direction of Durham, as far as Sunderland Bridge, and then abandoned the chase. Still advancing slowly, the army halted on the high ground above the Wear, and then, leaving Durham on the east, made their final advance towards the enemy. The respective divisions of the two armies were commanded as follows: Lord Percy led the vanguard which in the battle became the right wing, and was opposed to the rear-guard (*i.e.*, left wing) of the Scots army, under the High Steward of Scotland. The main body of the English was commanded by Lord Neville, and as centre, in the battle joined issue with the Scottish main body and centre under King David. The English rear-guard (*i.e.*, left wing), under Rokeby, was in conflict with the Scottish van, or right wing, led by the Earl of Murray. But the English had provided for that which the Scots had not, viz., a powerful reserve of picked cavalry, mailed horsemen all, which was under the orders of Edward de Baliol. Slowly the English advanced and deployed on the Red Hills, the Scots leaving their position on Durham Moor and advancing to meet them. The battlefield lies west and west by north of the cathedral and castle of Durham. It is a level ridge, now cut up into fields and partly built over. The ground dips on the west side and falls away steeply towards the river on the east. Northwards there is a sharp slope which forms a kind of trough into which a spur juts out. Hereabouts in those days the ground was covered with a thick wood, called Shaw Wood, and the name survives. In the trough, and in what were then the recesses of this wood, there is a little pear-shaped hillock known as the Maiden's Bower. On the top of this hillock the ecclesiastics from the city clustered to pray around the sacred corporas cloth of St. Cuthbert. This holy relic had been brought from the shrine and affixed to a spear to act as a sacred banner. From the top of the hillock it is just possible to see the tower of the cathedral (*vide* initial), and the tradition holds that during the course of the battle the different vicissitudes thereof were signalled from the monks with

The Maiden's Bower.

the standard to those on the tower. The tradition is a pretty one, and from the fact that its truth is possible, as an examination of the ground shows, it may well be here repeated. Albeit that the English ought by rights to have been the attacking force, in actual fact they were on the defensive. Halted, the archers, who according to custom formed the front rank, poured most destructive volleys, at long range, into their advancing enemies. In the Scottish ranks the spearmen fell thickly, and without hitherto having been able to inflict any injury on their opponents. William Graham, furious at this loss of men, and being possessed of good sense enough to perceive that archers at long bowls had a terrible advantage over men armed with sword, axe, and spear, besought David to give him but one hundred mounted men, and to permit a charge to break that line of bowmen. David refused, and the gallant fellow, then at the head of a few personal attendants, rode straight for the enemy. Down on the archers he

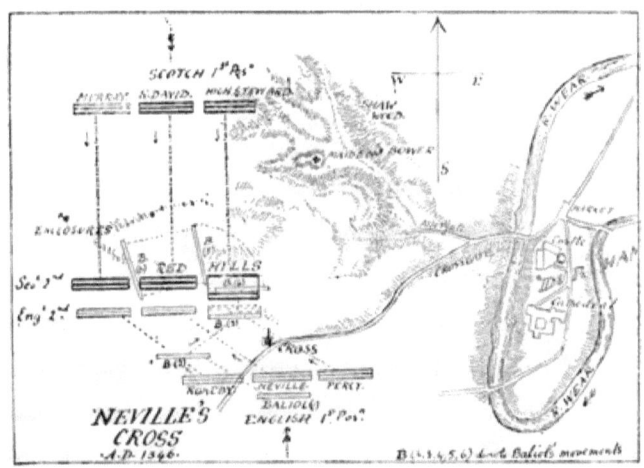

charged and proved the wisdom of his advice, for the little band actually broke through and dispersed them. At short range Graham's horse was shot by a broad arrow, and he himself was wounded. Still he managed to regain the Scottish line. The High Steward at once grasped the situation, and ordered a charge of men armed with swords and axes upon the partly disordered right wing. This charge was successful, the archers were broken up and driven not only back on to the second line, but through it. Lord Percy's wing was then in danger of rout. The value of possessing a reserve of cavalry, and a reserve with a capable commander, now became apparent. Edward de Baliol, comprehending the danger which threatened Percy, charged the Scottish troops with great spirit. Not only was the successful attack on the right wing repulsed, but that repulse was converted into a complete rout, and within a brief space the division of the High Steward were fugitives. Baliol was neither a Goring, nor a Lucas, nor a Rupert, hence he did not pursue the broken Scots; other methods of employing his troops, and to greater advantage, occurring to him. The battle between the centres had meanwhile been proceeding on equal or nearly equal terms. Baliol took in the position at a glance, and wheeling his men he executed a flank charge on the left flank of the king's division—a left flank which, through the flight of the left wing, was practically defenceless and at his mercy. This soldierly move was executed with expedition, and proved simply disastrous to the Scots. Their centre, attacked in front by Neville and on the left flank by Baliol, was thrown into confusion, began to give way, and finally fled, taking a direction to the right. The manœuvre was repeated with the right wing. Rokeby redoubled his efforts, and was victorious. But the men of the Scottish right, hampered by the nature of the ground, could not retreat. Caught in enclosures and between hedges they were slain without mercy and died in heaps. David in vain tried to restore the battle. At last—and it was almost a precursor of Flodden—the knights available formed themselves into a ring around their sovereign

NEVILLE'S CROSS.

and stood at bay. Many were slain, but at length the remnant of this human shield, some eighty in number, surrendered. David, wounded sorely, some say by arrows others by spears, was taken prisoner. He had lost his sword, or broken it, and was absolutely defenceless. His captor was John Copeland, the then Governor of Roxborough Castle. Tradition holds that in an endeavour to exasperate his captor into slaying him, David struck Copeland with his gauntleted hand, knocking out two teeth. Among other captives of note were the Earls of Fife and Monteith and Sir William Douglas. On the English side Randolph, Lord Hastings, was the only man of rank slain. Murray, Lord Strathmore, both John and Alan Steward, and a host of noble Scots perished on the field. Out of 30,000 French and Scots that entered into the fight, nearly half perished on the spot and many others in the subsequent pursuit. On the battlefield a beautiful cross was erected as a memorial; a fragment of this is yet retained in the present monument, of which an illustration is given. The original cross had seven steps surmounted by a large square stone, to which was fastened the socket stone. The shaft of the cross was 10 feet 6 inches to the boss, which was octagonal in shape. For decorations the Bull's head badge of the Nevilles and their coat-armour, gules, a saltire argent, were carved on the cross; a Rood with Mary and John completed the ornamentation. The little of this cross which is now left serves as a socket for the present shaft, and the structure is protected by a strong iron railing. It seems that certain

NEVILLE.

religious fanatics destroyed this most interesting relic as long ago as 1589. With the subsequent *Te Deum* at the cathedral we have here nothing to do, nor need the valuable spoils offered to the shrine of St. Cuthbert be enumerated. The banners of the slain and the captives long hung in the cathedral above the shrine, to which was specially offered the cross known as the "Black Rood of Scotland," a precious relic picked up on the field. The pursuit of the fugitives was pressed with ardour; it was considered needful to inflict as much punish-

NEVILLE'S CROSS.

ment on them as possible, and, having their king in captivity, a period of comparative tranquillity might then be looked for. Percy became ill after the battle, and was unable to join in the pursuit. The lives of both Neville and Percy are full of interest, as showing what men of action were needed in those troublous times on the Scottish borders. Percy died in 1352, and was buried at Alnwick; Neville died on August 5, 1367, and was buried in the south aisle of Durham Cathedral. It is interesting to read that he was the first layman ever permitted to be buried within the building. The tomb is still visible in the second bay eastwards but terribly mutilated—this the work of the Scotch prisoners confined in the cathedral in 1650. Mowbray, who fought in Rokeby's wing, was also a great soldier, and did good service to the State. He died of the Plague, at York, on October 4, 1361, and was buried in the Franciscan Church at Bedford. His arms were, gules, a lion rampant argent. Sir Thomas Rokeby became eventually Lord Justice of Ireland. His coat-armour was, argent, a chevron sable between three rooks proper. Edward de Baliol, the eldest son of John de Baliol by his marriage with Isabel, daughter of John de Warenne, Earl of Surrey, died in 1363, after a very adventurous career. The Baliol family belonged to Barnard Castle in Yorkshire—coat-armour, gules an orle argent. Sir William Douglas, Knight of Liddesdale, was born circa 1300. He was the eldest lawful son of Sir James Douglas of Lothian, and not the bastard son of the "good" Sir James. Perpetually engaged in warfare with the English, he had suffered a two years' captivity in Carlisle Castle subsequent to his defeat at Annandale. Having been ransomed, he at once took the field again. Time after time he performed most daring exploits, but sometimes unfortunately degraded by ferocity and inhuman barbarity. A murderer, he was eventually murdered in Ettrick Forest by his kinsman the Lord of Douglas. A cross, called William's Cross, long marked the spot. His body was buried ultimately in Melrose Abbey, in front of the altar of St. Bridget. Coat-armour—argent, on a chief gules, two mullets of the field. John Copeland, the Northumbrian esquire, who took prisoner King David, was a man of considerable independence of spirit. Queen Philippa, it is related, demanded the king from his captor. Copeland replied that to none other but his master would he deliver him up. Edward III. was at Calais, heard of the reply, and sent for Copeland. Copeland obeyed the summons, but first securely caged his captive in a Northumbrian castle. Edward knighted the man, and pensioned him to the amount of £100 per annum, dismissing him with a request that David might be delivered up to the queen. Copeland complied at once. King David was in prison for no less than eleven years in the Tower, being eventually ransomed by his nephew, Robert Stuart, for a payment of 56,000 marks.

CHAPTER VIII.

OTTERBURN.

August 19, 1388.

SIR HENRY PERCY.

IN the month of August, 1388, after a preliminary meeting of the leaders held at Aberdeen, the Scots mustered in force in the forest of Jedburgh. The exact date of the muster was St. Oswald's Day (August 5th). A large army collected, numbering, if we accept the lowest computation, 30,000 men. In order to hold their deliberations in the most private manner possible and to concert finally the plan of campaign, the leaders with a few followers adjourned to a small church in the forest at Southdean, ten miles south-west of Jedburgh. The name of this church is variously given as Zedon and Salom. A very retired spot, it had in addition the merit of being but four miles distant from Redeswire, at which the invaders would enter England as previously agreed. A spy was detected at the consultation, secured, and forced to disclose all he knew of the power and intentions of the English, his employers. His information was of importance, and was in substance this : The English, he said, knew the numbers of the Scotch, knew also that a most valuable supply of modern arms—1,000 stand of complete mail from the castle of Beaute, near Paris, had been recently forwarded by the French king—and that in numbers they were inferior to the invaders. What they did not know and what they wanted to know was, whether the invasion was to enter England *via* Carlisle, or *via* Redeswire along the great road. If by Carlisle then the English, he averred, had determined to embark on a counter invasion of Scotland *via* Redeswire and *vice versâ*. This was an imitation by England of the Scotch policy on a former occasion. The mind of the Scottish leaders was soon made up—they determined to invade England by both

James, Earl of Douglas.

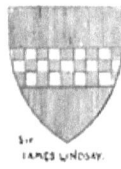
Sir James Lindsay.

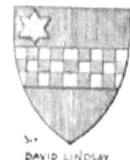
Sir David Lindsay.

Ramsay.

routes. The largest division was to march *via* Carlisle, the smaller, amounting to four hundred knights, squires, and men-at-arms, with some two thousand infantry, a picked body and well equipped, were to take the Northumbrian route. James, Earl of Douglas, was in chief command, and was accompanied by his brothers. With him were associated George, Earl of March and Dunbar, and John Dunbar, Earl of Moray. Renowned knights under his command were Sir James and Sir David Lindsay of Glenesk (one account gives three others of this name, *i.e.*, William, Alexander, and John), Sir Alexander Ramsay, Sir Patrick Hepburn and his two sons, Sir John Swinton, Sir John Montgomery and his son Sir Hugh, Sir

Henry Preston, and Sir William Dalzell. The entire expedition with Douglas including followers, pages, &c., would probably amount to about six thousand all told. The design of the Scots by their double invasion will be apparent—it would puzzle the enemy. Rapidity was of course needful, and as events showed rapidity was attained in the march southwards. With the movements of the large army under Sir William Douglas we have nothing here to do.

Lord Douglas started southwards on or about August 7th, and without collecting spoil passed rapidly through Northumberland, entered Durham and penetrated as far as Brancepeth—four and a half miles south-west of the city of Durham. The story that he continued the raid as far as the gates of York is probably untrue, at least it cannot be in any way substantiated. Arrived at Brancepeth, where, by the way, the Nevilles had a castle, the object of the Scots was achieved. Looting everywhere, driving away cattle, killing, burning, and destroying, they then turned their faces northward, leaving Durham county in a sad plight. Meanwhile Sir Henry, the Warden of the Marches, and Sir Ralph Percy, his brother, had collected within the walls of Newcastle an army which they destined to overthrow the invaders on their return journey. The Scots, it may be observed, had marched southwards partly along Watling Street, and had crossed the Tyne above Newburn—probably at Corbridge. There are fordable places at several spots, notably Ovingham, Corbridge, and at Newburn, but Corbridge is the locality which with the greatest amount of probability may be selected. Returning to the crossing and collecting an enormous loot by the way, the Scots reached the north bank of the Tyne and then marched along it eastwards right up to the walls of Newcastle. Their expedition having up to date lasted from seven to eight days, the distance covered being rather over one hundred miles exclusive of side excursions—a very remarkable performance. Douglas at Newcastle took up a position on the high ground on the north side, possibly with a view to taking the place. It was, however, too strong; still, parties sent out from his camp skirmished with the garrison at the gates, and in one of these skirmishes in which both Douglas and Henry Percy chanced to be engaged, the Scot had the good fortune to unhorse his opponent, Percy, and to capture the pennon from his spear. This he carried off in triumph, Percy vowing to recover it while Douglas dared him to try. An attempt was on the same occasion made by the Scots to storm the town, but this failed owing to the scarcity of the ladders at their disposal, the great width of the ditch (22 yards), and the height of the wall. The site of the encampment of Douglas outside Newcastle is to the north-west of St. Andrew's Church, and on the highest part of the Leazes. Before daybreak on the morning after the capture of the pennon, Douglas resumed his homeward march, passing by Ponteland, where he destroyed the tower, or pele, then the possession of Sir Aymer de Athol, whom he took prisoner and carried to Otterburn. A few fragments of this pele yet remain. From Ponteland Douglas proceeded still in a north-westerly line, crossing the burn (Otter Burn) late in the afternoon above the tower of the

Umfravilles. This tower, some relics of which are incorporated in the present Otterburn Tower, they left unmolested till the next day, passing onward to a hill to the north-west of Holt Wood, where, on the site of some old prehistoric earthworks, they pitched their camp, erecting temporary booths and huts, and with rough improvised palisades and brushwood strengthening as best they might the ancient ramparts. Loot and camp-followers were collected together in a separate place and protected by a guard. In addition to sacking and burning

SCOTCH CAMP, OTTERBURN, LOOKING NORTH.

Ponteland pele the Scotch army had marched thirty-two miles since daybreak—a fine performance. There was reason to make for Otterburn, for just below it, on the north side of the river Rede, Watling Street passes, and that would naturally be the road by which to return to Scotland. By crossing the country Douglas compelled his pursuers to do likewise, and he had a start of at any rate a few hours. Had he returned by the north bank of the Tyne he would have been liable to have been cut off, or at best to have fought in a position not selected by himself—an obvious disadvantage. From the old camp, the battlefield and a wide expanse of country are now visible. To the south-east, whence the English might be expected, the river Rede winds through the dale to the right for some two or three miles. Down to it in the front and to the point of junction of the Otter Burn, the ground falls gradually with here and there an undulation. Behind and on the left there is high ground, while in the immediate rear just over the crest of the hill a ruined pele is yet to be seen. It

FIELD OF BATTLE, LOOKING SOUTH-EAST, DOWN REDESDALE.

was beyond this high ground to the left and eastward of it that Percy came in pursuit. On that night the Scots slept quiet in their camp, but on the morrow, marching down to Otterburn Tower which stands buried in woods close to the junction of the Rede and the Otter, they endeavoured to treat it in the same manner as they had Ponteland Pele. For the greater part of the day they beleaguered the little fortress, and in vain. Late in the afternoon they retired to their camp both wearied and discomfited. It was proposed to break up the encampment at once and resume their northward march, but the authority of Douglas overruled this—perhaps from motives of chivalry he wished to give Percy another chance to regain the lost pennon. The Scots remained, but increased the strength of their camp by an earthwork on the north side, where it was weak, and by various felled trees which were disposed so as to form a breastwork. They impeded the track road to the camp by similar obstacles, and collecting the loot placed it in charge of the armed servants and camp-followers, to which a guard was also added. Meanwhile Percy, whether fearing a trap or for some reason, had not started in pursuit at the first withdrawal of the Scots. That he was rash in war is usually admitted, and that he should have hesitated to pursue even an hour seems almost incredible. To one thing, however, the delay can never be ascribed, viz., to fear. It must be noted that the Scots, though merely a small army, had with the utmost confidence marched through the greater part of two counties, had plundered, burnt, and destroyed, and had marched back, going out of their way to sit quietly down before a strong walled town, garrisoned by a large number of men. They had meant to puzzle the English, and had done so. Where all this time was the rest of the Scottish force, some 25,000 strong and up to date unaccounted for? Was this demonstration of Douglas's before the walls of Newcastle intended as a lure? Rash as Percy was he, at any rate for nearly thirty-six hours, acted like a cautious commander, forgetting his private quarrel in the performance of the duties of his command. Now the Bishop of Durham was expected to arrive at Newcastle in the evening of August 19th with a large reinforcement, spearmen and archers for the most part. Percy had already under his command some six hundred knights, squires, men-at-arms, and infantry, totalling between eight and nine thousand men. Accurate information came in during the morning of the exact position of the Scots at Otterburn, their numbers, their camp, and their disposition. On this information, particular as it was, Percy determined to act, feeling that the reinforcement under the bishop would be ample to secure the town of Newcastle, and that his own command was more than strong enough to deal with Douglas. By this time it had been ascertained that the raid, though part of the same plan, was not being co-operated with by any larger force. Percy, well informed as he thought, started at noon on August 19th, having with him his brother Sir Ralph, William, Lord Hilton, Sir Thomas and Sir Robert Umfraville, Sir John Lilburn, Sir Robert Ogle, Sir Thomas Gray, Sir Matthew Redman, the Governor of Berwick, and others. Following almost the same line of march as the Scots, Percy hurried on, reaching the neighbourhood of the Otter in the evening, where, concealed by the trees from the Scots, he made his final preparations. What, however, he did not know was that considerable changes had been made in the disposition of the Scotch camp since his intelligence had been received. To spy out the place would not have been easy, as both the camp of the Scots and the troops of Percy were hidden away from one another by thick woods. Sending a detachment under Sir Thomas and Sir Robert Umfraville,

Sir Thomas Gray, Sir Robert Ogle, and Sir Matthew Redman, to work round to the north of the Scotch position, and if possible hem them in, he cautiously, with the main body and in strict silence, stole through the woods till he reached the ridge above the Scotch camp. But the camp to which he made his way was that tenanted by the men told off to guard the loot and not the strictly military camp. Both were surprised, but the attack coming on the non-combatant camp gave time to those in the other to arm. For a time it went badly indeed

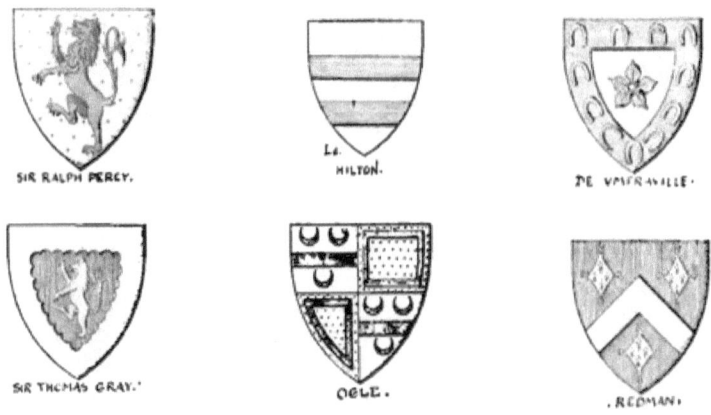

with the guard of the baggage and loot, who, despite their desperate defence, were slaughtered. Douglas ever wary in war had, meanwhile, gained the high ground north of the camp, missing by good luck the detachment under Umfraville— these last went too far north. Seeking shelter in the trees, Douglas worked round till in close proximity to the fight, but on the right flank of the English. Fighting was now general in and around the camp, and the Scots, hard-pressed and outnumbered, were on the verge of ruin. Suddenly their antagonists were assailed in the flank by Douglas and his most doughty companions in arms, the pick of the army in fact. The sudden appearance by moonlight of a hostile mailed force from the woods on the hillside was enough to cause disorder

in the English ranks, and did so. Little by little they began to give way, then rallying, managed to regain some semblance of military formation in the way of a fighting line. Meanwhile Umfraville had discovered his error, and had made himself master of the camp unopposed. For, be it remembered, that by this time the tide of battle had rolled down the hill, nearly half way to Otterburn Tower. Umfraville left a guard in the camp—a guard subsequently butchered by the Scots—and proceeded in search of the battle line of his friends. Shouts he had to guide him in plenty; but in the moonlight his task was not quite easy. Had he cut his way through the lower camp and fallen on the rear of the Scots the victory would, in all probability, have been with the English. As it was, he skirted round the battle on the north-east side, till he came in contact with the extreme of the English right wing—at that time well

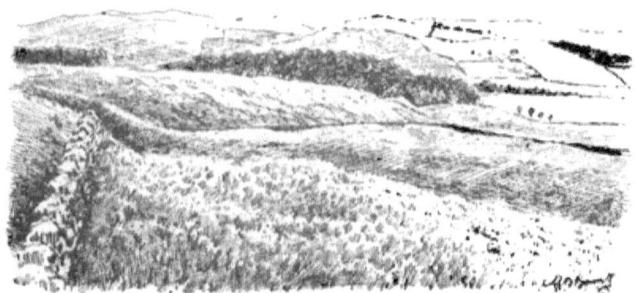

FROM CAMP, LOOKING SOUTH-EAST BY EAST. THE ARMIES MARCHED OVER HILL.

down the hill and not remarkably steady, though the restored fighting line was not yet broken. It is related that at this juncture the moon was obscured by a large passing cloud, and that for some few minutes fighting was suspended. When there was sufficient light again, a determined charge was made on the banner of Douglas, and so far succeeded in that the banner was nearly beaten down. Douglas himself, with a battle-axe or mace, by his personal prowess restored the battle in this part—

a heroic effort in which he was ably seconded by Sir Patrick Hepburn and his son.

Douglas pressed on, hewing his way, and at length got too far into the English ranks. Three spear-wounds in the body and a stroke from a battle-axe on the head brought him to the ground. But he had succeeded not only in restoring the battle but in turning the tide completely from defeat to victory. Over the body of the wounded Douglas the English ranks were pressed gradually back. Sir Ralph Percy, while performing a similar exploit to that of Douglas, was severely wounded, and finally taken prisoner by a Scottish knight, Sir Henry Preston, one of those serving under the Earl of Moray. Douglas, mortally wounded, was found by Sir James Lindsay and Sir John Sinclair as soon as in the course of the fight they could reach the place where he lay. Near him, beneath his banner, was his bastard son Archibald, wounded and faint. Both his squires were killed, one by name Robert Hart by his side. Richard Lundie, his chaplain, wounded but yet able to stand, with a spear had defended his master till help came. To Sir John Sinclair, Douglas gave the charge of again raising his banner, and recalled to him the old prophecy. The banner raised, formed a rallying-point for the Scots. All semblance of a battle line had now vanished. Detached groups, some small some large, were hewing at one another with sword or axe, or thrusting with spear. In the centre, where the Percys fought, the elder Sir Henry shared a similar fate to his brother by being taken prisoner. Sir Henry, though wounded, was not seriously hurt. His captor was Sir John Montgomery. This was the beginning of the end.

Hitherto the fighting on both sides had been continuous and equal in its obstinacy. Now on the English side that resistance began to slacken, finally it ceased, and a general flight ensued ere the day broke. How men, after marching thirty-two miles between noon and sunset on an August day, could fight with desperate courage through twilight and night till dawn is simply a marvel—but that feat was accomplished by Percy's beaten army at Otterburn. Fugitive chasing, with a view to obtaining ransom, was carried on with much spirit by the victorious Scots, so much so that hardly an Englishman of rank escaped either death or capture. The day following the battle was spent in the Scottish camp in preparing for the possible renewing of the combat, and in this wise: The Bishop of Durham, Walter Skirlawe, reached Newcastle on the evening of August 19th, and heard at once of the departure of Percy at noon. Ordering his troops to sup he at once started on the track of Percy. The bishop had a force of 5,000 foot and 2,000 horse, and by moonlight made his way in the cool over the moors towards Otterburn. Early in the morning fugitives were met, and, appalled at the news brought by them, nearly four-fifths of the bishop's army deserted. The old churchman, however, insisted on the advance of the faithful few, and almost reached the field of battle. Here a halt was made, and on deliberation the bishop, with the remnant of his force, returned to Newcastle. But the Scots were aware of his approach, and in their camp took precautions accordingly. The bishop returned to Newcastle where he found more reinforcements had arrived during his absence.

On the morrow, August 21st, he again started, this time at

the head of nearly 10,000 men, horse and foot. The army reached Otterburn in safety, and drew up some two bowshots from the hidden camp of the Scots. These, who all carried a large horn slung round their necks, at a given signal blew them in concert, and as loudly as possible, creating, as may be expected, no little surprise and perhaps consternation. The sound of a few thousand horns blown at once would indeed be a strange and unwonted noise. But the bishop did not at once withdraw— not indeed until he had caused the defences of the hostile camp to be reconnoitred. Closer inspection proved these defences to be strong, the camp well placed, and the entire military position selected with the greatest care if not genius.

The bishop and his forces elected to retire, and did so. The next care which occupied the Scots was the burial of the dead and the arrangements with regard to their prisoners. These numbered 1,040 men, and the feeding of them was a serious factor. Many were dismissed on a verbal promise to pay ransom, some (the poorest) were dismissed free, the remainder, to wit 40 knights, some squires and men, in all nearly 400, went into captivity in Scotland. The spot where Douglas fell was marked by a battle-stone. Of this battle-stone the socket survives and is employed to support the modern pillar of the present so-called "Percy's Cross." The site of the battle-stone was from 180 to 200 yards to the north-east of the present cross. It is understood that the lower part of the upright shaft once formed part of a fireplace at Otterburn Tower, to which a pointed extremity was added on its re-erection. Mounds covering the bones of the slain were common enough on the battlefield half a century ago, but in these days are not easily to be identified. A hut circle near to the camp has for some reason or other hitherto passed for a grave. By a pure chance the writer happened to visit this most interesting spot on the anniversary of the morning after the battle. It seemed curious to contrast the quiet Northumbrian hills of 1895 with the scenes which they must have presented just 507 years previously. In the battle on the English side 1,840 men either lay dead, or perished in the subsequent pursuit, while more than 1,000 were wounded. This may be an exaggeration, specially when coupled with the Scotch bill of a like nature. This owns only to 100 slain and 200 prisoners. These prisoners were mainly captured in their too eager pursuit after fugitives, *i.e.*, ransoms ! A few days after the battle the Scots resumed their march homewards,

bearing with them the bodies of Douglas and his squires, and within two days had reached Melrose.

One or two points in connection with this famous battle may well be raised. Why was it that the Scots selected for their camp the position they did—that is to say, on top of a hill and shrouded in trees? Only a few miles northward, right on the Roman road, stood the Roman camp of Bremenium, which in those days had mighty bulwarks indeed, whereas the little camp at Otterburn required much to be done to it. The answer is simple. At Otterburn, in their woody retreat, they were safe from the effects of the only English weapon they dreaded—the longbow. Yet the longbow was just the very weapon which Percy brought not against them, trusting rather in spear, sword, and axe, in the use of the first named of which the Scots were ever superior. At Bremenium, enormously strong entrenchment though that was, had Percy found the Scots and attacked them with archers, not a Scot would have lived to tell the tale across the border. Want of due rest was also a factor against Percy's army. They had performed an incredible march, while their opponents (in better training) had had at least a few hours' rest and food. The assault on Otterburn, ending in the afternoon, left them free to rest. Beaten though the English were, the feat of marching followed by a protracted night battle is one the parallel of which will not be easily found.

SIR JOHN LILBVRN

CHAPTER IX.

HOMILDON HILL.

September 14, 1402.

THE battle of Homildon Hill claims brief notice from the peculiar way in which it was fought and won. It may be remarked that to quell the rebels in Wales Henry IV. had issued writs for a muster of men at Lichfield on July 7th. The men arrived at the appointed time, but had to wait until late in the following month before the king took the field. His army was divided into three separate divisions : one commanded by the king in person, the second by the Prince of Wales, and the third by the Earl of Arundel. As a military expedition this triple invasion ended in complete failure, mainly owing to the tempestuous weather which rendered active hostilities almost impossible. Henry abandoned his design and returned to London towards the end of September. Meanwhile the Scots, ever on the lookout for an opportunity to profit by the occupation of England in other directions, had prepared to raid the northern counties. News of their intention either leaked out or was suspected by the king, hence he determined upon a counter-stroke, and on August 4th despatched troops to the Border. The Scots in force duly crossed the Border and penetrated as far as Newcastle. Their exact road southwards is not known, but that they were evidently returning by the Roman road and making for the Tweed at Coldstream is manifest from what subsequently occurred. The Scottish leaders on this occasion were Murdoch Stewart, the heir of the Duke of Albany, and Archibald, 4th Earl of Douglas, and their force had been gathered far and wide, being not only composed of the raiding Border families and their adherents, but also of contingents from more distant parts of the kingdom. To oppose them the house of Percy, with whom was Dunbar, the Scotch Earl of March, put forth their power, and having succeeded in placing their army between the returning Scots and the Border, quietly took up a position at Millfield on the river Till, a spot about five miles north-west of Wooler, and there awaited the enemy. For purposes of scouting it is to be presumed a body of 500 archers had been detached, and these suddenly came in sight of the Scots, who were occupying the terraced hill known variously as Homildon, Humbleton, or Homildoun. This hill is about two miles west by north of Wooler station. Humbleton village, with the usual ruined pele tower, is not far from the hill. All around are traces of prehistoric works.

Humbleton Hill itself is terraced in three successive tiers, and has an elevation of nearly 1,000 feet above the sea. Its top is flat and still shows its rude fortification fairly perfect. Within this earthwork traces remain of prehistoric dwellings. Burial mounds are visible on the slopes beneath. There is another camp westward known as Harehope, close to a craggy hollow and separated from Humbleton by a steep ravine. The whole district is full of deep interest to those who care to study the fortifications of such early times. It was on the terraces of Humbleton that the Scotch took up their position, and, according to tradition, numbered 10,000. This estimate, however, is probably an exaggeration. There was, nevertheless, admittedly a great disparity in numbers, but, nothing daunted, the 500 bowmen opened fire at long range into the crowded ranks of their hereditary foes.

Thick and fast the volleys of arrows flew, and though replied to by the Scottish archers the little body of Englishmen remained practically unharmed. This is to be accounted for in the following way: An English archer had a long strong bow and pulled his arrow to the ear; the Scotch bow, on the other hand, was smaller and weaker, and was only pulled to the chest. Many of the defenders of the hill fell either killed or wounded. An attempt was then made by the Scottish spearmen to charge, but without avail. The 500 retired in sections, firing volleys in succession, and the baffled spearmen pressed on, losing men at every step. The mounted Scots then attacked, but equally failed to come to close quarters. This manœuvre of the archers lured the enemy from the hill for about three-quarters of a mile till they reached a field known as Red Rigg, on the other side of the river Till. This was near enough for Percy and March to act, and after a few more volleys, which completed the disorder of the invaders, the English mounted men fell to work. In a brief space the Scotch fled and were pursued as far as Coldstream, the old crossing spot over the

Tweed. The loss of life in the battle was great, and in the pursuit even greater. Douglas lost an eye and was wounded besides in five places, being then taken prisoner. The men of rank who shared his ill-fortune were Murdoch Stewart, the Earls of Moray, Angus, and Orkney, Sir William Stewart of Jedburgh, two barons, eighty knights, and certain Frenchmen. Among the slain were Walter Sinclair, Roger Gordon, Ramsay of Dalhousie, and Livingston of Calendar. North of the hill, in the Red Riggs, is an old stone pillar known as the Bendor Stone, which was erected to commemorate this archers' victory. It had been the intention of the author to have sketched both this stone and the camps at Humbleton and Harehope. Unfortunately, after perambulating the field, a terrific storm of thunder, rain, and hail entirely prevented the accomplishment of his design, and it became needful to immediately seek more shelter than the barren moors afforded.

JOHN RAMPOLE

DVNBAR.

MVRDOCH STEWART.

LIVINGSTONE.

CHAPTER X.

SHREWSBURY.

July 21, 1403.

ON July 6, 1403, a treaty was signed at Bangor between Glyndwr on the one hand and the Earl of Northumberland and Sir Edmund Mortimer on the other, by which it was agreed to divide the kingdom of England. Three days later Sir Henry Percy (Hotspur) had crossed into Cheshire, where he ordered a general muster for July 17th. Hotspur was Justiciar' of the county, and, in addition to his authority by virtue of office, used the expedient of appealing to popular sympathies by the repetition of the old tale that Richard II. was yet alive. The "White Hart" badge of the late king was freely distributed, and seemingly with success, to judge from the losses among the Cheshire men in the battle which ensued. It is curious, however, to note that in the furious defiance which was sent to Henry IV. by the rebels, one of the charges laid to his account is that he had, by cold and hunger, done Richard II. to death at Pontefract. Henry IV. at once proceeded to take measures, both active and strong, to quell the revolt. He was at Burton-on-Trent on July 15th, and on the morrow, before he marched to Lichfield, issued writs to the sheriffs for a levy. The same course was adopted at Lichfield on July 17th. At the cathedral city the king remained until the 19th, occupied in organising his levies as they arrived. Speed in striking a counterblow was all-important; that the king himself felt, and that was the course strongly advocated by Dunbar, the Scotch Earl of March, who accompanied Henry as a species of military Chief of the Staff. Hotspur, in company with his old enemy, the Earl of Douglas, had entered Cheshire on July 9th. He is stated to have marched thence to Stafford, where his uncle, the Earl of Worcester, arrived to join him, and intended to proceed towards the army of Glyndwr, even then well on its way to meet him. Shrewsbury, the appointed place of meeting for the confederates, was the goal. It became a question whether Henry or Hotspur would first reach that town. Whoever did so would be able not only to hold it, but also to command the passage of that important river, the Severn. Henry won the race by a few hours, reaching Shrewsbury on the night of Friday, July 20th. Hotspur arrived at the Castle Foregate, on the north side of the town early on the morning of the 21st, having slept the preceding night at Berwick, a village near. It would be most interesting to know more accurately the exact period of time occupied by Hotspur on his long march of over 250 miles. All, however, that we can understand is that, probably proceeding south by Watling Street, he entered Cheshire on July 9th, and between then and the 20th had collected the bulk of his army, marching from Stafford through Newport, then *viâ* High Ercall and Haughmond Hill to Shrewsbury. Documentary evidence shows that Henry on the preceding day marched from Lichfield, a distance of nearly forty-five miles—a fine performance. On Percy's demand for admittance to the town, a demand coupled with a request for a supply of stores and provisions, a refusal point-blank was the response—a refusal, moreover, emphasised by the display of the royal banner from the walls. Percy found himself face to face with the following uncomfortable circumstances. Henry, with a vastly superior force, held the town, thus securing the passage over the Severn. Glyndwr had not arrived from Oswestry, and, even if he had, a junction could not have been effected between the two armies without one or the other first obtaining possession of the town. The Welshman, giving his version of the matter, subsequently stated that he had been delayed by floods, and he deprecated the notion that he had been but lukewarm in the expedition. According to tradition he actually arrived at Shelton, where, from a lofty oak, distant one and a quarter miles west of Shrewsbury, he viewed the proceedings, and waited anxiously to see which way fortune went before finally adhering to either party. Percy, finding himself denied at the Castle Foregate, fell back northwards in the direction of Whitchurch. At a distance of rather more than three miles he halted and formed battle array in that which, for his slender army, was a singularly advantageous position. That his selection of a fighting ground was fortuitous we can hardly think, so admirably adapted was it for increasing the difficulty of attack. Possibly, in expectation of some such eventuality, the district had been surveyed by him on the previous day, for that he slept at a place called Berwick on the night of July 20th, seems undoubted. Berwick, near which is "Bull Field," the camping-spot of his army, is situated close to the Severn, and distant two and a half miles north-west of Shrewsbury. In those days an almost complete lozenge-shaped bend of the river existed on the north of the town. This would have rendered Bull Field a well-protected camp, as it was practically surrounded on three sides by water and backed by well-wooded ground. Here at Berwick, in the house of a family named Betton, Percy is said to have left his favourite

Hateley Field Shrewsbury. Battlefield church stands on centre of site

sword. The battle line of the rebel army was due east and west, and occupied the north side of the church and churchyard along the line of an old track-road to Hussey Albright (now called Albrighton Hussey). In the front was a field of peas, and beyond this were certain ponds—both very useful in those days as additional defences. A general hostile advance from the south would thus be necessarily split up into two or more parts by the ponds, and these passed, the enemy would be incommoded by the field of peas. During the consequent disorder, the Cheshire archers could play havoc with their oncoming foes. The left centre of Percy's position may be taken as the present church, how far east and west of that the extremes of his lines extended it is not easy to say; but probably he so managed as to have ponds in his centre and on each flank. Henry IV. was not slow to follow the retreating force, and with all possible speed marched on to the ground by the field now known as King's Croft, through which the railway passes. The two armies were then drawn up facing one another, but in lieu of the ordinary right wing, centre, and left wing, the royal troops were in two divisions. Presumably half the centre was added to the right and half to the left wing, a gap being left where the pond protected the rebels. This was in all probability an accident of the ground, and the statement that Prince Henry was sent out with one detachment while the king followed with the other is hardly probable. Prince Henry, however, in the battle itself, ostensibly commanded the division on the left and his father that on the right. Before the actual battle began there appears to have been a good deal of preliminary discussion. The Abbot of Shrewsbury, sent out from the royal lines, went over to those of the enemy, and in his master's name offered pardon and redress of grievances. Percy certainly entertained the proposition, inasmuch as he sent back with the abbot, his uncle, the Earl of Worcester, formerly the governor of the young Prince Henry, and the man whose recent defection from the royal party had caused more astonishment in the land than the rebellion itself. Worcester seems to have conducted himself with no little arrogance on the occasion, but a species of truce to extend over two days was apparently entered into, and Worcester returned to his place. Whether the whole discussion was but a blind to gain time for the unwonted change in the formation on the part of the Royalists, or whether the Earl of March for his private reasons insisted on immediate action it is not easy to decide. Certain, however, it is that the left division, under the Prince of Wales, commenced active hostilities even before the actual word

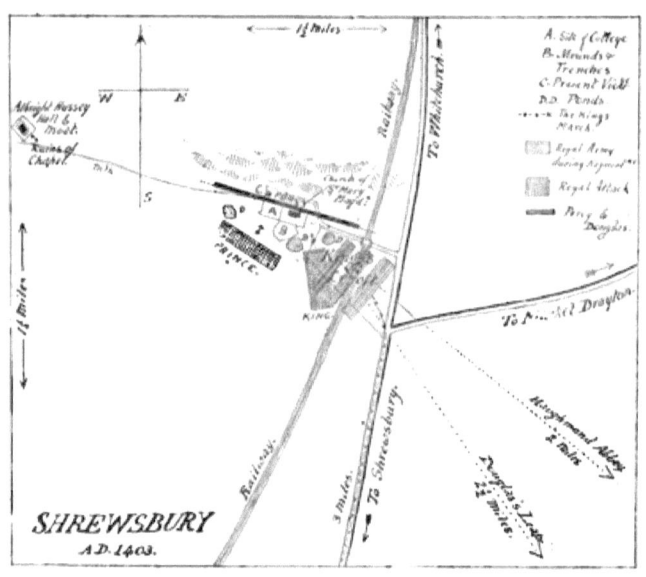

was given to advance standards. Percy was strong in archers, than whom in those days none were better than the men of Cheshire. Opening fire at their opponents—a fire speedily returned by those advancing—the Cheshire volleys of flight arrows prevailed, so much so that the prince was wounded and his bowmen put to the rout. This result, the nature of the ground would lead one to expect. Better posted, and on higher ground, the defending force had everything in its favour as long as the battle was but an archery duel, and, as has been said, in this arm the rebels were superior. When, however, it came to a charge of mailed men and those armed with sword, spear, axe, or maul, matters were different. Prince Henry, on the left, by a charge delivered at an angle, rolled back a part of the right wing of the rebels. At the same moment the king, having succeeded in getting his division between the ponds and up the slope, delivered a similarly oblique attack on the rebel left, possibly in column instead of in the usual line. It should be remarked that the distance between the ponds on the royal right was far less than that on the left, and to this cause must the king's delay be ascribed. It took longer time to get his men through the intervening space. His charge was successful, and the rebel left was rolled back to become intermingled with the disordered right. It seems reasonable to suppose that the extremes of the rebel line were undisturbed, the confusion only attaching to the centre, the left of the right, and right of the left wings. Of the actual disposition of the rebel forces—*i.e.*, of the respective commands held by the leaders—no records remain, but on their side the battle of Shrewsbury was a "personal prowess" fight. Hewing their way through the serried ranks with some twenty or thirty tried adherents, Percy and Douglas made a vain attempt to retrieve the day. Right up to the Royal Standard they fought, slaying in their passage the young Earl of Stafford, Sir Walter Blount, and also, it is alleged more than one groom in assumed royal attire. Henry had been for the time withdrawn by the Earl of Dunbar. During this terrible *melée* Percy fell, slain either by a chance blow or by an unknown hand, he having penetrated the royal line till completely surrounded by enemies.

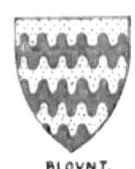
BLOVNT.

This shook the confidence of the rebels, who until now had given a very good account of themselves despite the disparity in numbers. The line, or what was left of it, began to waver as the news of Percy's death spread. Then a retreat began, which, being energetically followed up by the victors, soon became a rout. Douglas burst through the crowd, and rode direct for Haughmond. Here, hotly pursued, his horse, in leaping over a precipice, threw the earl, and broke his knee-cap. A few

hours later, in company with the Earl of Worcester, Sir Richard Vernon, and Sir Richard Venables, Douglas was a prisoner. Worcester, Vernon, and Venables were beheaded the next day at the High Cross, Shrewsbury. The head of Worcester decorated London Bridge, and his body is believed to have been buried in the Holy Trinity Chapel of St. Mary's, Shrewsbury, a tomb of one of the Leyburn family being used for that purpose. Douglas was in the most politic manner set free by Henry.

The body of Hotspur was removed to Whitchurch and there buried. After a short interval, however, the king revoked his permission for the funeral. By royal order the body of this brave man was exhumed, then exposed between a pair of mill-stones in Shrewsbury, and finally dismembered. Of the church built on the site of the grave-pits where the slain were buried, but little need be said here. Allowed to fall almost into ruin, to be robbed of its ancient commemorative glass, and to suffer various other kinds of ill-treatment, it has now been restored, but in a most unsatisfactory manner. The death-roll of this battle was extremely heavy. On the rebel side some two

Mounds and trenches outside Battlefield Churchyard

hundred knights and esquires, mostly from the county of Cheshire, fell, while the numbers of yeomen and archers is unrecorded. Of the royal army ten knights were killed, many esquires, and a large number (admittedly) of private soldiers. The wounded amounted to three thousand. Henry IV. has often been credited with founding the church now standing over the grave-pits as a memorial of the victory and in gratitude therefor. He cannot, however, claim that honour. The real founder was a certain priest, Roger Ive, the rector of Fitz, in

1399, and of Albrighton Hussey (close to the battlefield) from 1398 to 1447. He was a Lancastrian. The site of the church was given by Richard Hussey, of Albrighton Hussey. A license dated October 28, 1406, was issued by the king to assign two acres of land in Albrighton Hussey to Roger Yve and John Gilberd, chaplains, "situated in Hayteleyfeld in which a battle was fought between the king and Henry Percy lately his adversary deceased." A new chapel was to be built and masses said for

the salvation of the king during his life, and after death for his soul and for the souls of his progenitors and of those who were slain in the battle and there buried. But there is no record of who were buried on the field. Some of the dead of note were carried elsewhere. A few relics of the fight have been found in outlying places, and there is a story that a much-corroded knee-plate was found not far from Douglas's Leap about a century since. The main difficulty in treating the subject of this battle is the impossibility of reconciling the numbers said to have been engaged with the extremely narrow nature of the ground. Either all the existing accounts, old or new, are erroneous, or there were not one-third of the combatants engaged. It is impossible to get thirty or forty thousand men into a six-acre patch, let alone to execute either charges or manœuvres of a complicated nature in so small an arena.

VERNON.

CHAPTER XI.

ST. ALBANS.

May 22, 1455.

IN the month of May, 1455, Richard, Duke of York, having raised a force in the north marched on London. His army, principally composed of his personal retainers at starting, was augmented by the men of the Earls of Salisbury and Warwick and Lord Cobham, till on arrival (May 20th) at Royston, on the Cambridgeshire border of Hertfordshire, he found himself at the head of 3,000 men.

On the following day the Lancastrian leaders, taking with them the king, marched out from Westminster to give him battle. There was a good and sufficient reason for not awaiting the Yorkist attack in the metropolis, since there, the partisans of Richard formed a considerable proportion of the population, not a majority indeed, but still a minority which would have been an awkward factor to be reckoned with in case of a siege. It would appear that the comparatively close proximity of York to the city was unknown in the Lancastrian army, for we find that Leicester—where a council had been appointed to meet—was the destination of their force. From Royston Richard sent a letter of explanation to Archbishop Bouchier—a letter practically a manifesto, and signed not only by him but by Warwick and Salisbury. This document, professedly humble but in reality arrogant in its contents, put as a query the following proposition. An extraordinary council has been summoned to meet at Leicester to provide for the safety of the king as if some persons were suspected of having designs against him. Who are these persons? We are loyal and dutiful subjects. If supposed and wrongly so to be otherwise, who originated the suspicion?  This was aimed at Somerset, and was in fact a hint, nay almost a demand (backed as it was by an armed force), for his dismissal.

On the 21st of May, the day that Henry left Westminster, the Yorkists, marching seventeen miles due south, reached Ware, from which place they sent off a letter to the king and a copy of their previous document. The first document reached Westminster after the king had set forth for Leicester, but the messenger overtook the army at Kilburn. The second letter was delivered in the Lancastrian quarters at Watford on the night of the 21st. Henry in his first march covered a distance of nineteen miles, passing through Edgeware and Stanmore. As Richard's messenger probably came by the direct road through Waltham Cross, Edmonton, and Tottenham, it is not to be wondered that he missed the Lancastrian army.

On the morning of May 22nd the royal army marched from Watford to St. Albans, a distance of eight miles. At Ware, Richard presumably ascertained the direction in which the royal army was progressing, and forsaking his intention of marching on London, turned off south-west by west along the St. Albans road with a view of coming to conclusions with the Lancastrians. When Henry reached that city Richard was already at hand.

Ware is distant from St. Albans fourteen miles, and a portion of this march was cross-country. Richard appears to have halted in a field about half a mile from the city on the east side—a field still known as Camp Field. It seems reasonable to suppose that the Yorkists performed this as a night march, for they were even nearer the city as early as 7 a.m., by which time they had formed up in a piece of ground known as Key Field.

Henry had with him a scanty army amounting to no more than 2,000 men; but if leaders went for anything he was well supplied as far as blood goes. The aged Duke of Buckingham, the Duke of Somerset, and their eldest sons, the four Earls Northumberland, Pembroke, Wiltshire, and Devon were there, and the Lords Dudley, Clifford, and De Ros. Of these Somerset was the leading spirit, and being the man who in reality had most at stake, he had suppressed the documents sent to the royal army by York, and it would appear that no hint of their contents reached the king until the fight was over.

In numbers, however, the king was obviously overmatched, and hence the aged Buckingham was sent out to the Yorkist camp to negotiate—or at any rate to ascertain what the leaders of that force demanded. Richard, Warwick, and Salisbury, must have then perceived, even if they did not previously know, that they were in a measure able to dictate terms; and throwing off the mask they demanded the delivery to them of certain persons "to have as they deserved." With their numerically superior force and with the speedy expectation of a reinforcement of 2,000 men under the Duke of Norfolk, they could afford to take high ground. Buckingham returned to St. Albans and reported to Somerset, who saw before him two courses only—to fight and take the chances of the battle, or to surrender and of a certainty lose his head. He decided on fighting.

The old road to London in those days entered the city from Key Field by Sopwell Lane, and here there were bars. Other bars existed at Butts or Shropshire Lane, now called Victoria Street, and both these were closed and guarded. Somerset's force was therefore divided into two bodies, between which lay a considerable gap. The Royal Standard was set up in St. Peter's Street, probably at the cross-ways north-east of the market-place. The Yorkists attacked by the two lanes already mentioned, advancing at the outset to the Tonman Ditch, between which and the houses of the city were certain gardens known as the Town Backsides. This old ditch existed also on the other side of the city, where more gardens bore the same name. At first the defenders held their own, being able to repulse all attacks on the bars in the narrow lanes. Warwick then, in what we must call the centre, crossed the ditch and undefended rampart, rushed the houses in his immediate front, entering them from the gardens, and penetrated into the street. The exact spot where he effected his entry is stated to have been a house between the Cross Keys Hotel and the Queen's. These ancient hostelries were in 1455 known as the "Keye" and the "Chekkere" (Chequers). He now had pierced the royal position at a point where it was destitute of defenders. The attacks of his right and left on the bars in Butts Lane and Sopwell Lane were pressed, while he, dividing his troops, fell on the two separated bodies of Royalists, attacking the right flank of one and the left of the other. Henry, remaining by his banner, was wounded in the neck, it is said, by an arrow, and would probably, despite his rebukes, have been slain had not he been hastily removed to a cottage by his servants. It is a strange picture, the imbecile or almost imbecile king standing quiescent beneath his banner and mildly telling those who were attacking him, "Forsothe, forsothe, ye do fouly to smyte a Kynge enoynted so." Victory, within half an hour, lay with the Yorkists, Northumberland and Clifford were slain, and Somerset, perhaps luckily, shared their fate. Lord Stafford was mortally wounded, Lord Dorset not severely, Buckingham and the Earl of Devon slightly. Not more than one hundred perished, but of these the majority were of high rank, thanks to the order given by Warwick to spare the rank and file and smite only the leaders.

STAFFORD.

Immediately the fighting was over York, Salisbury, and Warwick sought out the king in his place of retreat (a tanner's cottage), and with hypocritical humility tendered their allegiance with bended knee, the which the poor king duly accepted. Passing the night at the abbey, which was not plundered, the king was taken back to London on the morrow, being *en route* treated with ostentatious respect. Northumberland, Somerset, and Clifford were buried in the chapel of the Virgin within the Abbey Church, and elsewhere in the building some forty-eight other men of gentle blood found their graves. St. Albans, as a town, paid dearly for having been defended, being devoted to pillage. With the loot thus obtained and the king's baggage also a prey to the victors, the Yorkist soldiery did not fare badly on this occasion.

BOURCHIER.

CHAPTER XII.

BLORE HEATH.

September 23, 1459

THE events immediately preceding the small but sanguinary battle at Blore Heath are as follows: Warwick, after a meeting with the Duke of York and Richard Neville, Earl of Salisbury, at York, had retired to Calais. York then went into Wales to raise troops, and Salisbury betook himself to Middleham Castle, where he set to work to equip a force.

Middleham Castle, now in ruins, stands on a hill about two miles south-east of the village of Leyburn, in the North Riding, and ten miles south by west of Richmond. The design of the Yorkists was that Salisbury should advance on London. So, when his force amounted to between 4,000 and 5,000 men, the earl started from Middleham and marched through Lancashire, Cheshire, and the north of Shropshire. James Touchet, 2nd Lord Audley, was then despatched by Queen Margaret with instructions to levy troops and oppose the earl on the earliest possible date. The route taken by Salisbury through Lancashire, Cheshire, and Shropshire seems circuitous, but there was a reason for selecting it, in the fact that the emissaries of the Red Rose had been most active in those parts; nay, Margaret herself, by keeping open house in Cheshire and distributing the silver swan badge of her little son, had done much to render her cause popular.

Early in September Henry VI. was at Nottingham, whither he had been brought by the queen. From Nottingham he was removed to Eccleshall. This manœuvre was planned

with a view to intercept Salisbury, who was rumoured to be making for Ludlow. Salisbury, however, managed to give the queen's army the slip at Eccleshall; and, on September 22nd, marching rapidly westwards through Newcastle-under-Lyne and Market Drayton, he camped just beyond that town on a hill south of it, to this day known as Salisbury Hill. But though he had the luck to avoid Margaret, Lord Audley, with a strong body of Lancashire and Cheshire bowmen, was that night encamped within three miles of him on an eminence due north-west, now called Audley Brow. The sole obstruction to an attack was the river Tern, which flowed westwards at the foot of Salisbury's camp.

On the morning of September 23rd Salisbury broke up his camp, moving off for the Nantwich road in a south-west direction. Having gained the road at or near a house called

BLORE HEATH.

Four Alls, he then made straight for Market Drayton, but before reaching the town turned off eastwards to Blore Heath, where he drew up on the rising ground beyond the Hempnill

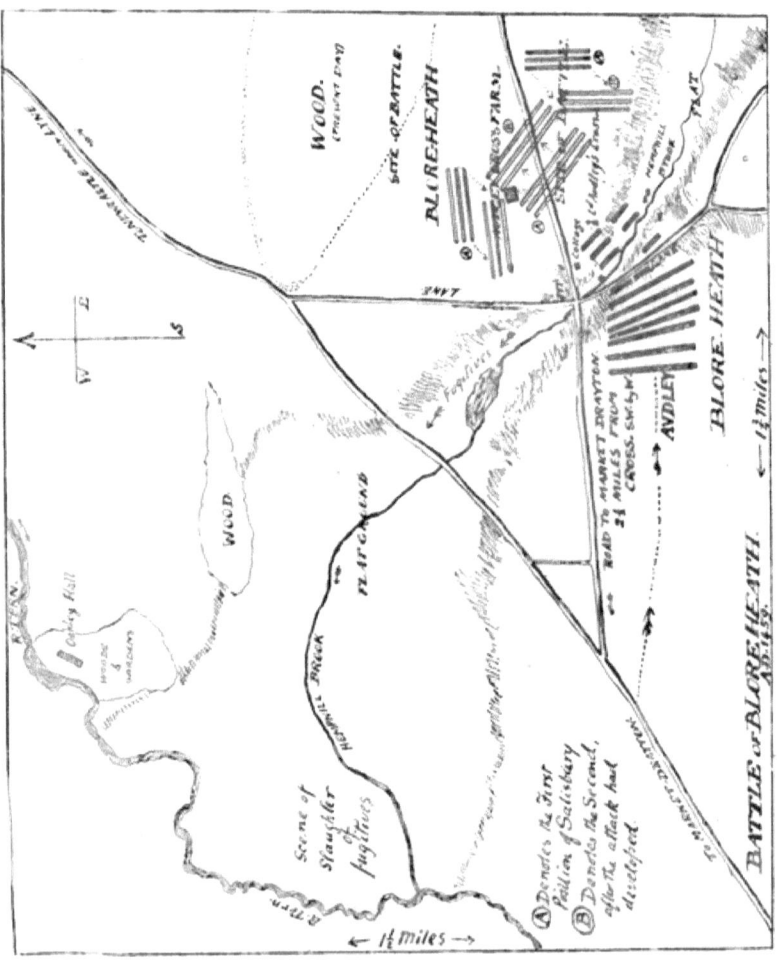

Brook. Audley, on discovering what had happened, at once started in pursuit, and, seeing that his force greatly outnumbered that of the earl, this course of action was more than justifiable.

BLORE HEATH.

Salisbury is said to have had better disciplined troops than his opponent, but the latter had certainly the flower of the Cheshire yeomen.

Salisbury, from beyond the Hempmill Brook, now awaited attack, and determined to deal his counter-stroke at the moment of crossing, when Audley's troops were of necessity in disorder. He likewise appears to have disposed his army in a formation somewhat resembling half a hexagon, the two wings being as much concealed as possible. His centre, as Audley's troops pressed on, fired a volley or two and then made a feint of retreating. On rushed the Lancastrians, their disorder increasing till they had reached and crossed the brook. Salisbury then faced his centre about, the concealed wings opened fire, and a huge slaughter resulted. More and more Lancastrians were hurried over the brook to meet the same fate. No accounts remain which lead us to conclude that Lord Audley attacked in the usual formation of centre and wings. The balance of evidence goes to prove that his men at once rushed on against the enemy probably in some semblance of line, but so mixed were the different arms that their archers were useless. The Cheshire bowmen, of whom a large number had been enlisted by Audley, got no chance to use their bows. Troops from behind kept pressing on, and in the act of crossing were shot by the two wings, which had by this time closed up. The reverse became a complete rout; a wretched remnant fled away along the flat swampy banks of the stream till, caught in a meadow where it joins the river, they perished.

Tradition states that the brook was completely dammed by

the bodies of the slain. Lord Audley fell on the hillside, and a stone cross, repaired in 1765, marks the spot. The main line of flight taken by the fugitives was along this stream, the archers rendering it difficult for them to retreat over the higher ground on the east of the brook. Two thousand four hundred men were slain on the Lancastrian side, and the battle is stated to have lasted from three to four hours. The Cheshire bowmen were conspicuous by the little silver swans, the badge of the

THE CROSSING-PLACE OF THE HEMPNILL BROOK.

Prince of Wales, worn by them. Of knights there fell Sir Hugh Venables of Kinderton, Sir Thomas Dutton of Dutton, Sir William Troutbeck, Sir John Legh, Sir John Done, and Sir John Egerton—all Cheshire men. Sir Richard Molyneux of Sefton in Lancashire, Richard Done, and John Dutton, esquires, were also slain. A pardon dated April 29, 1460, *i.e.*, about six months after the battle, is extant. It was granted by Henry VI. to a number of persons in consideration of the "good service done at the battle of Bloreheth." The names of those pardoned show that of sixty-six who accompanied Sir Thomas Fitton of Gawsworth, county Chester, thirty-one were slain. According to Drayton, in this battle the Cheshire men were much divided in their allegiance, relations fighting against relations in the most determined manner. A passage in the "Polyolbion" mentions several of the names of those slain in the battle, but suggests that they fell by the hands of their own kindred.

Salisbury's victory opened the road to Ludlow, and thither he went, with the results known to all students of history. The victory of Blore Heath was, as events proved, perfectly fruitless, a sad and profitless loss of human life. Juggled by a royal proclamation of pardon and betrayed by the treachery of Sir Andrew Trollope, who deserted with the Calais troops, the conjoined force of the Yorkists melted later on into air. Before December had passed York was an exile in Ireland, accompanied by the Earl of Rutland, his second son. Warwick had already fled to Calais, where he was shortly joined by Salisbury and the young Earl of March (afterwards Edward IV.).

DUTTON.

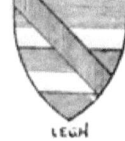
LEGH.

VENABLES.

CHAPTER XIII.

NORTHAMPTON.

July 10, 1460.

IT has been related how the battle of Blore Heath was fought in vain, and that before the end of October, 1459, the leaders of the Yorkist party were for the most part in exile. Without entering into the details of the operations between Salisbury and Warwick on the one hand and Somerset on the other outside Calais, it will suffice to mention that the latter suffered a severe repulse at Pont de Neullay on April 23, 1460. Warwick had despatched early in the year a small force, commanded by Sir John Dynham, to make a descent on Sandwich, then held by the Lancastrians under Lord Rivers (Wydeville) and his son. Dynham succeeded, captured both father and son, and took them off prisoners to Calais.

In no direction were the military operations of the Lancastrians successful. Richard, Duke of York, in Ireland was well received, and his authority as lieutenant recognised, though the Irish Parliament at the same time declared itself independent. The unfortunate bearer of a warrant to arrest

the Duke of York, who arrived from England, was arrested
and executed. Warwick now went from Calais to Ireland
and endeavoured to incite the natives to take up arms and
invade England in the Yorkist interest. His mission failed.
On his return journey he met and passed, without fighting, a
fleet under the Duke of Exeter. Sandwich was now seized
in earnest by the Yorkists, who thus obtained command of a
port. The governor, by name Osberne Mundeford, was
shipped off to Calais, where he
was executed, and Falconberg, as
Yorkist governor, reigned in his
stead.

Queen Eleanor Cross, a few yards from the old demesne near the spot where it meets the present road to Northampton.

On June 26th Warwick, Salisbury, and the young Earl of
March (Edward IV.) landed at
Sandwich with a scanty following,
among whom were the young Lord
Audley (a converted prisoner) and
also a person of far greater importance—the Papal Legate Coppini.
At Sandwich they were joined by the Archbishop of Canterbury,
Bourchier, and then a start was made for the metropolis. *En
route* their following grew, as armies were wont to grow in the
days of the Wars of the Roses. Lord Cobham came and with
him, or influenced by him, the men of Kent flocked to
Warwick, Salisbury, and the young earl. London, ever Yorkist
in its sympathies, went out to meet the approaching army, while
the Lords Hungerford and Scales, who held the Lancastrian

warrant to keep the city, shut themselves up in the Tower, whence they wrathfully shot "wildfire into the town every hour, laying great ordnance against it." To Salisbury and Cobham were committed the charge of reducing the city fortress, and in this they were aided by the Lord Mayor and a prominent mercer named Harrow. Their batteries were mounted from the side of St. Katharine's Wharf.

Warwick's army, swollen by recruits from Sussex and Essex, started north on July 5th by the trunk road through St. Albans and Towcester. Henry was at Northampton

NORTHAMPTON BATTLEFIELD.

when the Lancastrian leaders in his name were levying and organising an army to repel the Yorkist attack. It was, however, with quite a feeling of panic that the news of Warwick's northward march was received. Henry, himself a man devoted to the Church and most scrupulous in all his religious observances, now found arrayed against him not only an army but also the archbishop, the legate, and four other prelates, not to mention the prior of the hospital of St. John—a military prior. It is doubtful, however, whether the knowledge, if it ever reached the king, was fully comprehended by him, so weak in mind was he then. Still some

NORTHAMPTON.

soldiers and men of action remained true, and did not resign as the chief officers of the household did. The queen and the Prince of Wales were safe and at a distance, having been sent to Eccleshall from Coventry when the king and the army left that town for Northampton.

At Northampton active soldiers pitched the royal camp in a field outside the town and entrenched it strongly. There have been several sites suggested for this camp, but the most probable is the meadow, north of Delapré Abbey and south of the river Nene, locally called Hardingstone Meadow.

NORTHAMPTON BATTLEFIELD.

The morning of July 10th was occupied in marshalling the Yorkist army at the old entrenchment known as Danes Camp. Edward, Earl of March, led the right wing, Falconberg the left, and Warwick the main body or centre. A short time was spent in a sham attempt at negotiation, in which the Bishop of Salisbury from the Yorkist camp offered the mediation of the clergy from that camp. Warwick also proffered a request for a safe conduct to visit the king, but this attempt, never intended seriously, came to nothing. From Danes Camp by the old drove road the Yorkists marched to Hardingstone Fields. On their left, at a short distance from the spot where the new road cuts the drove they passed the beautiful Eleanor's Cross. Then skirting the boundary of Delapré Abbey a wheel to the left brought them to the Lancastrian entrenchments.

Two hours after noon an assault on the entrenched camp began. The Lancastrians were well provided with artillery, while their opponents had none; the guns, however, were useless, owing to the powder having been drowned in a

Danes Camp near Northampton
Yorkist Camp prior to Battle much destroyed this excavation

heavy storm of rain. Hardingstone Meadow — a water meadow—was flooded, and there were in addition two large and full ditches, or dykes, which hampered the Yorkist attack. The first assault on the rampart failed; the six-feet ditch full of water was too deep for men in armour to scramble out of and then to surmount a rampart slippery and wet. At that moment the force within the entrenchment, which was opposed to the attack of the Earl of March, turned traitor. It was under the command of Lord Grey of Ruthin. This worthy assumed the badge of Warwick, and his followers, leaning over the rampart, pulled up with their hands the storming party. The subsequent fighting was but small. Orders had been given by Warwick to spare the common herd, while smiting the leaders. Many who would have been unharmed fled, and while trying, as they thought, to escape over the river near a mill, were drowned. The slaughter of nobility and gentry was great. Near the king's tent Buckingham, Egremont, Beaumont, and Shrewsbury fell, while the poor

king, smiling at a scene he hardly comprehended, was captured by an archer. The total number of slain is stated not to have exceeded three hundred in the camp, but gathered importance from the rank of those who fell. The king was conducted into Northampton with respect, though rather ostentatiously; and after a stay there of three days was removed to London, where, in the "bysshop's paleys" he was "loged" on the 16th of July. Margaret and her son escaped to Wales. The Tower surrendered on July 18th, two days after the return of Warwick to London. The conditions of the surrender were shamefully broken. Lord Scales chanced to be recognised after being secretly released, and, being personally unpopular with the citizens, was slain when in a boat on the Thames.

CHAPTER XIV.

WAKEFIELD.

December 30, 1460.

ON July 10, 1460, the Lancastrian army suffered a signal defeat at Northampton. Henry VI. was taken prisoner, while Queen Margaret and her son, Prince Edward, fled to Scotland, where they found refuge. Richard, Duke of York, then a fugitive in Ireland, on receipt of the news, returned to London in October, occupied the royal residence, and, by a stretch of authority, called Parliament together. The remainder of the year was occupied in an attempt on his part to obtain recognition of his claims to the throne. Parliament demurred, but it was eventually agreed that on the death of Henry VI., Richard, Duke of York, should succeed to the Crown; an arrangement which was, of course, most detrimental to the youthful Edward, Prince of Wales. Such was the state of affairs in London in December, when Parliament adjourned. York, it may be observed, had brought with him a force of 500 men, nominally his attendants, "as a retinue," it is stated, but really the nucleus of an army and intended by its presence during the negotiations, to exert moral suasion.

Roughly speaking, the feeling of the country was this: In the large towns and in the places where there was any commerce, especially in the south, the Yorkist faction was supported by the majority. In the north the Lancastrians were in the ascendant then as ever.

At this juncture the Lancastrian nobility determined again to resort to arms. Assembling at York, Henry, 3rd Earl of Northumberland, Ranulph, Lord Dacre of Gilsland, John, 9th Baron Clifford, and John, Lord Neville of Raby, proceeded to raid the estates of the Duke of York and of Richard (Neville), 1st Earl of Salisbury. They were joined by a force of 8,000 men from Wales and the west, under the leadership of Henry (Beaufort), 2nd Duke of Somerset, Henry (Holland), 2nd Duke of Exeter, and Thomas (Courtenay), 6th Earl of Devon. The Lancastrian army, it is said, then amounted to about 20,000 men. The Duke of York, leaving Henry VI. at the palace of the Bishop of London, collected troops in haste, and on December 2nd marched north, accompanied by Salisbury, and taking with him his young son Edmund, Earl of Rutland; his eldest son Edward, Earl of March, being at that time in or near Shrewsbury, engaged in raising a force.

Proceeding northwards with speed, the expedition met with a serious check at Worksop, in Nottinghamshire. There the Yorkist advanced guard was surprised and very severely handled by a detachment under Somerset. How the army came to march through Worksop is not apparent, nor are there any authentic records of its subsequent progress until Sunday, December 21st, when it is known that Sandal Castle was reached. Details of this gap in the story would be interesting, for the following reasons: The Lancastrian army, which outnumbered York's little force by about four to one, lay at that time at Pontefract, distant only some eight or nine miles to the east. They had already succeeded in cutting up a detachment of the Yorkists at Worksop, and must therefore have been aware of the presence of a hostile army. It seems reasonable to suppose that the numbers of that army would have been spied out, and that its course would have been followed by scouts. This, however, does not appear to have been the case, for, eight days later Yorkist foragers sent out from Sandal, approaching too near the Lancastrian camp, were observed and hotly pursued right up to Sandal Castle, within the walls of which they and the whole army were forced to take refuge.

Sandal Castle, the possession of Richard, Duke of York, an extremely strong place of arms, survived until the Great Civil War, when, after surrender to the Parliament in 1645, it was demolished the following year. A few fragments of walls and the mighty entrenchments, specially the keep mound, are all that remain to tell the tale of its former magnificence. The castle stood about two miles to the south-east of the town of Wakefield, and commanded from its lofty keep a most extensive view. Even from the bare mound of these days miles of country can be seen. At the time of the battle open ground separated it from the river Calder, down to which the land gradually slopes. Wakefield bridge, with its celebrated chapel, stood there; and the site of the battle, between the bridge and the castle, was known as Wakefield Green. Thickly wooded ground lay to the south of the castle, and it is needful to remember this in order to understand the course of the fight.

To York the retreat and failure of his foragers was a matter of the greatest moment, as supplies were all but gone. There cannot have been great Christmas cheer in Sandal that

season, though the statement that the Duke "kept his Christmas" there has survived. Edward, Earl of March, had been implored by urgent messages to hasten northwards without delay. It became a question whether, considering the lack of provisions within the castle, it would be possible to hold out until his arrival. The capture of the castle by storm was an impossibility; it might be blockaded, and starvation was the only foe that in this case the garrison had to fear. In debate Richard decided to march forth to give battle, ignoring the prudent advice of Sir David Hall to endure blockade and await reinforcements.

The Lancastrian army soon covered the distance between Pontefract and Sandal, and marched in three divisions, only one of which, the main body or centre, was drawn up in battle array on Wakefield Green. The van- and rear-guards, which under ordinary circumstances would have formed the right and left wings of the army, were ambuscaded instead in the woods which lay to the rear of the castle, *i.e.*, south of it. The device was a clever one, because the ostensible fighting force of the Lancastrians did not, as thus seen from the walls, appear to very greatly outnumber that of the Yorkists—an inducement to the latter to come out. Of artillery the Lancastrians were destitute, and even had they possessed it they might have pounded Sandal with the guns of those days for months without making any impression on its massive walls. Probably also the lack of provisions within was unknown to them, and if victory was to be theirs they considered that they must either lure out the garrison or commence a protracted siege with, in the latter case, no slight chance of failure.

York was completely deceived, and on Tuesday, December 30, 1460, out through the gateway of Sandal and down the hill into the plain marched the doomed garrison. The battle in the onset began according to the usual tactics, with flights of arrows from the Lancastrians—they remaining as it were on the defensive, while the Yorkists ostensibly were the assailants. Charging on their opponents' line, the Yorkists were soon engaged in a fierce hand-to-hand encounter. The desired result was produced, and York was simply entrapped ; as closely netted, perhaps, as any commander has ever been in a comparatively open country ; for this was no case of a defile.

No sooner had the lines joined battle, than, from the woods behind the castle, and passing on both sides of it, came the hitherto concealed remainder of the Lancastrian force. The men in ambush were chiefly composed of light troops, both horse and foot. They had of necessity to be mobile, to perform a given thing at a given moment, and in concert. The horse is said to have been commanded by Thomas, 10th Baron de Ros, then a staunch Lancastrian ; the foot by James Butler, 1st and only Earl of Wiltshire of that creation. One account names Clifford and Wiltshire as the leaders. These two bodies, advancing with speed and acting perfectly in concert, delivered flank attacks in rear of the Yorkists. A desperate resistance was made by the luckless army, but within half an hour the battle was at an end. There is no need here to enter upon the conflicting stories as to whether York died fighting, or was after capture, insulted, and butchered in cold blood. Rutland, a mere boy, in company with his chaplain and tutor, "Sir" Robert Apsall, either perished in the pursuit or was murdered in the traditional way by Clifford. These traditional tales are probably little warranted by fact. Margaret, for instance, could not have received the head of York on the battlefield, she being in Scotland. A house near that building called "Six Chimneys," in Kirkgate, Wakefield, is locally supposed to mark the site of Rutland's death ; but this, too, is open to question. The "Six Chimneys" itself, however, stands where it did on the day of the fight, and is the only contemporary building remaining in the city. On the left hand of the road leading from Sandal to Wakefield, near a lane variously called Many-gates Lane and Cock and Bottle Lane, the spot traditionally the scene of the death of York is pointed out. Formerly it had the reputation of being haunted. A cross, destroyed in the Great Rebellion, marked the place of death. Relics of the

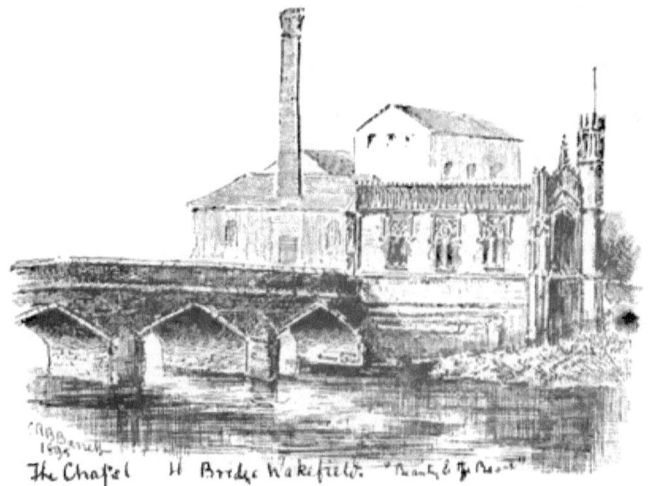

The Chapel H Bridge Wakefield.

fight, in the shape of bones, scraps of rusty armour, spurs, and a few gold rings, have been from time to time dug up on the battlefield. The chapel on the bridge has not the least connection with the battle. It was not founded by Edward IV., nor can it be proved to have been enriched by him. The real founders were William Ferry, of Wakefield, and Robert, of Heath, who in 1356–1357 endowed a chantry there with two priests.

A long list of distinguished dead can be extracted from

various chronicles and also from the Paston letters : Sir William
Parr, Sir Thomas Neville, son of the Earl
of Salisbury, Sir John, the son of Sir Thomas
Harrington (the father, being wounded severely,
died the day after the battle), Sir Edward
Bourchier, Sir Henry Rathford, Sir John
and Sir Hugh Mortimer, Sir J. Pickering, Sir
Hugh Hastings, Sir David Hall, Sir Richard Limb-
riche, Sir John Gedding, Sir Eustace Wentworth,
Sir Thomas Pykering, and Sir James Strangways.
Four gentlemen were knighted on the field by
Henry, Duke of Somerset, viz., The Lord Clifford,
James Lutterell, Robert Whittingham, and (? Nicholas)
Latymer, of Somersetshire. The Earl of Northum-
berland knighted eight, viz., Richard Percy (his
brother), Sir Will'm Gascoigne, Thomas Metham,
Will'm Bertram, Richard Alborough, Thomas Eldre-
ton, John Malev'er, and William St. Quintyn. The
Earl of Devon knighted his brother, Sir John
Courtenay, Thomas Fulford, Alexander Hoody,
(? Hody) and Richard Cary. Lord Clifford dubbed
his brother Sir Roger, Sir Richard Tempest, and
Sir Henry Bellingham. Lord Ros one only, viz.,
Sir Thomas Babthorpe. In the Parl. Rol., 1st ed.
iv., vol. v. p. 477, is an act of attainder—a subsequent act of Yorkist retaliation. It names a
number of those present at the battle, and is interesting as
showing in many cases the localities to which they belonged.

PARR

HARRINGTON

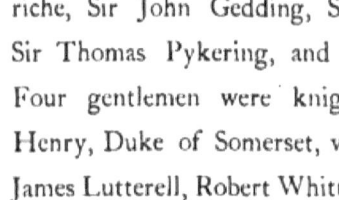

GASCOYNE.

METHAM.

BERTRAM

According to a well-substantiated tradition, the Wakefield Tower, in the Tower of London, owes its name to having been used as a prison for some of the captives taken in the fight. The prison room is never shown to the public, being as it is beneath the present Jewel House. The Wakefield Tower adjoins (on the east side) the so-called Bloody Tower. Its basement room is entered through a small, low, and narrow-arched door, concealed by one of the huge gates of the Bloody Tower, which when open are locked back to the wall on either side. On obtaining admittance, the front room, which is beneath the Bloody Tower, is seen to be furnished with one or two cupboard recesses in its walls. This was in former times the dwelling of the executioner. A smaller room off it contains the remains of a circular stone stair, leading to the upper part of the Bloody Tower. By a door, entrance is gained to the basement prison room—a room with a vaulted roof supported by a central pillar. The Wakefield Tower is circular on the outside but polygonal within, some sides being pierced by deep embrasures and lighted by tiny windows. Into this hole the wretched captives were probably thrust. The present Jewel Room above has in its wall an interesting little oratory, with a piscina on the south side of the space where the altar once stood. This room is traditionally the scene of the murder of Henry VI. On the upper floor of the Bloody Tower the portcullis, with its machinery, is still to be seen. A few interesting prisoners' carvings are there in their original position. The top part of the small circular stair is also remaining. If this tower (really a gateway) was the scene of the murder of the princes, by that stone stair it is reasonable to suppose that the assassins ascended. But a mystery attaches to the origin of the name "Bloody Tower" —a mystery as yet unsolved. More dark deeds than one have occurred within its narrow and gloomy limits. Who can say whether it is to the supposed murder of the princes or to the murder or suicide of Northumberland that the gruesome building owes its equally gruesome name?

DABTHORP.

FVLFORD.

S' QVYNTIN.

HODY.

CHAPTER XV.

ST. ALBANS.

February 17, 1461.

LANCASTRIAN BADGE, ASSYNED BY MARGARET FOR HER SON EDWARD.

THE Yorkist victory of Mortimer's Cross, related in the next chapter, was won on February 2, 1461, at which time Margaret in York was preparing for her southward march—a march of which the possession of London was the object.

Her force was large, and consisted of at least four nationalities, *i.e.*, English, Scotch, Welsh, and some French. Lacking in discipline, and devoted chiefly to pillage, the excesses committed by this unruly host south of the Trent did more to ruin the Lancastrian cause than any previous reverses. Outrages of all kinds marked the passage of Margaret and her army; churches, ecclesiastical establishments, towns, villages, and private dwellings alike were plundered during the time (about fourteen days) which was occupied in covering the distance between York and Dunstable on the borders of Hertfordshire. Here the Lancastrians arrived on February 16th, and in a slight skirmish with a Yorkist post met with success.

Four days previously Warwick, who took the king with him, started from London and duly arrived at St. Albans, where he pitched his camp on Bernard's, or Barnet, Heath, an open tract on the north-east side of the town. Barnet Heath was a good position, assuming that the attack came from the north, since on that side the ground slopes away considerably. Warwick here fortified himself with some care, and a list of quaint "gynnes" of war is extant, showing that his preparations were, for those days, elaborate. Nets of great cords, eight yards long and four feet wide, were stretched on iron poles; door-shaped shields, known as pavises, supported from behind, with holes pierced for arrows, were set up. Lastly, a spiked lattice, which was expanded or contracted at will and used to hamper cavalry, is mentioned. This curious device seems to have been a magnified and mechanical caltrap. Warwick had also some artillery and men who shot "wildefire."

On February 17th Margaret advanced on St. Albans from Dunstable, apparently perfectly well informed as to the whereabouts and arrangements of Warwick. With her came the Dukes of Somerset and Exeter, the Earls of Northumberland, Shrewsbury and Devon, Lords Ros, Grey, Greystock, Willoughby, Welles and FitzHugh, and Sir John Grey of Groby. With Warwick were the Duke of Norfolk, the Duke of Suffolk, the Earl of Arundel, Lord Bourchier, and Lord Bonville.

Warwick committed a grave error in his dispositions, in that he neglected to guard all the approaches to the town.

In fact, beyond his fortified camp he had no outposts save a single body of archers stationed without supports in French Row, adjoining the market-place. These archers commanded the approach to the town from Dunstable *via* Watling Street, St. Michael's Bridge, Fish Pool Street, and Cook Row; but the alternative route, on the north side, which passed along Folly Lane and Catherine Lane, and entered the town half way down St. Peter's Street was left totally unguarded.

Margaret, for some reason, adopted the first-named route for her first attack, and this attack failed. Massed archers, as usual, were too much for any troops advancing to attack. Repulsed, therefore, from French Row, Margaret retreated to the bridge of St. Michael, where, instead of crossing, her troops turned east down Folly Lane, and passed over the Ton-man Ditch into Catherine Lane, and so into St. Peter's Street. Warwick's position was thus completely turned—a fact he discovered while the fighting was going on in the streets. He therefore moved his whole army to the east, a distance of nearly three miles. Margaret in pursuit passed northwards through Bowgate, and out on to the heath, where she fell on the unsupported rearguard of Warwick's army. Warwick's rearguard fought well, but it was the third of an army against a very superior force. Neither the main body nor the vanguard came to its assistance—they were indeed too far off, it may be assumed. The rearguard, overcome, broke and fled headlong down the slopes of Barnet Heath. Warwick had, however, when too late, sent his main body back to the assistance of the rearguard, and these arrived just as the rearguard was routed. Panic seized them, and they incontinently fled without offering the least resistance. The vanguard, to whom their terror was communicated, followed suit. Henry VI., with one esquire-in-waiting, was left in almost sole possession of the camp.

The adventures of Henry after various battles ever seem to have been singularly strange. The esquire, whose name was Thomas Hoo, quietly brought his royal master to the Lord Clifford, where he was at once restored to the queen and the Prince of Wales. As after the first battle of St. Albans, the ensuing night was spent at the abbey. But few prisoners of note were taken, the chief being Lord Montagu (Neville), Lord Bonville, and Sir Thomas Kyrielle. The first of these was spared, but Bonville and Kyrielle were brutally executed, and a like fate befel William Gower, who had carried one of the king's banners in the fight. Henry knighted his son on the same evening, and the newly made knight then dubbed Lord Shrewsbury and thirty others. Loss of life in the battle seems to have been mainly confined to the rank and file, no lists of important names occur. One, however, a Lancastrian, is mentioned, viz., Sir John Grey, of Groby, who was mortally wounded.

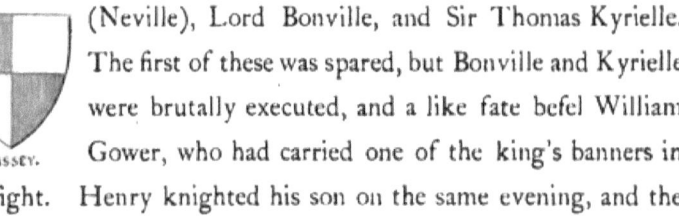
MASSEY.

Obviously Margaret ought at once to have repressed pillage and marched on the metropolis. This, unfortunately for her cause, she did not do. An edict against plunder was issued and was disregarded. Time was wasted, and after pillaging as far as Barnet the opportunity was lost, and lost for ever.

CHAPTER XVI.

MORTIMER'S CROSS. | TOWTON.

February 2, 1461. | *March* 29, 1461.

ROSE-EN-SOLEIL.

THE position of affairs in the month of February, 1460-61, was as follows: At Wakefield the Yorkists had been defeated, and the Duke of York, and Salisbury lost their lives. The Lancastrian forces, joined by Queen Margaret and the Prince of Wales, were marching on London. At St. Albans they were opposed by Warwick and the men of Kent, in whose custody was the old king. Here, on February 17th, victory again declared itself on the side of the house of Lancaster. Henry VI. was rescued, and the march was resumed after some delay. The delay and its cause—pillage and excess of all kinds—were fatal to the enterprise, for the Londoners refused, in dread of similar treatment, to either admit the Lancastrian army or to supply it with provisions. Margaret and her army lay at Barnet, unable either to obtain aid from the city or to attack it.

At Gloucester Edward, now Duke of York, heard the fatal news of the battle of Wakefield and of his father's death, while he was there employed in collecting an army.

Starting with all forces at his command, he at once proceeded to Shrewsbury with the intention of intercepting the queen on her march southwards. But a body of Lancastrians under Jasper, Earl of Pembroke, and Sir Owen Tudor

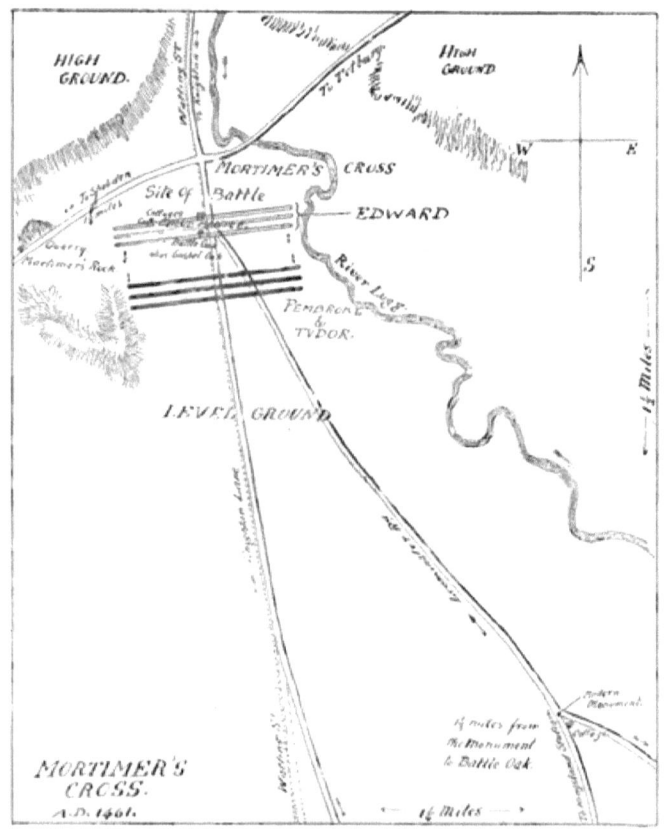

started in pursuit of him, though in no very large force. His own troops were not particularly numerous, and it was obviously the wiser course to turn on his pursuers and, if possible, to defeat them before trying conclusions with the main Lancastrian army under the queen. The third body of

Lancastrians, who had been victorious at Wakefield, were flushed with success, and greatly outnumbered him. Assuming that he prevailed against them, he would yet have Pembroke to deal with, and with weakened forces. Hence he elected to turn off to the west, meeting Pembroke at Mortimer's Cross, a place two miles north by west of Kingsland, and at that time traversed by Watling Street.

The battlefield, a flat plain, is but small. It is bounded on the east by the river Lugg, behind which is a low ridge of hills. The present road, now called Knighton Lane, runs

The Battlefield of Mortimer's Cross. Viewed from the modern monument.

due north and south. North of the battlefield hills also rise, and there are some low ridges for a short distance on the west; a small break to the north-west leads up a valley which beyond is blocked by more hills. To the south the ground is perfectly flat, and though quite open at the time of the battle is in these days cut up into regular parallelograms by hedges. Rather more than a mile away to the south-east, along the Leominster road, at a fork in the way, a stone was erected in the eighteenth century to commemorate the fight. On the battlefield there yet remains a noble old oak, much split by age but carefully protected from other injury by an iron bar. This oak is known as the "battle oak" (sometimes as the Gospel Oak). From its size at the butt and general appearance it certainly appears to have quite the antiquity that is claimed for it. Near to this oak are two ancient cottages which bear the quaint name of "Blue Mantle." It has not, however, been possible to ascertain whether the name has any connection with some tradition as to the fight. The battle takes its name of Mortimer's Cross from the tiny hamlet at the cross-roads where the ways to Hereford and to Tetbury intersect.

The young Duke of York turned off on his march to Shrewsbury, and, as it were, doubled on his pursuers who were on Watling Street. Pembroke's army consisted of Welsh and Irish, and were, it is said, inferior troops. The opposing forces came into collision on the morning of Candlemas Day, 1461. Edward was superior in numbers and attacked with vigour, employing the ordinary dispositions of the time. His superiority, especially in archers, soon told, and the Lancastrians were quickly overcome. Three thousand eight hundred men perished either in the fight or in the brief pursuit. Pembroke escaped, but Sir Owen Tudor, his father, was taken, and shortly afterwards beheaded. The Yorkist loss was very slight, thanks to the effect of the archers. According to a legend there was an appearance of three suns in the sky on the morning of the battle. Edward hailed this as an omen of good fortune, and henceforward added the rays of the sun to the old White Rose badge, thus forming the well-known rose-en-soleil (*vide* initial).

MORTIMER'S CROSS AND TOWTON.

This fight took place on February 2nd, thirty-four days after the defeat and death of Richard, Duke of York, at Wakefield. The victory at Mortimer's Cross, however, changed the plans of Edward. A few days had been lost, and the queen was nearer to her goal, the city of London. Hence, abandoning his first design, Edward marched with as much speed as he could on the city. On his way through Oxfordshire

he was joined by Warwick, who at Chipping Norton had reorganised his troops. Warwick's defeat by the queen at St. Albans took place on February 17th, and it must therefore have taken Edward nearly three weeks to traverse the sixty miles between Mortimer's Cross and Chipping Norton. It may be noted that the latter place is not ten miles north of the direct line between Mortimer's Cross and London, and is equidistant from both. With augmented forces he was now sixty miles from the city, while the queen was little more than twenty. As has already been explained, the Lancastrians never got further south than Barnet. Edward pressed on without turning aside to give battle, rightly deeming the possession of the capital of far greater consequence. He entered London on February 28th, where he was received with acclamation.

Disheartened and not awaiting the Yorkist attack, the Lancastrian army retreated to their northern stronghold, York, and prepared for the battle which was inevitable. The possession of London gave Edward a considerable increase in men, and, what was even a greater necessity, money. The Duke of Norfolk set forth on March 5th to raise troops among his retainers. Two days later Warwick, with the vanguard of the Yorkist army, started northwards, to be followed after an interval of four days by the main body of the infantry, and on the 13th the rearguard, commanded by Edward in person, left the city. The retreat of the Lancastrians, following as it did on the excesses committed by them when victorious, soon bore fruit, and large accessions of men flocked to the Yorkists as they marched.

A rendezvous had been appointed for Pontefract, about twenty-one miles south-west by south of York, and there the army, which numbered 40,660 men, encamped near the Bubwith Bridge—a spot adapted for a large encampment, being well watered by the Pontefract Beck. When the news of the Yorkist approach reached the Lancastrians at York, immediate preparations were made for battle, the only point requiring

MORTIMER'S CROSS AND TOWTON.

decision being, where the stand should be made. A position was selected on Towton Heath, about two miles south of Tadcaster and twelve from York. The precise date of the arrival of Edward at Pontefract can only be inferred, but it may be reasonably set down as being between the 20th and 25th of March.

The first care of the Yorkist leader was to secure the important ford over the Aire at Ferrybridge, a village two and a half miles north-north-east of Pontefract, to effect which a detachment of men was sent thither under the command of Lord FitzWalter. The passage was secured and duly guarded. At dawn on March 27th Lord Clifford, having made a rapid night march from the Lancastrian camp at Towton—a distance of ten miles to the south—surprised the guard, almost exterminating them, FitzWalter and the bastard brother of the Earl of Warwick both being slain. Clifford, *alias* "The Butcher," on this occasion commanded a picked body of the men of Craven, composed of his own vassals, for in Skipton of Craven the Yorkshire stronghold of the Cliffords stood.

CLIFFORD.

News of this reverse caused great consternation in the Yorkist camp, and, according to ancient accounts, led to a strange declaration on the part of Warwick, who, to emphasise his oath of fidelity, dismounted and slew his horse. Edward at the same time by proclamation gave license to depart to all those who preferred running away to fighting. Traditionally, not one man is reported to have availed himself of the offer.

Active measures were at once taken to, if possible, regain the ford, at first without success. On the failure of a direct attack the Yorkist detachment was divided. One portion marched to Castleford, a village four miles north-west by north of Pontefract, where it crossed the river Aire and turned back along its banks towards Ferrybridge, the remainder awaiting their arrival to deliver a double attack. Meanwhile the bulk of the Yorkist army marched *via* Castleford towards Towton, and by the following day (March 28th) the advanced guard had reached Dintingdale, a spot between Scarthingwell and Saxton, and distant about a mile to the east of the latter. Clifford had, however, been watchful, and, either through becoming acquainted with the manœuvres of his opponents or suspecting them, found it wiser to fall back on the Lancastrian army at Towton. But he was hemmed in, and in the skirmish which ensued on Saturday evening, March 28th, between his retreating force and the Yorkist advanced guard at Dintingdale Clifford fell, and, with two or three exceptions only, his entire force perished with him.

John de Clifford, 9th Baron Clifford, was born in 1435 or 1436. He is first heard of at the head of a body of troops outside the walls of London, clamouring for compensation for the death of his father at the first battle of St. Albans. He obtained his petition, the Yorkist leaders being compelled to establish masses for the souls of the slain, and also to pay a sum of money to their representatives. Clifford now became Yorkist in his sympathies, and was attainted after Blore Heath. Restored to favour, he was appointed commissary

MORTIMER'S CROSS AND TOWTON.

general of the Scotch Marches. In 1460 he was summoned to parliament as a peer. At Wakefield in December of that year he was a Lancastrian leader. Tradition credits him with the murder of the Earl of Rutland and the decapitation of the dead body of the Duke of York; hence his name of "the Butcher." Clifford fought at the second battle of St. Albans, and was slain six weeks later, the night before Towton. By the corner of the road leading from Scarthingwell to Saxton at the present time stands the socket of a wayside cross. Can this be a relic of some long-forgotten memorial to "Butcher" Clifford? Traditionally, his body was never found, but is believed to have been buried in a common pit close to the road at Dintingdale. The discomfiture and death of Clifford at Dintingdale brings

SOCKET OF THE WAYSIDE CROSS.

us to late in the day of March 28th. During the evening the Yorkist army reached Saxton and took up its position on the south side of the village on a rising ground. It may be well here to consider the respective marching performances of the two armies. December 29, 1460, found the Lancastrians at Pontefract. Thence they marched some nine miles to Wakefield, fought there, and obtained the victory. After the battle as a plundering horde they marched southwards, reaching St. Albans and fighting there on February 17th. From St. Albans they proceeded no farther south than Barnet and then retreated to York, reaching that city some few days before the battle of Towton. The march southwards, accordingly, must have been performed in a leisurely manner, for it occupied at least six weeks. Of the rate of progress northwards there are no records, but as the Yorkists entered London on February 28th and the Lancastrians were then already in retreat, it may well be assumed that about three weeks was occupied in the retrograde movement. And at this computation a few days' rest would be allowed to the army on its arrival in York. Consequently the troops were fresh when the battle took place at Towton. The Yorkists, starting from Gloucester, marched some distance northwards, turned off to fight and defeat Pembroke at Mortimer's Cross, and immediately after the battle marched, *viâ* Chipping Norton to London. The march between Mortimer's Cross and London occupied twenty-six days, an average of rather under five miles per diem. But it is to be remembered that the season was winter, the roads in those days bad, bridges scarce, and not a few rivers flooded. In London the halt occupied from February 28th to March 13th, and the northern march after the Lancastrians, therefore, was accomplished in thirteen days, for by March 26th, at the latest, the Yorkist army was encamped at Pontefract. The rate of progress, therefore, averaged nearly ten miles a day. This northern march was accomplished under far more favourable conditions than the march from Herefordshire. In the first place the trunk road was a good one. Secondly, the people by the way for three-quarters of the distance were friendly, and although undoubtedly supplies of food were not to be had—the Lancastrians having eaten up the country for miles on either side of the road—yet having London as a starting-point and the south of England in general friendly, it is reasonable to suppose that little was lacking to the Yorkists on the northern march. On one point there appears to be doubt, and that is whether the Duke of Norfolk, who left London on March 5th, was able to overtake the army in time to join in the battle. One account tells us that he was sick and unable to lead his troops, another that he managed to bring up a reinforcement at noon on the day of the fight. His march, however, must have been hurried at the last, and it is questionable whether the contingent was in good fighting condition. No details as to the numbers or composition of his force are extant, consequently the Pontefract strength of the Yorkist army, viz., 40,000 men, must be taken as fairly representing their strength, though one estimate puts it as high as 49,000. The Lancastrian force outnumbered their opponents by possibly 20,000 men; one estimate puts their strength as high as 66,000. This, however, is probably an exaggeration —still it may fairly be assumed that a number not far short of 100,000 men were engaged in strife on Palm Sunday, 1461.

The next considerations are the scene of the fight and the disposition of the armies. The village of Towton lies on the York and Doncaster road about three miles south of Tadcaster. North of it a stream called the Cock Beck or Cock River curves round in an easterly direction, running into the river Wharfe near Tadcaster. In ancient times the old London Road branched off to the north-west just north of Towton and crossed the beck by a narrow bridge. The ground both to the north and east of Towton is high and the descent to the beck is very steep. South of Towton and in the direction of Saxton the ground slopes, and at one spot there is a depression known as Towton Dale. A wood called Renshaw Wood crowns the heights above the beck on the east side for nearly half the distance between the villages. A detached wood, by name Castle Hill Wood, in former times called Mayden Castle, fills in a bend of the beck on the same side. The beck then turns to the west, or rather has come from that direction where the little chapel of Lead still stands; and near to it the ruined Lead Hall. The Cock Beck, which plays a most important part in the disaster which befel the Lancastrians, is a narrow, slowly running stream, in no place wider than ten or twelve feet, but with low, level banks of varying width along its course, especially on the east side. These flat banks are liable to flood and it is reasonable to suppose that at the time of the battle they were in flood. Through Renshaw Wood runs a path down to the Cock ford—a ford nearly opposite to which is Cockford Farm and quite opposite to which are traces of long mounds in the field. Cockford bore this name long prior to the battle of Towton, as deeds testify, and was then, as now, belonging to the Vavasours of Hazlewood. Between Renshaw Wood and Mayden Castle, on the opposite side of the river, the fields are known as Hazlewood Ings. Saxton village stands on the Castleford Road. Due east of it is Dintingdale and Scarthingwell, while to the south-east is Barkston.

The Lancastrian army was drawn up south of Towton in

a line which is improbably stated to have extended over a mile in front. The right of the line rested on the heights of Renshaw Wood and with the beck flowing beneath. The centre occupied the ground which is traversed by Towton Lane and the Doncaster Road, while the left wing spread out in the open fields eastward. It is stated, upon no probable ground, that a strong outpost held Mayden Castle, and inspection of the field negatives the idea. The Lancastrian army, it may be observed, was on the defensive and was well posted, with these exceptions: that its line was too extended, and there was a danger, should disaster occur, that the beck might prove the ruin of all concerned. The Yorkist army was, naturally, under the circumstances, the attacking force, though considerably less in numbers.

In the early morning of Palm Sunday, March 29, 1461, the Yorkists marched down to give battle, the Lancastrians quietly awaiting attack. Falconberg, it would appear, commanded the centre or main body, while Edward and the Earl of Warwick divided the wings. With the wind in their backs and in a heavy snowstorm the Yorkists attacked their foes. Falconberg ordered his archers to the front, practically as skirmishers. Curiously enough, it does not appear that the archers of the wings were also sent forward. Aided by the wind their arrows had a greater range than those of the Lancastrians. A few volleys of flight arrows sent at high elevation did great execution and effectually drew the Lancastrian fire. The Yorkist archers were then withdrawn, and the movement being unseen, owing to the blinding snow, volley

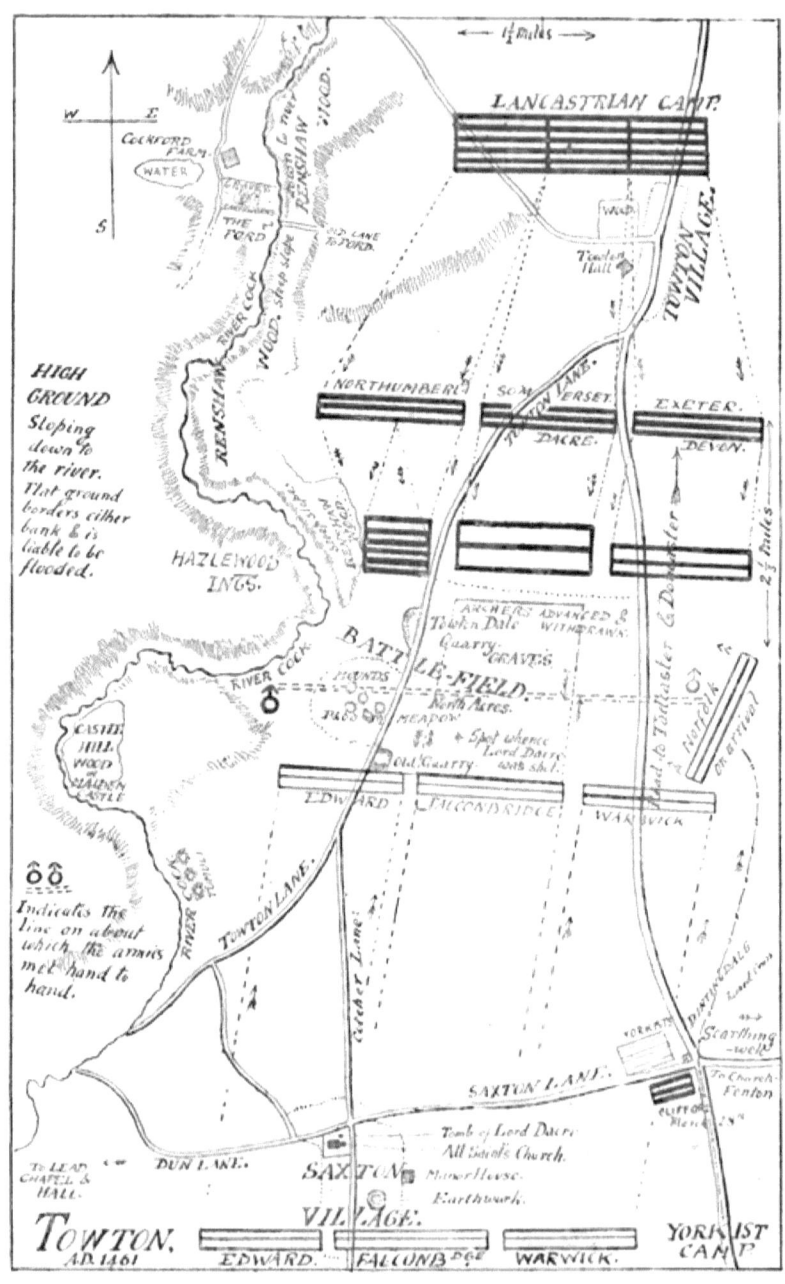

after volley poured from the Lancastrian ranks till the quivers were empty, but not a Yorkist fell. In the snowy field the uselessly expended shafts were sticking up like porcupines' quills. Falconberg then gave the word to advance, and at short range the Yorkist archers not only expended their broad arrows against their luckless antagonists, but also used against them their own wasted shafts which had been gathered as they advanced. A terrible slaughter took place and completely changed the course of the battle, since the Lancastrians were compelled to march down themselves to attack in lieu of acting on the defensive. Bows were laid aside by both armies, and, furiously charging one another, a terrible hand-to-hand conflict ensued. Quarter on either side had been strictly forbidden, and the carnage was appalling.

The chief part of this conflict took place in a field between the two quarries in the present Towton Lane. Here on one side of the road tumuli mark the graves of the slain, while on the other is a patch of ground also traditionally the site of death-pits. The field itself to this day bears the name of the Bloody Meadow, or Vale. Of the part which the Lancastrian detachment at Mayden Castle took in the fight there are no records, and its very existence may be doubted. From its position it should have been able to have attacked the advancing Yorkists on their left flank. Tumuli however, near to the edge of the wood and on the banks of the beck, would point to fighting having taken place in this part of the field. It will be remembered that the advance of the Yorkists began in the early morning, but allowing for the time needful to manœuvre so large a body of men as 40,000, it could hardly have been earlier than eight when the archers were at work. Probably the hand-to-hand conflict began an hour later. As to how long it continued indecisive, accounts differ; some say that not until darkness was coming on were the Lancastrians in full flight; another version, and probably the true one, is that Norfolk, approaching with his troops at noon, managed to fall on the left flank of the Lancastrians, and that after this they began to give way.

At first the Lancastrians, though falling back, did so without disorder, but the narrow extent of the battlefield to the north was a factor which had not been calculated upon. One road alone—that to Tadcaster—existed, and the country eastwards was perfectly open, rendering pursuit a matter of little difficulty. Probably for this reason the line of retreat was deflected westwards towards the Cock River. A bridge which, it is said, once stood here has been described as the spot at which the passage was intended to be made and where the great slaughter of fugitives took place. The existence of this bridge in 1461 is, however, doubted. An alternative spot suggested is the ford at Cockford Farm, and the mounds in the field opposite give some corroboration to this view. How the retreat became a rout is as follows: The wings, especially the left wing, gave way before the centre and were gradually bent back on Towton. They began to retreat and became intermingled. At this juncture the centre gave way, pressed on the already retreating wings, and all three became inextricably mixed up. The baggage guard, which does not appear to have taken any active part in the fight, now being north of Towton, blocked the way to Tadcaster and hence the turn westwards towards the Cock Beck. To have sought the Cock Bridge (even if it existed) the fugitives must have safely passed through Towton, which they do not appear to have done. The Cock ford is situated now, and was then existing, at the same spot, due west of the village. Fugitives running along the flat banks or attempting to cross the beck stepped suddenly

into the deep channel. Wounded, weighted with weapons or armour, it is not to be wondered that the stream was soon blocked and that a bridge of drowned or slain enabled pursuers and pursued alike to cross. During the whole night and during the following day the pursuit of the fugitives was continued, mainly in the direction of York, whither all seemed to go. How many in all were slain at this fearful battle, how many in the flight, and how many at the beck, has been variously estimated. More than 30,000 bodies were by tradition buried near to the field of battle. The heralds, it is stated, "numbered" 28,000 dead. Of these not more than a fourth belonged to the victorious party.

The traditions, most of them worthy of credit, which yet linger around the field of Towton, are not without interest. In Saxton Churchyard the restored tomb of Ranulph de Dacre—Baron Dacre of Gillesland—is still to be seen. He was buried there with his horse, a fact proved without doubt. The mouldering original heraldry on its sides is interesting, and its blazon is

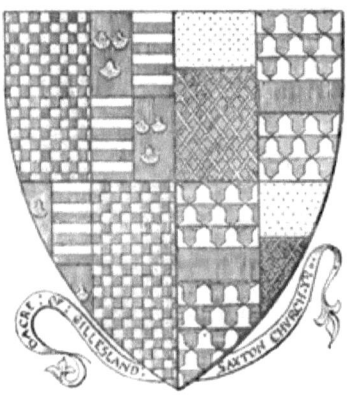

as follows: "North. Quarterly 1 and 4 chequey, or and gules (Vaux); 2 and 3 Quarterly, 1 and 4, gules, three escallops or (Dacre); 2 and 3, barry of eight, argent and gules (Multon); impaling Quarterly, 1 and 4, azure, fretty or, a chief of the second (Fitzhugh); 2 and 3, Vair, argent and azure, a fess gules (Marmion). The south side bears Quarterly, 1 and 4, Vaux; 2 and 3, Dacre. The east and west faces are alike and bear Quarterly, 1 and 4, Vaux; 2 and 3 Dacre. The original inscription is now not to be deciphered, but is reported to have been: "Hic Jacet Ranulphus dominus de dakar et gillesland verus miles et strenuus in bello pro rege Henrico VI. anno domini MCCCCLXI die mensis marcii videlicet dominica ramis palmarum cujus animae propicietur deus amen." Tradition tells that Lord

MORTIMER'S CROSS AND TOWTON.

Dacre was shot by a boy "hidden in a bur tree," *i.e.*, an elderbush. He had taken off his helmet to drink. The spot where this took place is yet pointed out in the field called North Acres. Rude incised crosses now built into Saxton Church Tower are said originally to have marked tombs of the slain. Round and about the graves in the field the little white and red roses even yet grow, though it is a vulgar error to suppose that this "Rosa spinosissima" only flourishes on the battlefield of Towton. It is a pretty little flower (now, alas! growing scarcer each year), with white petals, each flaked with a crimson dash. At Towton, on a spot now known as Chapel Garth, Richard III. began to build a great chapel "in token of prayer" and for the souls of the slain. Bosworth Field was fought, Richard slain, and the chapel was never completed. Bones in large quantities have been found on the site and also a few relics of carving. Sir Leo de Welles, 6th Baron Welles, was killed and his body conveyed to the church of Methley, a distance of eleven miles south-west of Saxton. Lord Welles had married as his first wife the heiress of Sir Robert Waterton, the founder of a chantry at Methley in 1424. The existing Welles tomb is of alabaster and bears the effigies of Sir Leo and his first wife, Jane Waterton. The second wife of Sir Leo was Margaret, Dowager Countess of Somerset, the mother of Margaret, Countess of Richmond and grandmother of Henry VII. The arms of Lord Welles were or, a lion rampant double queued sable, armed and langued gules.

A curious fact relating to the battle is that no exact record exists which specifies the commanders of the various parts of the defeated army. The most satisfactory account is that the Earl of Northumberland and Sir Andrew Trollope commanded the van while the remainder was divided between the Earl of Somerset, the Duke of Exeter, Lord Dacre and the Earl of Devon. Of these the Earl of Northumberland fell sorely wounded and was conveyed to his house in the Walmgate, York, where he died. His body, in a stone coffin, lies beneath the floor of the north aisle of the church of St. Dionys in York. Henry Percy, 3rd Earl of Northumberland, was the grandson of the celebrated Harry Hotspur, slain at Shrewsbury in 1403. Curious and inexplicable stories are told to this day of the strange noises in the house in the Walmgate, where Northumberland died, which are heard towards the end of March each year and at no other time. Sir Andrew Trollope was killed John Holland, 2nd Duke of Exeter, took refuge in flight, accompanied by the Duke of Somerset. Arrived at York, they joined King Henry, Queen Margaret, and the Prince of Wales, and hastily fled thence to Scotland. The Earl of Devon, the only man of note who is recorded as having been taken prisoner, was subsequently beheaded at York. Thomas Courtenay, 6th Earl of Devon, was born about the year 1432. It is noteworthy that both of the younger brothers of the earl died for the Lancastrian cause, Henry being beheaded in 1466 and John being slain at Tewkesbury. Besides these leaders a long list of men of rank that fell at the battle is extant. From the Act of Attainder a much more extended list can be formed, since it gives the names of many of those of lower degree known to have taken part in the fight. This bill includes 12 noblemen and 153 knights, squires, and yeomen, &c. The names of a few of the clergy occur and that of a certain Thomas Litley, late of London, grocer.

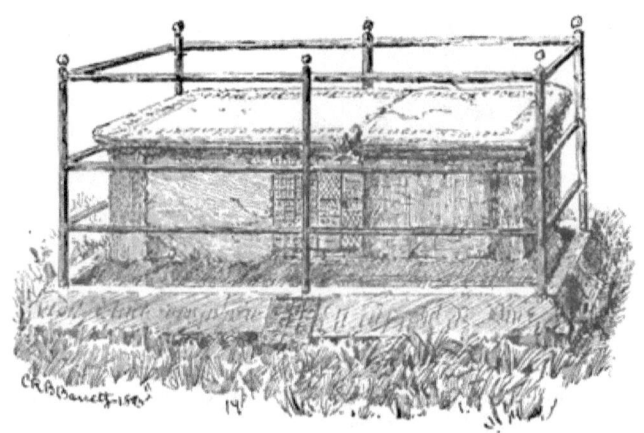

TOMB OF LORD DACRE, SAXTON CHURCHYARD.

CHAPTER XVII.

HEDGELEY MOOR.	HEXHAM.
April 25, 1464.	*May* 8, 1464.

THE details accessible in these days with regard to both these battles are unfortunately very scanty. Why this should be so is rather inexplicable, seeing that though the forces engaged were upon neither occasion very large yet the results were highly important, especially in the case of the victory on Hexham Levels. Both battles were won by the Yorkists, and both were won by the same commander, John, Baron Neville of Montague, the younger brother of the celebrated Warwick. In the battle of Hedgeley Moor, Sir Ralph Percy, through the treachery of Lord Hungerford and Lord Ros, suffered defeat, and met with his death. After the battle of Hexham, and within a few days, these two lords, taken captive, were executed. By some error, or rather through a series of errors, the date assigned to the battle of Hexham was for years variously misstated. Legend and tradition, entirely unwarranted by now known historic fact, has wound around the

Percy Badge. Carved by a prisoner in Carlisle Castle.

Lancastrian defeat strange and romantic tales, and for this, in all probability, the loose method in which the old chronicles were frequently put together is responsible.

The position of affairs in 1464 was briefly this: A truce had been entered into with France, which was to take effect until October 1st. A similar engagement had been entered into with Scotland. By these diplomatic means Edward IV. hoped to gain breathing-time to consolidate his own strength, and, what was even more important, to weaken the power for harm possessed by the Lancastrian faction. Better still, he might obtain opportunities to destroy in detail those Lancastrian leaders who had not sought safety in foreign lands. France and Scotland might yet afford them an asylum, nay, might even abet them in future attempts at the subversion of his rule; but for a few months at least could neither actively co-operate with them, nor even overtly supply malcontents with money, ships, men, or arms.

The three castles of Alnwick, Bamburgh, and Dunstanburgh, all situated in the Lancastrian County of Northumberland, were at the end of 1463 still in the hands of adherents of the Red Rose. Possibly also a few isolated strongholds in various parts of the country were similarly held. But it was in the north in the main, and in Northumberland in particular, that danger was to be apprehended, and to avert this danger and crush his foes while he had the time allowed him, was the task which Edward set himself to accomplish.

Parliament, already adjourned, was further prorogued until February 20th, and was summoned to meet on that day at York.

It met, but was again prorogued until May 5th. Before the date of session arrived, however, the battle of Hedgeley Moor had been won, while Hexham was fought three days later. Lancastrian resistance was thus crushed; so crushed that not until 1471 was it possible for the conquered again to place a force in the field; when the fatal defeat at Tewkesbury finally extinguished all hope.

In April, 1464, two bodies of Lancastrians took the field in Northumberland. United, their forces would not have

PERCY'S LEAP.

amounted numerically to anything like a respectable army; but Edward knew by experience how strangely armies grew in those days; knew, too, that if his own troops suffered defeat or even check, the consequences would be most serious. Hence his resolve was to destroy his adversaries in detail. His chance of so doing was greater, as the force at his command would have outnumbered the united Lancastrian bands, and these at the time had not effected a junction. Sending Lord Montague ahead towards Northumberland with a small but efficient force, and,

HEDGELEY MOOR AND HEXHAM.

promising a further reinforcement, Edward himself started for the north. At this juncture the Lancastrians seized the castles of Norham, in Northumberland, and Skipton, in Yorkshire. Matters looked more serious, and the movement was evidently spreading.

Montague advanced as far as Durham, where he waited for

PERCY'S ADVANCE. LEAP ON LEFT.

the promised reinforcements, and these duly arrived. He then proceeded on his mission. Further north he struck on to the old Roman road known as the Devil's Causeway, and thereon at Hedgeley Moor, not far south of Wooler, he came upon one of the two Lancastrian armies then in arms.

This force, commanded, according to one account, by Lord Hungerford, to another by Lord Hungerford and Lord Ros, to a third by Sir Ralph Percy, was drawn up facing south. The battlefield, which lies mainly on the west side of the present road, is small. One side of it is now bounded by the railway for some distance, and to the east of the railway the ground is flat and still marshy. On the west, undulating ground gradually rises till the extreme distance is bounded by lofty hills. No details as to the actual numbers engaged have come down to us, the formation and disposition

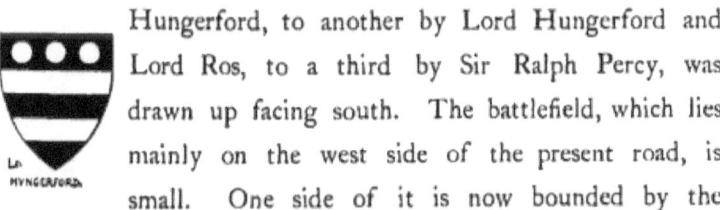

of the troops is unrecorded, and facts are sadly wanting. All accounts, however, agree in admitting that when the armies came in view of one another, the Lancastrians were greatly outnumbered by their foes. At the first

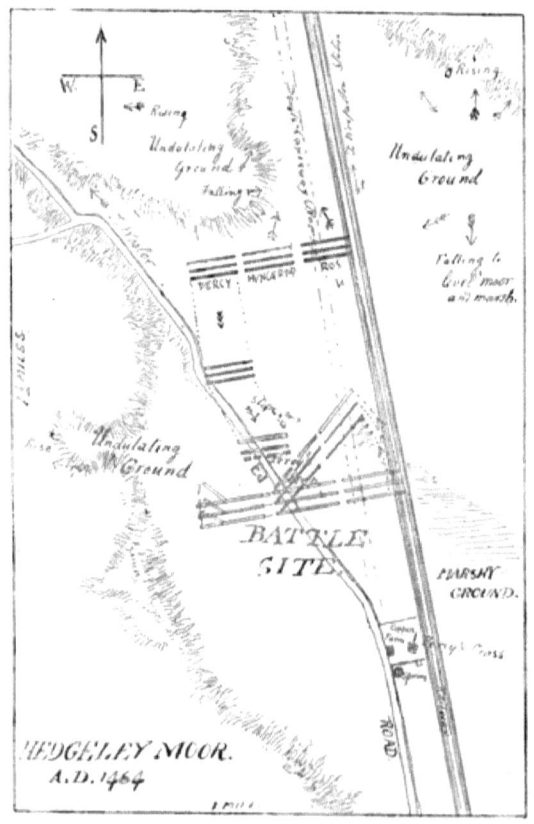

onset, either through cowardice, treachery, or for private revenge, the Hungerford and Ros sections of the force fled from the field with their leaders, leaving Percy to bear the brunt of the onslaught, supported merely by his personal retainers and scanty power. The Yorkists then attempted to surround the little band. Percy, with his wonted gallantry, charged in an attempt to cut his way through at all hazards. Had he succeeded in this he might have ridden along the Devil's Causeway to Hexham, where, or near where, at that time Somerset, with King Henry, was encamped. It is probable that he had partially succeeded when his horse unfortunately was wounded. According to tradition the animal made a gigantic bound at a spot still marked by two boulders. Percy was himself almost immediately wounded, and was afterwards dismounted. He died, or was despatched, at the place where

HEDGELEY MOOR.

now the interesting Percy Cross stands. The story goes that water was fetched from a well near to revive the fallen warrior. The relics of his band fell either near the leap or in the marshy ground.

The Percy Cross, now well protected by a strong iron railing, is full of interest, and is to be found at the edge of a little plantation. Among the various battle crosses in England, it is perhaps the most authentic and the best preserved, especially heraldically. Its tapering shaft is decorated with the Percy badge, "a shackle bolt within a crescent," and also with the Lucie badge, a "luce" or pike. This Percy badge, it may be observed, also appears among the prisoners' carvings in the keep of Carlisle Castle. It will be hardly credited that an enterprising antiquary once endeavoured to show that this Percy Cross was originally a Roman milestone! Brought, however, face to face with the Percy and Lucie badges, he appears to have held that they were subsequently carved thereon in relief. Imagine a Percy erecting in the fifteenth century a second-hand memorial on a battlefield! The Percy family came to adopt the Lucie badge in addition to their own in this way. The father of Hotspur married Maud, daughter of Thomas de Lucie, second Baron, and widow of Gilbert de Umfraville, Earl of Angus. On the marriage it was settled that if she, either by her marriage with Percy, or, if surviving him, by any subsequent marriage, should leave no children, then Hotspur should inherit her Lucie estates, adopting therewith the Lucie arms in addition to his paternal coat. The family honours forfeited under the attainder of the 1st Earl of Northumberland, slain in a skirmish at Bramham Moor, 1407-8, were restored in 1414 to his grandson, Hotspur's only son. This Henry, second earl, married Lady Alianore Neville, daughter of the 1st Earl of Westmoreland, and had "ix. sonnes and iii. daughters." Of these sons, Ralph, who perished at Hedgeley, was the seventh. Sir Ralph Percy died unmarried at the age of thirty-nine. He does not appear to have performed any great military achievement, or at least is credited with none. As the leader of the Percy faction he was much engaged in the family wars against the Nevilles.

After the victory Lord Montague presumably turned his

HEDGELEY MOOR AND HEXHAM.

face southwards and followed the Devil's Causeway, a road running south from Berwick-on-Tweed to the Roman wall near Chollerford, where it joins Watling Street. How far he

PERCY'S CROSS (RAILING OMITTED).

had proceeded on his march before receiving accurate intelligence of the Lancastrian camp on Hexham Levels, near Linnel's Bridge, and of the presence therein of Henry VI., is not apparent. The distance is forty miles, and this was covered between the 25th of April and the 8th of May, a very slow rate of progress indeed when compared with other marching feats at the same period.

The battlefield at Hexham Levels is a beautiful spot situated two miles south-east of Hexham, that interesting and historic town. On the haughs or fields the King and Somerset lay encamped, having at their back the celebrated Devil's Water, which curves round, and on the west of the position has its stream increased by the West Dipton Burn. These united, continue their course in these days beneath the early sixteenth century Linnel's Bridge (1530), passing thence in a north-easterly direction through the historically romantic Dilston Estate, memorable as the ancestral home of the luckless Earl of Derwentwater. Beneath the beautiful one-arch bridge belonging to the castle—a castle of which but an unimportant fragment and the tiny chapel only remain—the stream rushes on, passing next under Dilston Bridge, and thence into the Tyne at a spot one mile west of Corbridge. The whole district teems with poetic legend and romance, and the natural beauty of the steep wooded banks of these streams, though on a small scale, is full of charm.

In view of the Queen Margaret Legends, which, through chroniclers' errors, have come to be accepted far and wide as absolute fact, special notice should be paid to the course of these two streams. Somerset, whose forces were very scanty, had in the camp the old King Henry VI., who had accompanied the duke from Scotland. Queen Margaret was not at Hexham, neither was the "faithful" De Brezé, and hence the romantic legends of the well, the robber, and the Queen's Cave must be entirely rejected, despite the strong local traditions.

The facts are as follows with regard to the movements of Queen Margaret. In 1463 she was in Northumberland in sad poverty after the first surrender of Alnwick. De Brezé was also with her. These two, in company with some two hundred followers and seven of Margaret's waiting-women, sailed from Bamburgh in 1463 and landed at Sluys. The Queen was penniless, and the relics of the fortune of De Brezé were

HEXHAM LEVELS.

employed to keep her from starvation. From Sluys Margaret went to Bruges and finally to France, where for seven years she lived in poverty, until March 24, 1471, at St. Michel-en-Barrois.

Montague with his superior force appeared on the morning of May 8, 1464, on the ridge above the camp and to the south-east of it, having crossed the Tyne at the best available spot, viz. Corbridge, though Bywell has been suggested. There does not appear to be any other possible route open to him, for had he come *via* Hexham it would have been needful to have crossed the Devil's Water, which, with its precipitous banks, would have been no easy task. By marching as he did, on the other hand, he had not only no stream to cross himself, but he had in the rear of his enemy this steep-banked rushing torrent. The fight—it can hardly be designated a battle—was short and bloody while it lasted. Soon the Lancastrians were scattered in flight, though how they got over that stream

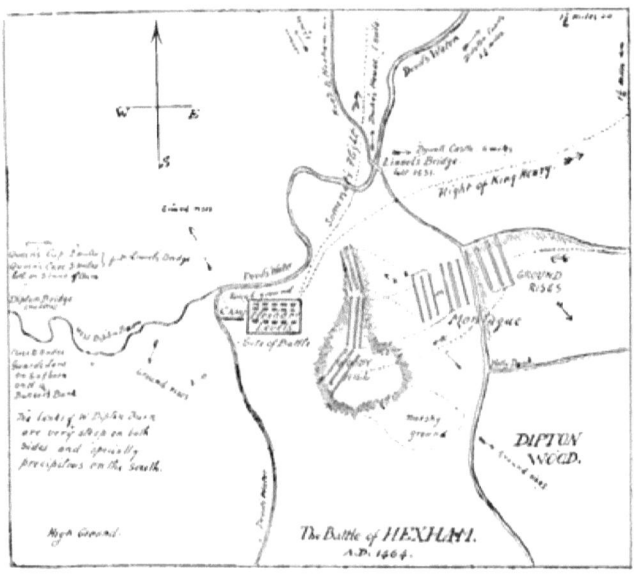

is somewhat a mystery. Somerset, wounded, was captured in a small house one mile to the north. Part of this house is said to exist, though modernised. The modern mansion "Duke's House" perpetuates the memory. Henry VI. rode off at full speed with a few attendants, and was hotly pursued. He, however, made good his escape, crossing the Tyne at Bywell, distant six miles due east of Linnel's Bridge. Bywell

Castle, of which the interesting gatehouse remains, was at that time the possession of Ralph, 5th Baron Neville of Raby and 2nd Earl of Westmorland. At Bywell there was at that period a Roman bridge, the last relics of which disappeared only a few years ago. In the pursuit of King Henry, some of his pages or followers were overtaken and captured, one of whom had in his possession the king's "bycocket," or cap of estate. This word has been corrupted into "abacot" by various writers; others call it "abocoked," others "avococket." The "bycocket," or cap of estate, of Henry VI. was "garnysshed with two crownes of golde and fret wyth perle and riche stone." The pages are described as having their horses "trapped in blew velvet." The "man-lion" from the Standard of Fitz-walter *temp.* Henry VII. wears a "bycocket," or what we now call a cap of estate or maintenance (*vide* tailpiece).

Now it will be observed that Henry fled due east, while Margaret's Cup and Cave lie due west, and to reach either of these the woody defile through which the rushing Devil's Water takes its course would need to be crossed. Then the even steeper West Dipton Burn would remain. That fugitives reached this West Dipton Burn may be conjectured from the place-names Guards Lane and Butcher Bank, which occur close to the present Dipton Bridge. But between the Burn, below the Queen's Cup and the Queen's Cave, it is needful to cross the stream more than a dozen times, when the water is low, on shaky stepping-stones, but when in flood by wading. Is it possible that a delicately reared woman with a child of tender years, even if accompanied by the faithful De Brezé, could

THE TRADITIONAL QUEEN'S CUP.

HEDGELEY MOOR AND HEXHAM.

have accomplished this feat? As it is, we know she did not. The spots are romantic, the little hollowed stone cup is ever full of fresh water which trickles into it; but the cave is now almost filled up, and to effect an entrance it is needful to crawl. In no place is it possible to stand upright therein. With the ascertained and romantic story of the wanderings of Henry VI. we have here nothing to do, nor need the story of his recapture be related.

THE TRADITIONAL QUEEN'S CAVE.

Somerset, captured, was executed at Hexham, and his body is believed to lie somewhere within the precincts of the grand old abbey church there. Lord Hungerford and Molines was taken prisoner, conveyed to Newcastle and there executed. Other sufferers were Sir Thomas Wentworth, Sir Thomas Hussey, Sir John Fynderne, and Sir Ralph Grey, the last-named having been degraded from knighthood before execution. His gilt spurs were hacked off, his sword broken and his shield reversed. In Metcalfe's "Book of Knights" is the entry: "Sr Rauf Grey was a Knight of the Bathe as it appeereth by his disgradynge in Anno 4 Edward IV., but where and when he was made inquiratur." Ralph Grey had deserted the Yorkists, for whom he had done good service in past years. In 1463, after the capture of Alnwick (first siege), he expected to be made governor, but was only made constable, Sir John Ashley receiving the superior post. Grey subsequently became Lancastrian. Sir John Neville (Lord Montague) was the third son of Richard Neville, Earl of Salisbury (new creation), by Lady Alice Montacute, daughter and heir of Thomas Montacute, Earl of Salisbury (old creation), and was the younger brother of Warwick. At first Yorkist, he was rewarded by the Earldom of Northumberland when Percy fled to Scotland, his previous title having been Baron Neville of Montague. Later on the king was reconciled to Percy and desired or thought it politic to restore to him his honours. Neville surrendered the earldom in consequence, and was recompensed by the augmented title of Marquis of Montague. In 1471 he sided with his brother in the attempt to restore Henry VI., and fell with him at Barnet on April 14th. Henry Beaufort, 2nd Duke of Somerset, K.G., served his king as governor of the Isle of Wight with the castle of Carisbroke, and also as governor of Calais. He accompanied Henry VI. in his flight from York after Towton, and is accused of abandoning him at Berwick. Having made his peace with Edward IV., possibly by the surrender of Bamburgh Castle, he was taken into favour. Again becoming

Lancastrian, he was in command at Hexham, defeated, captured, and beheaded May 9, 1464. His successor, after an interval, was his brother Edmund, the third and last duke of that creation.

CHAPTER XVIII.

BARNET.

April 14, 1471.

THE COAT-ARMOUR OF RICHARD NEVILLE EARL OF WARWICK & SALISBURY. "THE KING MAKER".

AS an immediate effect of the powerful coalition formed against him by Warwick, Queen Margaret, and the Lancastrian party, Edward IV. was compelled to go into exile. He fled from Lynn, where shipping was seized, accompanied by his brother Richard, Duke of Gloucester, the Lords Rivers, Say, and Hastings, and about 800 followers. After a voyage, in which they had the luck to escape from the pursuit of a fleet of Easterlings, the fugitives landed at Alkmaar well nigh destitute. Edward himself, being unprovided with money, rewarded the master of the vessel in which he had passage with the fur-lined gown from off his back. In Holland a kind reception was afforded by Louis de Bruges, the Burgundian governor, who succoured the party and conveyed Edward to the Hague. Politically the arrival of the fugitives was a source of great embarrassment to Charles, Duke of Burgundy, and for some months he declined to offer more than shelter. On January 2nd, however, a meeting took place between the brothers-in-law at Aire, and they were in close communication for five days : the upshot being that the Duke hired, or supplied the means of hiring, 300 German hand-gun men, collected a fleet of fourteen or seventeen Hanseatic ships to act as an escort, and in addition presented Edward with 50,000 florins in gold.

Edward now actively prepared for a descent on England, and fixed his base at Flushing. He had augmented his original following somewhat during exile, and, together with the 300 Germans, his force at starting amounted to 1,500 men. By March 2nd all was prepared, and the expedition embarked. Contrary winds sprang up and the fleet was unable to move. Propositions were made to disembark again, but these Edward refused to entertain. The men remained on board until March 11th, when at last a start was possible. Preparations of this nature, lasting as they had for a space of nearly two months, were of course known to Warwick, and both on land and sea he took every precaution save one to repel invasion. Warwick's position in England was full of difficulty. Henry VI., in whose name he was ruling, was a puppet. London was more Yorkist than Lancastrian—it had ever been thus ; and Margaret still delayed her return to England despite the various urgent messages sent to her to return. Between Margaret and Warwick any reconciliation could at the best have been but hollow, and mutual mistrust must have existed. Old animosities professedly stifled still remained, and in all probability it was to this that the absence of Margaret was due. But her absence in the event proved fatal to the Lancastrian cause.

Warwick's precautions were these. Under Falconberg a fleet acting from Calais patrolled the Straits of Dover and prepared to defend the Kentish coast. The Earl of Oxford was on the watch with a force in the eastern counties, where the Yorkist influence was strong. The Earls of Montague and Northumberland were expected to provide for the north between Hull and Berwick. Warwick himself, with Henry in his keeping, remained in London, the disaffected seat of government. Of the causes which led to the pronounced Yorkist feeling in the metropolis the following may be mentioned. It had always been the more popular cause there and was so still, but another and more potent reason existed, and this was the question of pocket. The expenditure of Edward had ever been profuse, and his debts there were large. The household of Henry VI had been cut down, and his expenditure was comparatively small. Trade was therefore bad; there was no probability that Edward's debts would ever be paid unless he came to the throne again, hence the empty pockets and unsatisfactory ledgers of the London merchants and traders became a powerful factor in the attitude of the citizens.

Warwick's great mistake was in the divided command in the north. Montague, the ex-earl of Northumberland, and Percy, the reinstated earl, were mutually jealous one of the other, and Percy both politically and from a military point of view was by far the stronger man. Percy's district was in the far north, while Montague had command of the West Riding of Yorkshire. The expedition from Flushing started on March 11th, and on the following day arrived off Cromer.

Here emissaries from the fleet landed, only to return on board with most discouraging intelligence. Oxford was on the alert, prominent Yorkists had been seized and either imprisoned or bound by sureties to remain quiet. Nothing could be done there, and the only course was to put to sea again — but whither? Edward's genius or boldness, or both, came to his aid, and he gave the order to make for the Humber, sailing as it were into the very lion's mouth, for Yorkshire, on that side at least, had always been a stronghold of the Lancastrians. The fleet put to sea only to encounter a heavy gale in the Wash, which scattered the vessels but luckily blew from the south. It took three days before a partial reunion could be effected, but eventually the expeditionary force was landed at various spots on the Yorkshire coast. Edward, with Hastings and 500 men, set foot on the shore at Ravenspur, and in the course of the next night was joined by the remainder of his little army.

It is doubtful whether Edward fancied that he would be received favourably. More probably he counted upon nothing of the kind. As a matter of fact, the population fled from the villages at the very rumour of his approach. But he had gained one great point, an unopposed landing. Hostile villagers without leaders might be neglected, and of Lancastrian leaders in the district there happened to be none. One squire, however, sent off an express to York, and himself with a small band followed the invaders at a distance; but beyond this nothing was done. Edward began his march through what must be deemed a hostile country, and arrived before Hull (sixteen miles), where he found the gates shut and admittance refused, despite the Lancastrian badges assumed by both himself and his followers.

It was then debated whether to cross the mouth of the Humber and march south, or to make for York. Edward determined on the latter course—to cross the estuary would have been as bad as a retreat. Turning due north he went to Beverley (eight to ten miles), and here his reception was equally cold, though he was not absolutely excluded from the town. Leaving Beverley, he marched north-west by west directly on York *via* Market Weighton, a distance of twenty-eight miles, giving out that he merely came to claim his father's duchy of which he had been deprived. Three miles from York, Thomas Conyers, the Recorder of that city, rode out to meet him, and endeavoured with many arguments, but without success, to divert him from his proposed visit. Edward, however, kept on his way, and on the morning of March 18th arrived before the city gates. These he found closed, and the citizens had manned the walls. After a parley in which the story of the recovery of his duchy was again repeated, and all hostility to the king disavowed, Edward with but sixteen followers was admitted into the gates. Proceeding to the minster, he then and there took an oath to the same effect upon the cross at the high altar. Perjury this, of a most inexcusable kind, seeing that he added a disclaimer of ever intending in the future "to take upon himself to be King of England," laying on Warwick the blame of his having done so in the past. The citizens were satisfied, and after some cheering for King Harry and the Prince of Wales, opened the gates, admitting the entire force. Edward remained within the walls of York for twelve hours, and in the early morning of March 19th set forth south-west for Tadcaster.

Meanwhile what had become of Northumberland and Montague? The former levied troops and remained otherwise quiescent, watching events; the latter, with between two and three thousand men, shut himself up in Pontefract, thereby barring the way south along the Trunk Road. Edward's generalship now showed forth. Leaving Tadcaster and proceeding some little distance along the road, he then turned to the south-west, and by means of country tracks reached Sandal Castle (Wakefield), distant twenty miles (about) south-west of Tadcaster and nine miles west by south of Pontefract Castle. He was thus on the left flank of Montague. No intelligible reason can be assigned for the neglect of Montague to prevent this manœuvre other than that he was incompetent. His force was superior by several hundred men, and hence weakness cannot be urged in excuse.

Hitherto Edward's success had been of the negative order, but at Sandal his force gained a most welcome addition, drawn from the men in days gone by his own retainers. Leaving Pontefract on his left he then started south-east for Doncaster (twenty miles), reaching that town on March 21st. Two days later he arrived at Nottingham (about forty-five miles), having gained various small accessions of strength by the way. At Nottingham Sir James Harrington and Sir William Parr brought him six hundred well-appointed men at arms.

The position was now somewhat favourable. Montague and Northumberland had done nothing active to stay the invader, and were apparently intending to do nothing. Warwick was in London, and Edward with a rapidly increasing force at Nottingham. Warwick realised his danger, and at once prepared to take the field. On March 22nd he started for Warwick to raise his own men, sending Clarence on a like errand to Gloucester and Wilts, and Somerset into the south-west. The Earl of Oxford had some 4,000 men at Lynn already raised from Norfolk, Suffolk, and Cambridgeshire. Warwick's plan was to march on Newark from Warwick and, if possible, meet Edward before his force assumed greater proportions. Oxford was ordered up from the east for a flank attack, and Montague from the north to fall on the enemy's rear: a reasonable plan of campaign under ordinary circumstances, but Warwick had to deal with Edward, and Edward was far and away his military superior.

Oxford, who, in addition to his own force of 4,000 men, had been joined by the Duke of Exeter and Lord Bardolph, duly marched to Newark, where he established himself, so that one of the Lancastrian trio of commanders at the outset followed the plan of Warwick. Edward foreseeing danger, and most imminent danger should the various forces of the enemy combine or make a combined attack, resolutely set himself to destroy, or at least check, them in detail. He had now between 5,000 and 6,000 men, and, leaving Nottingham, made for Newark. Oxford did not await his

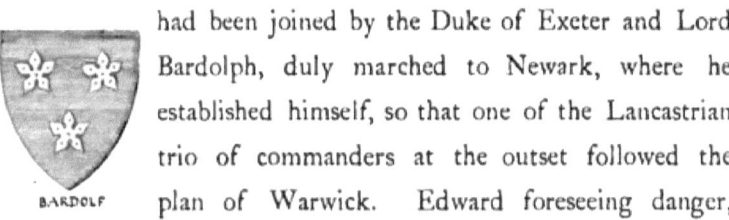
BARDOLF

attack, but retired thirty miles south-west by south to Stamford, on the borders of Lincolnshire. Edward did not pursue, but, satisfied with the result, returned to Nottingham. His route to Newark is not known for a certainty, but as speed was needful, it seems probable that he marched west till he cut the Roman Foss Way and then turned to the north-east. The line of retreat of Oxford would have been by way of Grantham.

By this time Edward had found it convenient to forget his oath at York and openly claimed the crown, announcing his intention to take it by force. Marching due south, he now made for Leicester, and here numbers came flocking in to join his standard. Hastings raised from among his own retainers no less than 3,000 men. The Yorkist army, already too powerful for Oxford on the left flank, now with increased strength advanced towards Warwick, and Warwick they outnumbered in the proportion of ten to six.

Edward left Leicester on March 28th, and on the same day Warwick advanced to the town of Coventry. On the morrow the opposing forces were nearer one another, in fact within sight, and both sides looked for a battle. Warwick, however, knew the superiority in numbers of the Yorkists, and probably in his heart admitted the military superiority of their commander. He declined battle and withdrew into Coventry, there to avail the reinforcements from the north now overdue. Edward tarried not to besiege the place, but by a rapid march slipped by Coventry, seized the town of Warwick, and then, marching south-west, drew up his force a few miles north of Banbury across the road which leads from Coventry through Banbury and Oxford to London. Warwick was thus not only cut off from the shortest road to the city, but Edward had a brief space in which to take breath.

Clarence, it will be remembered, had been sent by Warwick into Gloucester and Wilts to raise forces, and was now returning at the head of 7,000 men, ostensibly to join Warwick. The story of his desertion is well known and need not be retold; suffice it to say that he joined his brother at the camp on the London Road a few miles north of Banbury on April 3rd. News of his defection reached Warwick in Coventry on the following day. Oxford with his 4,000 men had meanwhile joined Warwick, but Montague was still some distance off. Edward returning northwards with an army now totalling about 18,000 men, accompanied by Clarence and his brother Gloucester, drew up in battle array on April 5th outside Coventry. Again Warwick refused to fight, though Somerset, with nearly 8,000 men from the south-west, was within fifty miles and Montague was now quite close. His decision was wise in one way, for the situation was critical; it was, however, fatal in another, as the result will show. Warwick undoubtedly was not strong enough to fight, but he might have so occupied Edward outside Coventry as to detain him there. As it was, by his entirely declining battle, Edward was enabled to turn south; and with the utmost rapidity marched along Watling Street to London. On April 7th he was at Daventry, on the 10th at St. Albans, and on the following day was again master of the metropolis. Of the intrigues within the city, just prior to his return, no mention need here be made.

On April 12th Bourchier, the Earl of Essex, Archbishop Bourchier and Lord Berners, with other notable Yorkists, arrived with a further contingent of 7,000 men, that had been raised in the eastern counties as soon as Oxford's force was withdrawn. The morrow saw Edward again in the field, as in the afternoon he sallied forth to meet the advancing Lancastrians under Warwick.

Warwick throughout this whole campaign had met with nothing but misfortune. Somerset had taken an unconscionable time in bringing up his levies, especially over the last fifty miles of his march. A detachment left by Edward on the road for the purpose of harassing Warwick's column had zealously performed its duty, and his march was hindered considerably thereby. He reached Dunstable, *via* Watling Street, on the evening of April 11th, where news reached him of the capture of London and the other events which had occurred there. At once Warwick made for St. Albans, and then turned south-east. His intention probably was to block the Ermine Street, thus preventing reinforcements from the Midlands from reaching Edward. All other portions of the kingdom had now done their worst, and this alone remained.

On the night of Saturday, April 13th, his army, drawn up in battle order, was at Monken Hadley. All that night the force was under arms, the men lying in their ranks behind a long line of hedges, beyond which on their front was an expanse known as Gladmore Heath. As a precaution a picket was placed in the town of Chipping Barnet, distant one mile on the road to London. During the night the Yorkist army reached Barnet, and, at once dislodging Warwick's picket, pressed forward. To Edward it was all important to find Warwick, and, what is more, when found to make him fight. The picket, chased by a party of Yorkists, fled back to the main body, and hence the position was discovered. Edward, on the arrival of his troops, drew them up in battle order immediately facing, as he thought, the army of Warwick, but in the lower ground beneath the road. The night, however, was dark, and it appears that Edward's right wing extended beyond Warwick's left wing, while Warwick's right wing similarly projected beyond Edward's left. In the obscurity Warwick opened a cannonade as soon as he discovered the enemy, but his guns were mainly posted on his right, probably because thence the first attack might be expected, and consequently did no damage to the Yorkists.

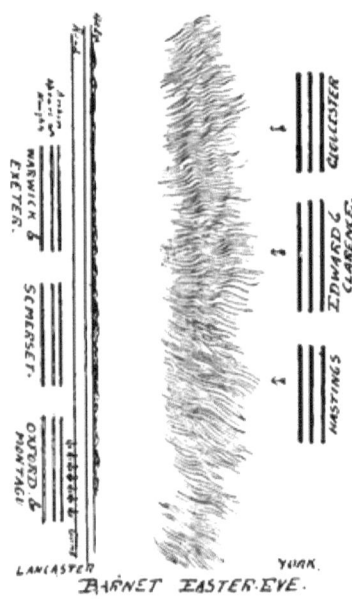
BARNET EASTER-EVE.

On the morning of the 14th (Easter Sunday) both armies were hidden from each other by a heavy fog, a fog which concealed friend from foe and almost friend from friend.

Edward, commanding Clarence's troops in the centre, and having Clarence with them (probably for prudential reasons), gave the right wing to Gloucester, his young brother, and the left to Hastings. Warwick with Exeter led the left wing of the Lancastrians, Montague and Oxford the right wing, and Somerset the centre. The composition of this line of battle was perhaps the most curious of all during the Wars of the Roses. Men who a dozen times had been ranged against each other, who had in cold blood executed one another's relatives, sacked one another's castles and houses, and ravaged one another's manors and estates, were now fighting side by side, and it must be admitted not without considerable suspicions of the fidelity of one another.

·VERE·

In the fog, at between 4 and 5 a.m., this extraordinary battle began, and, it must be added, with caution ; for the advance in lieu of a charge was on both sides at the slowest possible pace, the army of Edward having to ascend a rising ground. Presently those immediately opposing one another were dimly visible, and archers and cannon opened the ball. But at no time during this day was the whole of one line visible. Gradually closing on one another, at length the two lines met throughout their length in hand-to-hand fight. As was to be expected, Montague and the men of the north and the eastern counties were able to outflank Hastings, and did so. Not only this, but they routed him, chasing the fugitives in disorder down as far as Barnet. Gloucester, on the Yorkist right, outflanked Warwick, and forced him back somewhat. Both these events happened without even the commanders of either Yorkist or Lancastrian centres being aware that disaster had occurred. Such was the effect of the fog, and as far as Edward was concerned it probably saved him. No panic ensued; Oxford pursued the fugitive left wing without heeding the battle. Edward and Clarence pressing Somerset hard in the centre, were rather getting the better of their contest with the west country bowmen and billmen. Montague, with his men more in hand, appears to have skirted round and given assistance to the Lancastrian left. Oxford at length seems to have pulled up and bethought himself of the battle and a return to the field. Shouting—for of this there was plenty—is, however, not a sure guide on high ground in a fog. Oxford and his troops lost their way; it can hardly be wondered at, seeing that save by night or in the fog they had not seen the ground. By some unlucky chance, though intending to take the Yorkists in the rear, they absolutely found their way after nearly an hour to the rear of their own centre. The De Vere badge of a mullet argent, worn by his men, and appearing on his own banner either as a badge or a heraldic charge, was mistaken for the rose-en-soleil, the badge of Edward. The mistake was admissible in a fog, but by daylight would have been impossible. Facing round, the Lancastrian bowmen saluted their approaching friends with a volley of arrows. Mistrust, hitherto concealed, now blazed out, Oxford raised

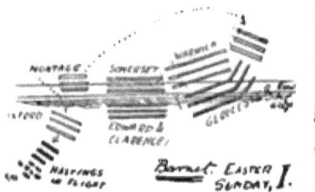

a shout of treason; in truth, there had been so many examples of such conduct during the wars that it was hardly surprising. At the head of his men he instantly quitted the field. But though his flight might have passed unnoticed, the shouts of his men did not pass unheeded. Down along the already hard-pressed centre and left of the Lancastrian army the cry passed from man to man, from mouth to mouth. Montague fell under suspicion, and his men were sharply attacked by comrades who believed themselves betrayed; Montague himself being slain. In the centre Somerset fled from the field, and Warwick's wing alone maintained the combat. Not, however, for long, as it was soon patent to the Earl that all was lost. Gradually he began to retreat, seeking the cover of the hedges in the rear of his position, and it may be was seeking his horse, as he had fought that day on foot. To run was impossible, nay, even to walk fast in his heavy armour, so that, speedily overtaken and surrounded near Wrotham Wood, he fell. By this time the battle was over, and that, too, before eight or nine in the morning.

Edward during the day returned to London in triumph. The dead bodies of Warwick and Montague were brought in and exposed for three days in St. Paul's, after which they were duly buried at Bisham Abbey. Exeter, sorely wounded and supposed to be dead, was succoured, and eventually took sanctuary at Westminster. Of Yorkists, two of the Bourchiers fell, and also Lord Say. Probably owing to the fog, the number of slain was small, *i.e.*, not more than 1,000.

There is no doubt that the mistake with regard to Oxford had a most unfortunate influence on the result of the battle, even if it did not absolutely cause the defeat. One explanation of his appearance in the rear of the Lancastrian line is as follows. It is ingenious, and well merits consideration. When the fight began, the two opposing armies lay practically north and south, the Yorkists attacking up-hill. The Yorkist right, outflanking the Lancastrian left, drove it back on the centre. The Lancastrian right chased the Yorkist left off the ground. When the two centres were closely engaged, Somerset being worsted slightly, bent round so as to face more towards the north, while Edward faced more to the south, the position of the Yorkist right and Lancastrian left having also similarly changed. Thus when Oxford returned from Barnet, whither he had gone in pursuit of the fugitive wing of the Yorkists, he would naturally come up in the rear of Somerset, *i.e.*, in the rear of the then Lancastrian centre. Another point in this explanation needing elucidation is this. How could the outflanked left wing of the Yorkists have fled in the direction of Barnet at once? Their obvious direction in flight would have been to the north-east, down the hill, and then by a circuitous road southwards. The mention of hedge sides, too, is rather puzzling. Hedges were infrequent in those days, and many years after were even the reverse of common. But such a boundary might with considerable probability have fringed the road; and along the road, according to tradition, the battle was fought. Edward on leaving Barnet, as soon as Warwick's whereabouts was fairly well known to him, turned east, through Monken Hadley, keeping to the low ground. Then, when he had advanced far enough, he marched due west up the hill and in full front, as he thought, of Warwick. As we now know, he marched too far, and hence his right overlapped Warwick's left, and *vice versâ*.

The tailpiece shows the mullet argent, the badge of Vere; a previous initial letter has given the most ordinary type of the rose-en-soleil, the badge of Edward IV. The rose was argent, seeded or, encircled by rays of the last. An immense number of types of this badge exist, as of the Lancastrian rose gules, seeded or. That the rose-en-soleil worn at Barnet may have been of a simpler nature than the specimen figured, is possible; and that it could have been mistaken in a fog for the mullet argent seems more than probable.

THE MULLET (VERE).

CHAPTER XIX.

TEWKESBURY.

May 4, 1471.

THE military events which immediately preceded the battle of Tewkesbury, the last of the long series of sanguinary combats known as the Wars of the Roses, are briefly these. Edward IV. had, on April 14th, defeated the Lancastrians at Barnet. Warwick and his brother were slain, and Henry VI., the old king, was in captivity in the Tower. On the afternoon of that day the energetic Queen Margaret with her son, Prince Edward, accompanied by a small band of exiles, landed at Weymouth, in Dorset. Among her followers, the chief appear to have been the Lord Fortesque, Sir John Langstrother, and Lord Wenlock. At Cerne Abbey, on the next day, she heard of the defeat at Barnet, the captivity of the king, and the deaths of Warwick and Montague. Tidings such as these were but poorly compensated for by the accession to her fighting force, which brought the evil tidings. On her own part, this intelligence seems for once to have daunted her usually indomitable spirit, and it is recorded that her desire was at once to return whence she came, and thus to remove her son, the Prince of Wales, from danger. By advice—reckless counsel it seems in these days—the Queen determined to continue her enterprise, and with her usual energy set to work to raise an army in Somerset, Dorset, and Wilts; counties in which the emissaries of Warwick and the Beauforts had already been hard at work spreading disaffection. A force was gathered, and an advance made as far as Exeter, where Sir John Arundel and Sir Hugh Courtenay joined the now increasing army. An important accession of strength this, as it was speedily followed by a fine contingent of the men of Devon and Cornwall. Moving out of Exeter, the county of Somerset was traversed, Taunton, Glastonbury, and Wells being in turn visited, and in the last-named city a halt was made to consolidate the force.

Edward, who had disbanded his army immediately after the victory at Barnet, heard of the arrival of Margaret two days subsequent to her landing; and at once took measures to combat this new danger. But at the time it was not apparent in which direction that danger would have to be met. Would Margaret march on the capital, or would she first make her way northwards through Wales and Cheshire? In the first case her road would lie through Salisbury and Reading; in the second case a junction with Jasper Tudor, and a large accession of strength would inevitably ensue. Moreover Cheshire, still Lancastrian, would next be visited—Cheshire, where the vengeance taken on the followers of the Red Rose after preceding battles was not yet forgotten, and a considerable increase in strength might be looked for to the queen's army. From Cheshire it became a question whether Margaret would not proceed still further north into Lancastrian Northumberland, and then turning south, through York, march on the capital. If all this were accomplished, her army, at present small, would in all probability become immensely large. Her march south would present rather the appearance of a triumphal progress than a military expedition on which the fate of a kingdom depended.

Edward IV. was a soldier, but more than that he was a general—a combination rare in those days of personal prowess. Grasping the situation, he appointed Windsor as his place of muster, seeing that thence in the most convenient way he would be able to strike the enemy on either line of march. On April 19th he reached Windsor, and tarried there collecting his troops till April 23rd.

Margaret and her advisers had considered both lines of march, and had determined on the route *viâ* Wales, where Tudor was professedly ready to effect a junction. Knowing Edward, and recognising his military talents, it became of importance to deceive him if possible as to their absolute intentions. To effect this, a very feeble, nay, more, a played-out device was resorted to. Messengers were sent along the Salisbury and Reading route to spread the news of the immediate advent of the queen and her army. Under cover of this ruse, the Lancastrian force was marched into Somersetshire, as before stated.

Edward, however, was not the man to be deceived;

probably, also, he had plenty of spies at work. The real intention of the queen then, either being divined by him or having become known to him some time between the 19th and 23rd, he started from Windsor on the 24th. On Saturday, April 27th, he reached Abingdon, that picturesque old town —picturesque even in these later days. Remaining at Abingdon till the 29th, he marched to Cirencester, where the intention of Margaret to occupy Bath that day was announced to him. The two armies were now only thirty miles distant from one another, and if both meant fighting, the looked-for battle might take place at any time within the next forty-eight hours. Edward immediately marched out three miles westward, where he pitched his camp and anxiously awaited news of the enemy. On the morrow, May 1st, having received no intelligence, he advanced eight or nine miles south-west to Malmesbury, and there obtained tidings that, avoiding Bath, Queen Margaret had proceeded to Bristol.

At Bristol the Lancastrians were well received, being feasted and supplied with provisions. But their object was as yet to avoid an engagement, and with this end in view they sent out small parties to pretend to take up a position at Sodbury Hill, a spot almost equidistant from both Bristol and Malmesbury. Under cover of this pretended assumption of a battle-ground, they marched off in the direction of Gloucester, by the way of Berkeley Castle. Berkeley Castle is distant eighteen miles north-east by north of Bristol, and Gloucester is fifteen miles beyond it in the same direction. Edward reached Sodbury Hill prepared to fight, but found no enemy. He, however, learnt the direction in which the queen was marching, and promptly despatched an urgent message to the Governor of Gloucester, Richard Beauchamp, to hold the city at all cost till relief arrived. And as this could be but little delayed, the task was one which Beauchamp under ordinary circumstances might well perform. Gloucester, as it commanded the only passage over the river Severn in that district, was of the utmost importance to Margaret. There was no other for miles. Lancastrians in plenty were within the city, and the queen hoped that the example of Bristol would there be followed. This would undoubtedly have been the case had not the premonitory message of Edward enabled the governor to take measures to preserve the city. Gates were closed, walls manned, and all preparations made when, on May 3rd, the weary Lancastrians, after a night march, appeared at the gates of Gloucester demanding admittance and passage over the river.

Beauchamp refused, and the queen was compelled to make for the next place of importance, which happened to be Tewkesbury. Tewkesbury is ten miles higher up the river than Gloucester, so that if it be true that the march from Bristol to Gloucester was made without a halt, the Lancastrian army covered nearly forty-five miles before encamping in the fields south of the old abbey of St. Mary, Tewkesbury. But at Tewkesbury there was no bridge, and the number of boats there was quite insufficient to convey an army across. Edward was known to be pressing on in pursuit, though not exactly in their track. Horse and man were tired out completely, and no wonder, after such a terrible march. Hence no other course remained but to stand at bay and fight.

Edward meanwhile had been marching along the higher ground, *i.e.*, the Cotswold Hills, in a direct cross-country line from Sodbury to Tewkesbury, and covered about thirty miles that day, a "right-an-hot day." Food for men and horses was not to be had, water was equally scarce, one tiny brook on the road being all that was available. Towards evening he reached Cheltenham, then a village, and distant eight miles south-west by south of Tewkesbury. Here he obtained definite news of the arrival of Queen Margaret at that town, and of the position and formation of the camp. Pressing on without delaying for more than a meal and a brief halt, Edward advanced a few miles further and then encamped for the night. This was a wise precaution, as there would be less ground to cover in the morning, his troops would be fresher for the fight, and, moreover, some scanty supplies had been obtained, so that his men would not fight empty. Margaret had approached Tewkesbury by the old road from Gloucester, and therefore on its south side. Somerset commanded the van, and would under ordinary circumstances have commanded the right wing, but appears, for some unknown reason, to have been posted on the left. The Prince of Wales, with Lord Wenlock and Sir John Langstrother, led the main body, and commanded the centre, while to the Earl of Devon was assigned the rear-guard, and subsequently the right wing.

The army passing the field now, for some unknown reason, called Lincoln Green, probably then turned eastwards, and encamped on Gaston Field, in those days of course unenclosed. To the west was the river Severn, to the south-west the high ground of Tewkesbury Park, and at that time a forest. North, the position was bounded by the Avon and the Swillgate river, the latter flowing round southwards, and thus enclosing the western side of the camping ground. Between the Avon and the Severn is a wide and perfectly level plain known as Severn Ham (in the west, "ham," is a frequent name for waterside fields). Between the Avon and the Swillgate river lies the

So Called Queen Margaret's Camp Tewkesbury

Abbey of St. Mary, and, trending in a north-east direction, the still quaint streets of the old town. So much for the main features of the ground. Of Holme Castle, though it must then have been in existence, there is no mention in any account of the battle. The small irregular entrenchment known as Margaret's Camp is altogether too small to have needed more than a few hundred defenders, but that it formed an important portion of Somerset's line of defence is very doubtful. Margaret's Camp, of which the real name is Camp

Ground, on inspection gives the impression of being a prehistoric earth-work. It has been erroneously suggested by some to be of Roman origin. Wearied men after a forty-five mile march could hardly have erected such a defence in one night. The queen, it appears, sought shelter in a religious house where she slept.

The position selected by Somerset was a strong one, owing to the nature of the ground, for any opposing force must necessarily have developed its attack from the south. All chroniclers definitely state that the Lancastrian army was drawn up with its back to the abbey and town. In their front were hedges, trees, and bushes, so that it was very hard to get within striking distance. But is it absolutely certain that "drawn up with its back to the abbey and town" means facing south? Careful inspection of the ground points rather to the conclusion that the Lancastrian line of battle was facing to the south-west, drawn up on the high ground at the foot of which now runs the modern road. Perry Hill and Holme Castle were in Somerset's rear, while the fields known as the "Vineyards," close to the castle, lay in the immediate rear of his right wing. South and west of the position all was wood.

Edward, on the morning of the battle, advanced from his camping place, through Elmstone-Hardwick and Tredington, crossing the Swillgate river at an old ford not far north of Prest Bridge. Richard, Duke of Gloucester, his brother, led the van, and commanded the right wing, Edward in person the main body and centre, Lord Hastings the rear-guard and left wing. There was no reserve proper, but in order to secure his right flank from attack *en route* to the battlefield, Edward left a body of 200 spears in a wood. Chroniclers put this wood as a quarter of a mile distant from the field of battle, but state that it was near a wooded lane. Now the only possible old lane on Somerset's left and Edward's right passed east of the Camp Ground along Perry Hill, and thence into the town. Two hundred men armed with spears were not a large body;

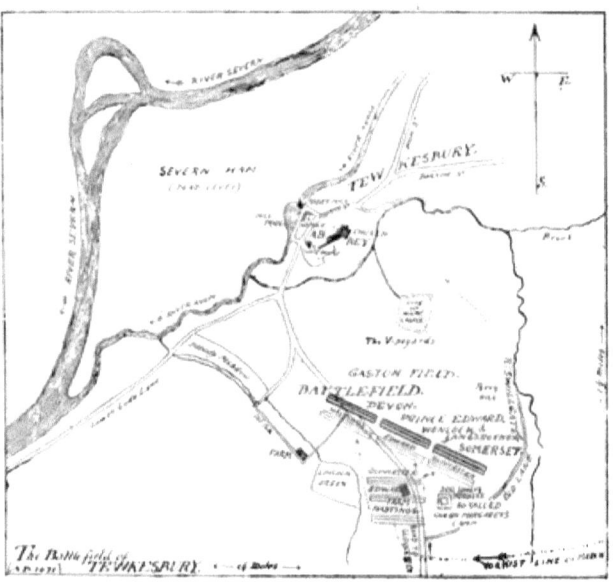

but within the so-called Queen Margaret's camp, and shrouded from observation by the trees, they would have been secure. And as a chance Yorkist defence at the battle of Tewkesbury this prehistoric earthwork must, we think, in these days be considered.

The two armies faced each other, and Gloucester, acting under orders, began the action with arrows and artillery. Gloucester, be it remembered, was on the right, the only open side. Any Lancastrian disaster there would have the effect of disordering both the centre and the other wing, and with Avon, Swillgate, and Severn running all round the rest of the position, the course adopted by Edward showed the best generalship. Somerset, strongly posted and entrenched, was able to hold in check his assailants, and did so until, in an evil moment, he determined on executing an offensive movement. Whether he conceived this design himself, or was provoked thereto by a feint at flight on the part of Gloucester does not appear. All we know is that he left his defences, passed into an old woody lane, wheeled round and attempted to outflank the Yorkist centre. Edward received the charge—he was not yet in action. Gloucester, who had either rallied his men after a real flight, or saw that from his ruse having succeeded the moment to strike had come, returned to the attack. Suddenly and simultaneously out from the wood rushed the hitherto concealed body of 200 spears, who charged the extreme left of Somerset in its new position. The supposition of a feint in the retreat by Gloucester appears the most worthy of credit, but only an incapable commander like Somerset would have been deluded by so transparent and well-worn a device. In a short time the Lancastrian left wing was routed and driven down the hill eastwards with great slaughter.

The position was this as regards the remainder of the armies. Somerset, by leaving his entrenchments, and by his subsequent defeat, had left the Lancastrian centre exposed. Edward instantly grasped the situation, and entering the enemy's line of battle by the deserted entrenchments, outflanked the centre, threw it by his attack into confusion, then routed it and pursued the fugitives through the vineyards towards the town. At the abbey mill a terrible slaughter took place. Here huge numbers of men coming along the Avon bank in full flight met, at the corner of the abbey wall where but a few feet of road separated it from the mill pool, the fugitives who had fled through the town. Caught in this cul-de-sac, they were hewn down without mercy.

The story only of the right wing remains to be told, and

that is of a similar nature. After destroying the Lancastrian centre the same movement was repeated, and the unfortunate right wing, caught between the Yorkist left and the victorious (or portions of the victorious) Yorkist right and centre, was discomfited, being pressed in a north-west direction towards the river in full flight. Some gaining an old ford, where now there is a modern bridge, were slain on the bank; but the bulk of the fugitives made off direct for the Avon, and were caught in a narrow meadow at the end of an old still existent lane. Here there was a terrible slaughter, and the place to this day bears the name of Bloody Meadow. Of the fate of Prince Edward, the last Lancastrian in the male line, there are no accurate records. He commanded the right wing as we know, and therefore in his flight would probably have taken a line towards the town, where he knew, or thought he knew, his queen mother was in a religious house. Probably he was cut down in the pursuit. Most of the stories told of his death or murder bear on their face the stamp of improbability. If he really fell into the hands of Richard Crofte, the king's old tutor, and sheriff of Herefordshire, when "fleinge to the townewards," then his death was murder. Margaret, it is said, left Tewkesbury either just before or during the battle, and retired to a neighbouring religious house, from which she surrendered three days later in company with the Lady Anne (Princess of Wales) and Lady Courtenay. Slaughter continued, according to local tradition, up to the very doors of the grand old abbey. After the battle Edward went there, and found the building (which was not a sanctuary) quite full of fugitives. These were removed; the common people taken prisoners were spared, but nearly all those of gentle blood were executed. Prince Edward was buried in the abbey, where in one of the chapels a fragment of his stone coffin is still shown (*vide* initial). Many others of the slain were also buried in the same place, but their graves are unmarked. Whether those fugitives who were taken within the building were all spared or not it is difficult to determine. It hardly looks like it in the face of the historic fact that from May 4th until May 30th the abbey church was closed, and that re-consecration followed.

A relic of the fight, and a curious one, may be seen on the inner side of the vestry door. This door is entirely lined with fragments of armour, sword-blades, &c., hammered out roughly and nailed to the wood, dents and notches being yet visible. Devon, John Beaufort, and Lord Wenlock fell on the field. Somerset, Sir John Langstrother (the late Treasurer and Prior of St. John's), Sir Humphrey Audley, Sir Hugh Courtenay, Sir Thomas Tresham, Sir Gervaise Clifton, and about a dozen others, were taken before the Dukes of Gloucester and Norfolk two days after the battle, and were tried and executed forthwith, but without mutilation forming a part of the sentence. A few gentlemen prisoners were spared, perhaps a dozen in all, including Sir John Fortescue. Metcalfe, in his Book of Knights, gives a list of forty-six persons knighted on the field of "Grafton besydes Tewkesbury" after the battle by Edward, who seems, on the 20th of May, on his return to London, "in the highway without Shordiche" to have also dubbed a batch of thirteen city aldermen. The old herald records that "all the which liberally payd their fees to the Officers of Armes."

Conjecture alone must be relied on with regard to the numbers engaged on either side, but they probably were not large. A large force could not in the time have covered the great distances which were traversed during the campaign, brief though it was. If from 9,000 to 10,000 were present at the battle it is an outside estimate. The Lancastrians,

TEWKESBURY.

according to all accounts, happened to be numerically superior. Edward is known to have had more than 3,000 "footmen," *i.e.*, infantry ; his proportion of cavalry would certainly not equal this number, and may be taken as 1,500. This would give him 4,500 men, a reasonable estimate. The absolute money cost in wages for the twenty days the troops were out was £1,718, and the number of archers is stated as 3,436. "Malles," leaden heads with wooden handles, and most deadly in effect, to the number of 1,650 were also paid for, and probably issued to the infantry.

CHAPTER XX.

BOSWORTH.

August 22, 1485.

BADGE OF RICHARD III (THE WHITE BOAR). A MUCH MUTILATED EXAMPLE EXISTS ON THE EXTERIOR OF A TOWER, CARLISLE C^{AS}.

ON August 1, 1485, Henry, Earl of Richmond, took ship at Harfleur with a following at most numbering 2,000 men. The expedition disembarked at Dale, near Milford, during the evening of August 7th, and on the morrow marched ten miles to Haverfordwest, starting early and proceeding with rapidity, so much so that the force itself brought the first news of its landing. At the outset the prospects of the expedition did not seem favourable, help promised by the Welsh not being forthcoming; nay, more, rumours reached the camp that Welsh friends counted upon to support Richmond were even arrayed against him. From the former retainers of Jasper Tudor, Earl of Pembroke, however, messages of welcome came in; and somewhat reassured, Richmond marched onwards to Cardigan. Still the news received was hardly of the kind to inspire confidence. An unfounded rumour held, to the effect that Sir Walter Herbert was hurrying in pursuit with a force from Caermarthen. A small body of Welsh under Richard Griffith now joined Richmond, and a message, friendly in its nature, but evidently sent with a view to exact a promise of liberal reward for service, was received from the powerful Rice ap Thomas. The negotiation with Ap Thomas was successful. Richmond then sent urgent messages to his English sympathisers and promised supporters, among whom were the Stanleys and Talbots. Shrewsbury he named as a place of rendezvous, and he besought all to join him there.

The march was resumed, Richmond taking a route *viâ* Cardigan, Machynlleth, New Town and Welshpool, till the banks of the Severn were reached. The bridge over the river, between Monford and Forton, was seized, and the expedition, augmented by the adherents of Rice ap Thomas, moved on to Shrewsbury, where they found the gates shut, the town being held by Thomas Mytton, the bailiff, for Richard III. Richmond then fell back to Forton, and thence entered into negotiations with Mytton, using what may be called the Bolingbroke plea. On the morrow Mytton, having been won over, permitted an entrance into the town, and here Richmond obtained a small accession of strength. From Shrewsbury he marched to Newport, where Sir Gilbert Talbot effected a junction with him at the head of some 500 men.

He had thus passed unscathed through Wales, had received accessions of strength there, and had reached a point on the border of Shropshire 19 miles east-north-east from Shrewsbury and about 140 miles from London. Thence he proceeded, *viâ*

Stafford, to Lichfield, 25 miles north-north-west, and there he encamped for the night outside the town, being well received on his entrance therein on the morrow. That day his army reached Tamworth, but Richmond, having missed his way, slept at Whittington, a small village not far from Lichfield. On the morrow, however, he overtook and rejoined his troops, and then hurried on to Atherstone, a market-town in Warwickshire. Here his army encamped in a field north of the church, afterwards known as the Royal Meadow. Richmond himself, according to tradition, took up his quarters at the Three Tuns Inn, and here, on August 20th, held the memorable interview with the Stanleys. Atherstone, an unimportant place enough as regards size, was important from a military point of view, being on Watling Street and therefore on the direct road to the Metropolis. A plan of action when the time came having been agreed upon between Richmond, Lord Stanley, and Sir William, the two intending traitors withdrew in the direction of Shenton and Bosworth, taking the precaution to keep their respective bodies of troops separate, though at no great distance one from the other.

Richmond remained at Atherstone till the 21st, when he advanced a short distance along Watling Street, till, taking to Fenn Lanes he passed through Fenny Drayton, a village in Leicestershire, six miles west-north-west from Hinckley. Then turning towards Shenton he encamped on a bridge, now known as Moory Leys, but then as White Moors, and distant nearly one mile from that place. Sir William Stanley had pitched his camp on the west side of the road to Market Bosworth and two miles north-north-east of White Moors, while Lord Stanley occupied an eminence one mile east of his brother Sir William.

Let us now trace the movements of King Richard III. The news of the projected invasion reached the king at Nottingham during the month of June. On the 22nd orders were sent forth in various directions to the authorities to muster their men to be ready to act at an hour's notice. Henry had not yet set sail, however, and Richard in reality had ample time to have equipped a force sufficiently strong as to have slain the invaders to a man. But of friends he had few —few, at least, worthy to be trusted. Nearly every man of rank was either lukewarm in loyalty or else preparing to join the enemy as soon as it could be done with safety. From Nottingham Lord Stanley, the Steward of the Household, early in August begged leave to go home to Lathom. Permission was granted on condition that his son and heir, Lord Strange, came to court as a hostage. On August 1st the Great Seal, fetched in haste, arrived at Nottingham from London.

When Richmond landed on August 7th Richard assumed an air of satisfaction, whether real or not no one can say. The sweating sickness, a new and unknown disease, had been ravaging the country during July and continued to rage. Sir William Stanley fell under the suspicion of treason, and not without cause, when news came to hand that Richmond had reached Shrewsbury unmolested. He was proclaimed a traitor, and Lord Stanley was at once summoned to Nottingham as a matter of precaution. Stanley, however, declined to go there, averring that he suffered from the prevailing malady. At this juncture Lord Strange made an attempt to leave Nottingham and join his father, but was discovered. Only by accusing his uncle and pledging himself for his father's loyalty did he save his head. It seems but reasonable to suppose that this sweating sickness was a great factor in the defeat of Richard III. Undoubtedly he should have brought far more troops into the field than he did. But how were large bodies of men to have been raised as early as the middle of July, and kept together, with a terrible pestilence raging through the land?

In August, however, without doubt the king acted with decision. The Earl of Northumberland was called on for his levy, and came. The Duke of Norfolk from the east brought his retainers, and Lord Lovell marched from the south. Brakenbury, ever faithful, conveyed to Nottingham a supply of arms and munitions of war from the Tower of London, and also certain gentlemen of dubious loyalty. These, viz., Sir Thomas Bourchier, Sir Walter Hungerford, and others, had the good fortune to escape by the way. Norfolk's contingent was summoned by him to muster at Bury St. Edmund's on August 16th. Three days later some troops from York had not yet started—nay, the number required was not yet known. By dribblets, however, an army of some kind, and, if loyal, sufficiently large, had been got together.

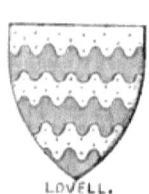
LOVELL.

On August 19th Richard arrived at the town of Leicester.

On this day, it will be remembered, Richmond marched from Tamworth to Atherstone. Remaining there till August 21st, and probably waiting for expected contingents, Richard then marched out in a south-westerly direction from Leicester, passing through Leicester Forest and Earlshilton, he then took to the fields, and encamped near Abraham's Bridge.

His position was this: on his right and north-north-east

Market Bosworth from the crest of Ambion Hill.

was Stapleton village, distant half a mile. On his left was the Tweed river, which also ran round in rear of the camp. Beyond the river and in the rear was the road to Hinckley, which crosses the stream by means of Abraham's Bridge. The site of the camp was a small spur which projected southwards from a longer ridge running east and west. North of this ridge, in the hollow runs a tributary of the Tweed, by name the Sence Brook. Beyond this again, and distant two miles north-west from Richard's camp, is a high ground, and here on the morrow the king drew up in battle order. The name of this hill is Ambion Hill. South of it is Radmore Plain, and south of that again Ambion Wood. Half a mile due east of the right of the royal line is the village of Sutton Cheney. Richard commanded the centre, Northumberland the right, and Norfolk the left.

Early on the 22nd Richmond marched out to battle, taking a direction northwards for nearly a mile to Shenton, and then

AMBION HILL.

bearing north-east for about an equal distance. His object was, firstly, to keep the Tweed between his army and that of Richard; and, secondly, to bring his force before the fight as near as possible to the troops of the two Stanleys. Having avoided a dangerous marsh which lay at the foot of Ambion Hill and at its north-west extremity, his column and that under the Earl of Oxford then wheeled so as to face to the south-east, being nearest the left wing and centre of Richard's army. Lord Stanley and his brother had meanwhile been summoned to occupy their destined place, *i.e.*, the left wing.

BOSWORTH. 219

Stanley returned for reply that Henry might go on fearlessly, adding that he would be at hand if needed. Obviously Richmond's intention was to bring the Stanleys into line while on the march, and then, facing directly south, to join conclusions with Richard. But Stanley, holding back, produced a change. When partly wheeled the force advanced, so that the armies came into collision, gradually starting from Richmond's extreme right under Oxford.

The advance was necessarily uphill, but from the very

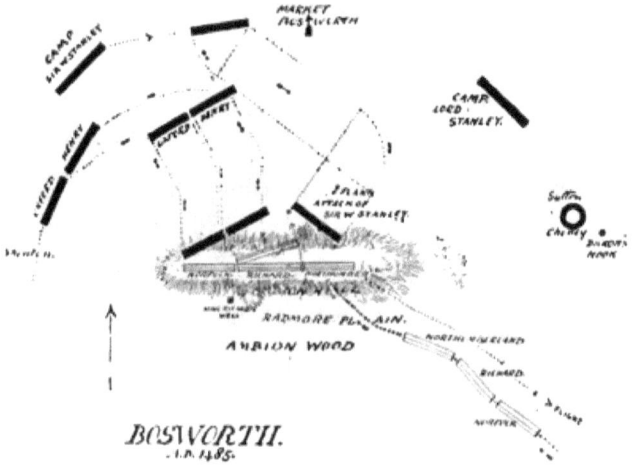

outset Oxford seems to have been successful. That he had carefully given his orders in order to preclude a rash pursuit in case of victory seems established. Slowly his wing gained ground on their opponents, but the battle was on this side confined to the archers. In the centre, however, as soon as Richmond came within charging distance, matters were different. Richard, mounted, made a furious attack on the advancing line—an attack first directed on the standard. To overturn this was the next best thing to killing Richmond. Sir William Brandon, the standard-bearer, was killed, Sir John Cheyney was overthrown, but Richmond's line, though hard pressed, doggedly fought on. Northumberland, with his right wing, must have had a good view of the fight. He had no opponent, and probably being but half-hearted in the cause, hardly desired one. His abstention would assuredly reap a reward. Lord Stanley, in the distance, anxious to save the head of his son, was also an onlooker; but not so his brother Sir William. The latter had been gradually approaching the line, having taken a direction which if persevered in would have brought his troops to their allotted place in the left wing. Seeing the condition of things in the centre, where Richard almost looked like succeeding, he threw his men forward in support of Richmond and delivered an attack on the right flank of Richard's centre, Northumberland still offering no opposition, though it was evidently his business

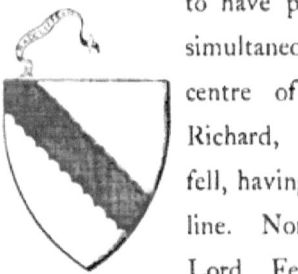

to have prevented such a manœuvre. Almost simultaneously it would appear the left and centre of the king's army were shattered. Richard, fighting with the utmost bravery, fell, having penetrated well into the enemy's line. Norfolk had also perished, as also had Lord Ferrers, Sir Robert Brakenbury, Sir Richard Radcliffe, and Sir Robert Percy. Catesby, Surrey, and Northumberland were taken prisoners, and it may be remarked that the men commanded by the last named left the field without having joined at all in the combat.

BOSWORTH.

On the field and in the pursuit, a pursuit which lasted for a couple of miles, a considerable number perished, but accounts vary, so that it is difficult to estimate either the total number engaged or the number of those who fell. Probably, including the force of Sir William Stanley, Henry had between 4,500 and 5,000 men engaged. Of Richard's army we can only say that it considerably exceeded this in size. It has been estimated as amounting to 10,000 men; this would, we think, include the forces both of Lord Stanley, Sir William, and Northumberland. Subtracting for these, the king may have had 6,500 at the very outside who fought at Bosworth Field.

Sutton Cheney, near which Lord Stanley encamped, is a small but picturesque village. It possesses an interesting old manor house and a small church, near which, westward, traces of entrenchments are visible. East, and rather to the south of the village church, is a field known as "Dickon's Nook." Local tradition connects this spot with Bosworth Field, but erroneously.  With far more probability the old well at the foot of Ambion Hill bears the name of King Richard's Well. This well has been covered over by a massive stone pyramid. On the inside there is a much mutilated, though comparatively modern, inscription. The name of Ambion, which belongs to both wood and hill, does not seem to be capable of any explanation. It is of greater antiquity, however, than the date of the battle.

CHAPTER XXI.

FLODDEN.

September 9, 1513.

THE political events which led to the Scottish invasion in 1513 need not be recapitulated. James IV., whether partly influenced by the French Queen, who, it is said, sent to him a letter, 14,000 crowns, and a turquoise ring, or merely to revenge certain grievances which he imagined he had against England on account of the Barton incident, had determined on war. The army which followed him across the border on August 22, 1513, was the most numerous of the many that had preceded it. At its setting forth it is recorded to have mustered near upon 100,000 men. Its leaders were all those of the highest rank in the Scottish kingdom, and it may be fairly said that no grown-up member of any family of position was absent from the expedition. But although ready enough to loyally follow the king whithersoever he led them in actual war, for some reason his venture was either unpopular or deemed unwise. Those among his trusted advisers who dared to give counsel gave it in favour of abstention from acts of war. Such advice, however, was rejected by the king. Next, it was attempted to influence his known superstition by trickery, and a " ghostly " visitor warned James not to set forth. This warning was, as it deserved to be, neglected.

Marching on Wark, Norham, and Etal Castles, the Scots laid siege to them and took them. There was as yet no army in the field to oppose their advance, and Northumberland lay at the mercy of the invader. Considering the magnitude of his preparations, the absolute amount of damage inflicted on the English seems very disproportionate indeed. Advancing to Ford Castle, the stronghold of the Herons, James took the place and burnt it, this being the sole other achievement of the campaign. It has been said that Lady Heron of Ford managed by an exercise of the arts of coquetry to keep James dancing attendance on her, though she was ostensibly at that time his captive. Be this as it may, it is certain that for some cause James loitered about in the neighbourhood of Ford and Flodden, while his army grew daily less and less. Some, gorged with plunder, betook themselves home again ; others, starved out—for the districts had been well foraged— also recrossed the Tweed, till in the day of trouble James found himself with hardly more than 30,000 men. In other words, two-thirds of his army had melted away. But this residue was the cream of the whole, and was perhaps the noblest body of fighting men that had ever been gathered together. Henry VIII., then in France, had left to the Earl of Surrey the charge of defending the kingdom. Surrey, naturally, on receipt of news that the invasion was imminent, mustered what men he could, naming Newcastle as the place of meeting. Advancing northwards, he gathered forces by the way, receiving a large accession of strength at Pontefract From Newbury, in Berkshire, it will be remembered that the famous clothier, John Smalwood, *alias* Winchom or Winschomb, better known as "Jack of Newbury," came to join the army, at the head of a hundred men armed and equipped at his own cost. At Durham the so-called banner of St. Cuthbert was given into the custody of Surrey—the banner that had been last displayed 167 years before at the battle of Neville's Cross. When Surrey reached Newcastle late on the 30th of August he was joined by contingents under Sir Marmaduke Constable, Lord Dacre, Sir William Bulmer, and others. Proceeding northward to Alnwick, his son Thomas Howard, the Lord Admiral, arrived with 5,000 men, who had been conveyed thither by sea. According to a letter, which is extant, to Henry VIII. from Cawarden, the Master of the Revels, who accompanied Surrey, this long march was attended by terrible hardships to all engaged therein, though it is not easy to understand why.

From Alnwick Surrey despatched a formal challenge to James, naming Friday, September 9th, as the day of the battle—a challenge which was duly accepted. Surrey, in this as in everything else connected with the campaign, showed himself more than a match for his adversary. At the time the challenge was received James was encamped in the low ground. According to the old rules of chivalry his acceptance from that spot implied one, and probably two, things—first, that he should give battle there, and second, that he should not give battle before the day named. Surrey required the Scots to be on a level ground if possible; he also needed time to strengthen his force. By this cunning challenge he obtained both. James, as has been said, accepted this challenge, but not without opposition from his adherents. One, the aged Earl of Angus, better known to history by his curious nickname of "Bell-the-Cat," was insulted by his master when imploring him not to accept the challenge of Surrey. James retorted by a doubt on the proved bravery of the earl. "If you are afraid, you can go home," quoth he; and the earl sadly departed, leaving his two sons, however, to perish in the fight.

On September 6th, having advanced to the village of Bolton, five miles west of Alnwick, Surrey received the answer of James to his challenge, and at once moved on to Wooler. But James had meanwhile removed his camp from the low ground near Ford, and had taken up a strong position on Flodden Hill, an eminence which lies due south of the castle, and runs east and west in a long ridge. When Surrey reached Wooler he found by spies that the Scots had changed their camping-ground, and that the change was detrimental to the object he had in view. It therefore became again needful to resort to diplomacy to lure his enemy back if possible to the plain. Writing a letter of reproach in which he pointed out that the arrangement had been made for a pitched battle, but that instead the chivalrous James had fortified himself in a very strong camp, he concluded by challenging him to come down on the day appointed and fight on Millfield Plain—a level tract south of Flodden Hill. James, it seems, refused to see the herald who brought this epistle.

Millfield Plain had quite recently been the scene of a sanguinary defeat of some Scotch raiders under Lord Home. Home's force consisted of 3,000 mounted men, and was returning laden with booty after a successful raid. Passing

FLODDEN FIELD.

through the road which crosses the Plain, the freebooters found themselves in an ambuscade. Sir William Bulmer, of Brancepeth Castle, had lined the tall broom on either side of the road with 1,000 archers and men-at-arms. Utterly demoralised at the suddenness of the attack, and encumbered with loot, the Scotch could make but a feeble attempt at resistance. Between 500 and 600 were killed, and 400 taken prisoners. On the English side about sixty fell.

From Wooler, Surrey marched on September 8th, and crossed the river Till, then keeping down the right bank, but so far removed as to be invisible to the Scots on the hill. His line of march was concealed by some high ground to the south of Doddington. On the night of Thursday, September 8th, the English army halted at Barmoor Wood, where it encamped. All this time James had apparently taken no steps to ascertain what the enemy was doing, whither he was going or what might be expected to happen. He may have been, nay he was, a most chivalrous knight, but as a strategist and tactician contemptible is a hardly strong enough term to apply to the luckless Scottish king.

Early in the morning Surrey broke up his encampment, marched straight for the bridge at Twizel, an ancient one-arch structure. Here his artillery, with the heavy baggage in charge of the vanguard, crossed the river, the main body and the rear-guard crossing higher up by two other fords, known respectively as the Willowford and the Sandyford. This movement appears to have taken James completely by surprise; at any rate it may be assumed that he did not foresee it, in that he took no precautions to prevent it. The only attempt which he made to protect the passage of the river was to point two guns at a crossing near Ford. Surrey had now thrust his army between James and Scotland; the Scotch position was one of danger on that account. Yet a few comparatively slight military precautions would, if taken, have prevented such a condition of things. Scouting appears to have been unused in the Scottish army with James—not one attempt at observation seems to have been made. A comparatively small force accompanied by artillery holding the Twizel Bridge would have secured the passage, and at the fords neither guns nor baggage could have been got across the river.

On observing the English debouching from the distant bridge, James conceived a new idea, viz., to occupy a neighbouring hill known as Branxton Hill, from the neighbouring village, and to abandon his strong entrenched position on Flodden. Evidently his notion hitherto had been that Surrey's attack would come from the south, on which side Flodden Hill is even stronger. And here was Surrey appearing on the north with only one weak point in his situation, that his army was enclosed between the Tweed and the Till. If James could have defeated Surrey, it would have been woe to the vanquished. James then gave orders to burn the rude huts which had been constructed within the lines of the old entrenchment which crowns the top of Flodden Hill. The King of Scotland did not "tent himself" in the elaborate kind of structures shown in a large modern *basso relievo* now exhibited in a certain northern museum. This work of art, designed by one celebrated artist and executed by another, offers one of the most amusing spectacles of historical blundering that is to be found. The huts being set on fire, James under cover of the smoke moved his forces towards Branxton Hill, and, concealed from them by the same smoke, Surrey continued to advance.

The two armies at length faced one another, James on the ridge above Branxton, and Surrey in the plain in front and facing south. It appears that the formation of the line of battle was somewhat different from that usually employed, as both sides were divided into four divisions, and both sides had a reserve (this last was also unusual). Beginning on the

English right, the first division was commanded by Sir Edmund Howard, the younger son of the Earl of Surrey. To him were opposed the Gordons of the north-east Highlands under

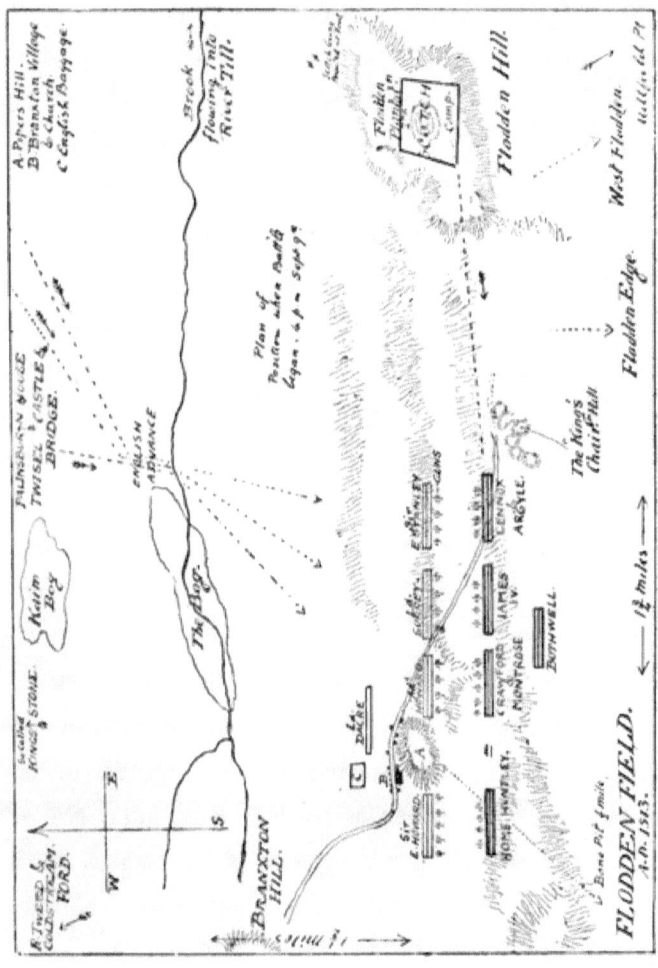

the Earl of Huntley, and the men of the border under the Earl of Home. The second English division was led by Admiral Howard, who was faced by the Earls of Crawford and Montrose. The Earl of Surrey, with the third division, was opposed by King James, while Sir Edward Stanley, with the fourth division, had to try conclusions with the Earls of Lennox and Argyle, whose troops consisted mostly of highlanders. The English reserve, mainly cavalry, was commanded by Lord Dacre, that of the Scotch being under Bothwell. Both reserves were posted in the rear of the centre, Lord Dacre rather on the right. In artillery the Scotch were superior, from the fact that their guns were far better manufactured than those of the English. Their gunner Borthwick, possibly through the assistance of skilled French artisans, had succeeded in casting one special battery of seven field-pieces, known as the Seven Sisters of Borthwick. These guns were at that date remarkable for the extremely small size of the touchholes, an improvement in make which naturally increased the force of the projectile. Other guns he had, but the remainder were of comparatively small account. The Scotch artillery was, however, badly served, and the men working the guns committed the error of firing at too great an elevation, the shots thus passing over the heads of the English and burying themselves harmlessly in the marshy ground beyond. Borthwick, with his guns, was stationed at the foot of the hill. No reliable account is extant as to the number of the English guns, but it is admitted that they were posted in front of the line and were well served.

The position at the commencement of the fight was as follows. The Scots, drawn up in the order already given, occupied higher ground than the English, and faced about due north. The right of the English position was south-west of Branxton Church (a church now rebuilt), and a baggage camp was formed in its rear; the two centre divisions lay eastward, and in rear of Admiral Howard, Dacre's horse, some 2,000 strong. The left took up ground to the south-east of Branxton village. A small hill known now as Pipers Hill appears to have so intervened as to prevent the right of the army as posted from being completely within view of the remainder—a somewhat curious method of marshalling even in those days. Various computations averaged, point to an equality in troops, or thereabouts, in both armies, and roughly speaking, 60,000 men were engaged in battle on that day.

Though the enemy had been within sight of the Scots since early morning, the two armies were not absolutely in position until the afternoon, and it was not until 4 p.m. that with shot of cannon (mainly harmless) the battle commenced. Even thus early the Scots had the misfortune to lose their chief gunner, Borthwick, who fell dead, killed by a ball, after which his guns were deserted. This supports the view that the English guns were fairly well served, or at any rate shows that the aim was not too high. Shots directed at a slight elevation presumably would have played some havoc in the Scottish lines on the higher ground. But it was not by an artillery fire that Flodden was to be won. An attack by the Scots was now ordered, and Lords Huntley and Home, with their border troops, appear to have been the first to come into collision at close quarters. It was remarked that the Scottish advance took place in complete silence. The Scottish left and the English right then entered into a hand-to-hand fight. Huntley and Home, with a powerful body of men armed with long pikes—the weapon in which for more than two centuries the Scots had put their trust as an infantry arm—charged Sir Edmund Howard's line with great impetuosity, and appear in this part of the battle to have achieved absolute success. Thrice was Sir Edmund beaten down, his banner was overturned, and it seemed as if disaster was about to overtake the English right. The fighting line was in disorder, a part of the troops fled (Cheshire archers these, who seem to have been offended at the position assigned to them). These Cheshire men were a contingent which had been separated from the bulk of their comrades, and added to Howard's force to strengthen it in its proportion of archers. The remainder of the men of Cheshire, who fought under Stanley, fought well. But the effects of this petty clannish feeling might indeed have been serious. Luckily there was a mounted reserve at hand, and it was acting under a capable commander, Dacre. A brave attempt under John Heron, usually known as the "bastard Heron," at the head of a body of Northumbrians, for a moment so far checked the Scottish success as to give time for Dacre to act. Dacre charged down, and though he did not restore the English line, nevertheless succeeded in putting Huntley to flight and in neutralising the force of Home. These last remained on the ground, but drew off to a slight distance. They had taken many prisoners, among others Sir Philip, the brother of Lord Dacre. Home's freebooters plundered the English baggage, and in the event got off clear to Scotland with but little loss and an immense loot. Admiral Howard with his division, hard beset by Crawford and Montrose, was compelled to send for succour to his father, the Earl of Surrey. Surrey at once moved up to come to his assistance, but was confronted by the division of Scots under James in person, and found the king gave him enough to do. Bothwell, in command of the reserve horse in the rear, seeing that the two Scottish divisions in his immediate front needed

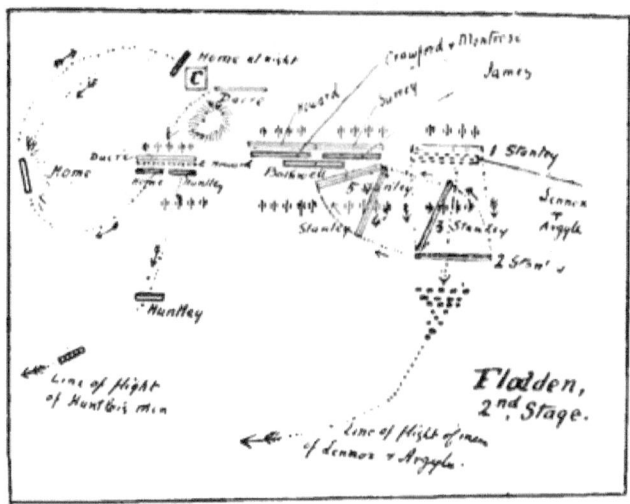

but a little support to prevail, brought up his force, and for a brief space it looked as if disaster must befall both the Admiral and Surrey. Hardly contested along the whole line, the battle now was at its height.

On the English left, which was specially strong in bowmen and pikemen from Cheshire and Lancashire, the volleys of arrows poured into the ranks of the Scottish right, mainly highlanders under the Earls of Lennox and Argyle. Galled by the hail of shafts which spitted their unarmoured bodies—not, indeed, that armour was a great protection—the circumstances of the battle of Northallerton were repeated. Abandoning every other consideration, casting aside targets, the clansmen in a wild rush hurled themselves on to the English ranks in a vain attempt to hew and hack their way to victory. But discipline prevailed; the bowmen and pikemen, though for a moment shaken, maintained their formation, the archers

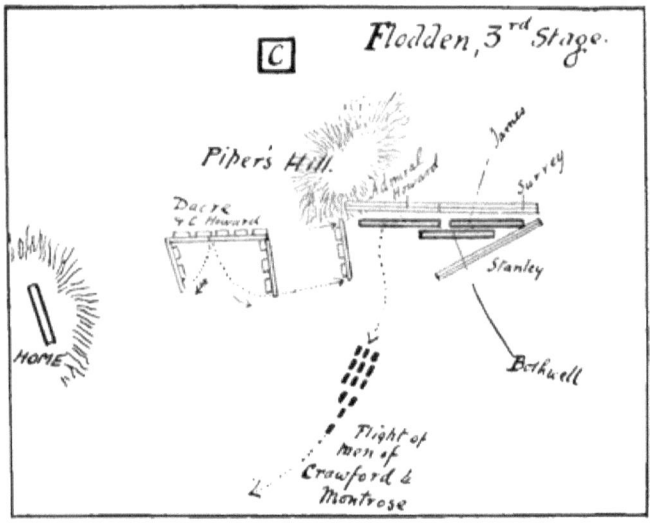

poured in volley after volley at close quarters, actual approach being prevented by the inner line of pikemen. After a terrible slaughter the clansmen gave way, at first fighting, but afterwards in complete rout, and Stanley victoriously won his way up and crowned the ridge.

Stanley did not then commit the error of pursuing from the field thoroughly broken troops, an error which, time after time repeated, had lost, and for years after continued to lose battles. Facing about on the ridge of this hardly-won hill, he charged obliquely downwards in a north-east direction, taking the two divisions of the Scots in the rear of their right flank. The battle in its course was now mainly at the foot of the little green hill close to Branxton Church—the hill known ever after as "Pipers Hill." Stanley's charge produced a terrible effect on the Scots. Hemmed in, they fell by hundreds, and the slain were the pick of the Scottish nobles and knights. Dacre finding that Home was by no means desirous of renewing hostilities (indeed it is stated that the latter was urged to go to the assistance of the Scottish centre, but declined on the plea that he had done his part and they might do theirs), leaving a part of his force to keep Home in check, then advanced to support the Earl and the Admiral. Admiral Howard now got the better of his immediate antagonist, Crawford, who was put to flight. Facing then to the east, Dacre completed the environment of the division of James by a flank attack on his left.

As a battle all was now over, and nothing remained but a slaughter. Surrounded by a solid ring of his knights, James, refusing to yield, at length fell, and with him to a man died his thirty human shields. It was a splendid example of personal bravery, but the day of chivalry (as the term is generally understood) was past. A king the leader of thirty thousand men needed to be a general, and not a knight errant. During the night, Home's men and other marauders pillaged the dead and dying of both armies indiscriminately, and, moreover, the baggage trains. In the morning the banner of this worthy was still to be discerned on the left flank of the English, and a small body of Scotch who had rallied in the night were collected on a hill fronting the English centre. These probably consisted of the relics of Crawford's men who had been routed by Admiral Howard. Surrey, by means of his artillery, broke these, and they sullenly withdrew towards the Tweed, crossing that river at Coldstream.

Ten thousand men fell on the Scottish side—the lowest computation says 8,000—and the English loss was at least 5,000. The body of James was found covered with wounds, and amid a heap of slain. His sword, dagger, and what is supposed to be the turquoise ring, were found on the field and are now preserved in the College of Arms. Seventeen guns were abandoned by the Scots on the hillside, and among them the "Seven Sisters." To attempt anything like a list of the slain would be almost to catalogue the ancient Scottish nobility. It was the most terrible and overwhelming blow that any kingdom has ever experienced. Except the heads of families of distinction who were either too old to fight or too young, there was hardly one of the first rank which did not suffer. Twelve earls, the Archbishop of St. Andrews and other churchmen, the bastard son of the king and innumerable heads of clans, smaller nobility, and knights fell on this fatal day. The body of James was wrapped in lead after being embalmed, and sent first to Newcastle and then to London. Rumour has it that it was subsequently buried at the monastery at Sheen; another story is that, having been consigned to a lumber room, it was eventually thrown into a parish common grave.

FLODDEN.

For years the Scots entertained a belief that the king escaped, and looked for his coming. Fiction has of course been busy with the locality. Sybil's Well is a myth, being situated in an impossible place. The King's Stone also has no historic significance whatever, being a glacial deposit, and far from the field.

Ford Castle, the most of which only dates from the 18th and 19th centuries, was originally built by Odenel de Forde in 1287. His heiress married Sir William Heron, who fortified the tower by license. Ford was demolished in 1385 by a party of raiders under Douglas. Since the days of Flodden the castle was rebuilt in part prior to 1549, when some Scots under a

THE KING'S STONE.

Frenchman bombarded it with four guns. With regard to the part which Lady Heron played in the tragedy of Flodden, it is unlikely that she would have been on any terms at all with the man who, despite all her efforts, persisted in destroying her castle. During the time James was occupied in besieging Norham and Etal, the lady was endeavouring to negotiate through Surrey for the castle to be spared. Surrey, it seems established, absolutely offered to restore two prisoners of note to the Scots as a price for abstention from damage to Ford—an offer which was not entertained. One point with regard to the camp of the Scots needs notice, and that is, that though well-nigh impregnable, it could only be held by a large body of men for a brief period. Water, that most needful adjunct, was lacking. Surrey, when once arrived in close proximity to Flodden Hill, could by the proper disposition of his troops have effectually cut off the water supply of his enemies, unless, indeed, they fetched it from a considerable distance on the other side, *i.e.*, from Palinsburn. Archers, aided by artillery, could have held the line of the Till with but little trouble, and the loss certain to have attended the daily watering parties for 30,000 men, who had to obtain supplies in the face of the enemy, would have been enormous. Thirty-five knights were made " at the battaile of Branston Moore, otherwise called Flodden Field."

NOX I.

HOWARD.

KELSY.

CHAPTER XXII.

NEWBURN.

August 28, 1640.

ABOUT the middle of July, 1640, the recently disbanded Scotch army was re-assembled at Dunglas, on the Clyde, a place distant about two miles and a half to the east of Dumbarton. Alexander Leslie, a soldier schooled in the German Wars and a popular Scottish general, was again placed in command. Another tried military man, William Baillie, was one of his subordinates. Baillie, the bastard son of Sir William Baillie, of Lamington, had seen a good deal of service under Gustavus Adolphus. Eight years previously, on the death of that king, Baillie's name occurs as " colonell to a regiment of foote of Dutch " in the list of foreign officers employed by him. Leslie's army amounted to more than 20,000 foot and 2,500 horse. Money, stores, and artillery were, however, lacking, and the methods employed to raise the two first-named were as follows :—Contributions of cash and plate were invited and freely given. Linen to make tents was supplied out of the household stores of the people, mainly in Edinburgh. Leslie's desire to have an adequate supply of tents arose from a wish on his part not to quarter his troops on the population of the districts through which he passed. Provided with tents at the start, too, there would be no need of predatory excursions when on the march to obtain the requisite materials, and less unpopularity, therefore, would attach to the invading army in its passage. Linen, too, made as it was then made by industrious Scottish matrons and girls, was as strong, nay, stronger than canvas, and lighter withal; a most excellent substitute, therefore, for the coarser and heavier stuff generally employed. To supply his deficiency in artillery, Leslie is said to have resorted to a curious expedient of which he had learnt the use in Germany. This was nothing less than the manufacture of temporary cannon, *i.e.*, cannon of small calibre, sufficiently strong to stand a few discharges but no more before becoming useless. These guns, two of which could be carried on a pack-horse, were manufactured in Edinburgh. Firstly a strong tube of tin (one account says bar iron) of the required bore, and heavily closed at the breech, was made. This was wrapped thickly in wet raw hides, the whole being then tightly and regularly bound with strong cord from muzzle to breech. A touch-hole bored completed this curious but ingenious instrument. True, such guns would stand but a few rounds before bursting, but the moral effect of a large number of them on an enemy which was secure in the notion that artillery was lacking to its opponents can be imagined.

On November 20th the Scottish army crossed the Tweed by the old accustomed ford at Coldstream. It is stated that lots were drawn by the various divisions of the army to settle the order of march through the water. The lot fell to the body commanded by James Graham, 5th Earl and 1st Marquis of Montrose—the Montrose whose subsequent adventures and sad end are well known. As a military commander comparatively scant justice has been done him. His skill in manœuvring a small force was indisputable, and as a tactician he was even greater. An innovator, or so considered by the military men of his time, Montrose almost habitually varied his plan of battle according to the circumstances under which he was about to fight, the troops of the various arms of which his force was composed, and the composition of his enemy. The old-fashioned hard and fast "plan of battle" was almost invariably eschewed by him. Hence, perhaps, the reason for his success four years later, when, within twelve months, he won six pitched battles against the Covenanters. Assuredly Montrose possessed military genius which for those days was of a very high order. In the passage of the Tweed, Montrose was conspicuous by the zeal with which he led his men. Detractors, and he had many, noised it abroad that this zeal was but a mask assumed to conceal intended treachery. From Coldstream the army marched southwards, arriving at Newcastle Moor without hindrance. Newcastle, a strong place, was found to be defended by a strong force, a detachment of 3,000 foot and 1,500 horse, under Edward, 2nd Viscount Conway, guarding the ford over the Tyne at Newburn, about five miles from Newcastle. It will be observed that as the city of Newcastle is on the north side of the river, and

Conway's post was on the south, the English commanded both banks, or intended to. Leslie had no siege guns, and Newcastle was too hard a nut for him to crack on the northern side. But if he could win his way over the river a different complexion would be put on the matter. Newcastle, less strongly fortified on that side, would be more easily attacked, or an engagement in the open field might possibly be provoked, in which case his veteran soldiers would have an advantage over the raw levies which, for the most part,

LESLIE'S POSITION BEYOND THE RIVER. CONWAY'S BATTERY IN FRONT.

composed the English army there at that time. Leslie therefore determined on forcing a passage over the river by one or both of the fords at Newburn, a passage which, if successfully achieved, would enable him effectually to turn the enemy's flank. The fords at Newburn were the first places above Newcastle at which the river was passable for foot. Leslie occupied Heddon Law, the heights above the village, mounting his rudely constructed cannon on the old tower of the Norman church, and also erecting batteries, masked amid the ragged bushes which then covered the hillside and grew down to the river bank itself, but which now do so no more. Beneath him the river wound its tortuous course to Newcastle. The selected spot for passage was a bend in the river where, owing to its width and the season of the year, there was hardly any water. King David, *en route* to Neville's Cross, had forded the stream at the same spot. On the other side, the ground, for some distance from the river bank, is perfectly flat. Here Conway erected batteries or sconces. The remains of one exist to this day—unless, indeed, the partly broken mound is a relic of the stronger fortifications which, four years later, baffled Leslie in a similar attempt to cross, and forced him to ascend the river as far as Ovingham before he was able to effect a passage. Traces of earthworks are also apparent on one side of the wooded dell or dene, and these, by their direction, appear to have been constructed in a line from the larger battery in the field beneath. Elsewhere, neither along the haughs nor on the hills, are there traces either of earthworks or batteries, though the hills were certainly fortified to some extent. The high ground at the back runs steeply down with more than one projecting spur, and at that time wooded. Conway headed one regiment of the defenders, Lord Wilmot another.

Conway, on the appearance of the Scots at the ford, opened fire with what guns he had chiefly at the church tower, and was astonished to find not only that his fire was replied to, but also that in the number of guns, if not in weight of metal, the invaders were superior. His troops were raw and undisciplined, while those of the Scotch were veterans. The action began in the afternoon. Colonel Lunsford, who was in charge of the greater sconce, finding that his fire on the church produced no appreciable effect, and that, on the other hand, his earthwork was breached, retired therefrom after ineffectual efforts to prevail upon his men to continue the defence. It is stated with regard to this evacuation that a captain, a lieutenant, and some other officers were there slain. The men, half mutinous, complained that all that day and all the preceding night they had been under arms at the guns without relief. To these remonstrances Colonel Lunsford replied by exhortations, but without avail, and a successful shot from the other side at this juncture, pitching among the men and killing some, decided the matter. Throwing down their arms, the fellows ran for shelter to the wooded ground in their rear. Leslie, from his position, could overlook the defenders, and this retreat was not, of course, lost to his eye. By this time the tide had fallen to its extreme low-water mark, and the moment to effect the crossing had come. A forlorn hope numbering twenty-six mounted men, gentlemen of the College of Justice troop, were sent to cross the river and to reconnoitre if possible, but ordered on no account to come into direct conflict with the enemy. Under cover of a heavy cannonade the little band crossed the river. This cannonade cleared the upper trench of its defenders. Their retreat was observed, and more horse under Sir Thomas Hope, supported by two regiments of foot commanded by Lord

Crawford, Lindsay, and Lord Loudon, at once passed the river. Leslie, on his side, was by no means idle; for he moved nine small pieces to a hill on the east and opened fire on the Royal Horse, which was drawn up in the flat meadows and might be expected to charge at any moment. The guns disordered the horse, and a retreat was sounded, before which Colonel Lunsford managed to withdraw the abandoned guns. A small cavalry skirmish took place between the rear-guard of the retreating force and the foremost of the Scotch; Wilmot, Sir John Digby, and Daniel O'Neil, according to one account, being the chief actors in this part of the battle. The English foot retreated up the hills (banks) towards Ryton and also towards Stella, *i.e.*, right and left of the position they had occupied. One account states that the rear-guard of the Scots then crossed the river and caught the cavalry of the English rear-guard between them and the main body of the invaders, taking Wilmot, Digby, and O'Neil prisoners, together with some of their men.

Another version is that the English horse, to the number of six troops, were ordered to charge the forlorn hope and did so, driving them back across the ford. They were then thrown into disorder by a brisk cannonade from Leslie's guns and retired in the direction of Ryton, where, amid the trees and over the crest of the bank, they would be unobserved. Their path must have been up the dene or glen. Near Ryton they met with some English infantry. The Scots now crossed successfully in large numbers, their horse in two divisions and accompanied by 10,000 foot. Proceeding up the hill past the now deserted batteries they came into collision with Wilmot and the infantry. Wilmot's cavalry fled, leaving him a prisoner, and the infantry, in like manner, made off. In their flight the cavalry rushed among Lord Conway's horse, which up to this time had not been in action, putting them into confusion and mingling both with them and the other foot. In a few moments the entire army was in full retreat in the direction of Newcastle. No other resistance was made save by a gallant little band of gentlemen armed with breastplates and well mounted. These in vain tried to stem

STELLA. CONWAY'S POSITION. RYTON.

the tide. As a forlorn hope they dashed into the van of the advancing Scots, where many fell.

As will be seen these accounts are somewhat conflicting, a fact which is perhaps due to the partisanship of writers of that date. Neither account reflects credit on Lord Conway, who appears to have been a thoroughly incapable if not an absolutely cowardly commander. Clarendon attacked Conway most bitterly for his conduct, implying that he not only ran away himself but refused to lead his men again to the charge when they begged him so to do. Conway, in his defence, pleads that his want of success was due to lack of time to properly fortify the position. He adds that his position was disadvantageous (this is probably true), also that his men did not fight as they ought to have done, " being the meanest sort of men about London and unacquainted with service," &c. His excuses, however, are very lame. The loss of life at this fight was indeed small ; it did not, in fact, total fifty on both sides. Conway got clear off as far as Durham. Newcastle was entered by the Scots from the south side without offering any resistance. Baillie in his letters tells us how, in the king's magazine there, the Scots found "good store of biscuit and cheese and five thousand arms, musket and pikes," besides other provisions. Conway's excuse must, in truth, have been a lame one, for Newburn Ford, in 1644, was held, and successfully, against the same commander, Leslie. A huge wheel found at Newburn is now in the Newcastle Museum. It purports to have belonged to a gun. If this be true, there must have been at least one very heavy gun on the English side that day, which, properly served, would soon have cleared the church tower opposite of its small makeshift pieces.

WILMOT.

LUNSFORD.

DIGBY.

CHAPTER XXIII.

EDGEHILL.

October 23, 1642.

ON August 22nd the standard of Charles I. was unfurled at Nottingham. Dover Castle had been surprised and seized by a party of Parliamentarian soldiers on the previous day. In Essex, notably at Colchester, Puritan mobs were plundering Royalists and the houses of inoffensive Catholics. Canterbury Cathedral suffered from the excesses of fanatical soldiery, its organ being demolished and altar desecrated. Nor did the Puritans elsewhere in the country suffer less at the hands of the Royalist troops, for all notable men of that party were plundered as opportunity arose. Within a day or two after the formal raising of the standard a slight Royalist reverse took place near Coventry. Early in September Rupert, already general of the royal cavalry, was scouring the country to raise supplies, specially of money, and had mulcted Leicester of £500; he asked a loan of £2,000. On September 7th Portsmouth surrendered to Sir William Waller. On September 9th the Earl of Essex took leave of

Cromwell's silver mounted leather bottle (Littlecote).

the Houses of Parliament and started for Northampton, reaching that town late on the following day. Among the baggage of the Parliamentarian commander was a coffin, a shroud, and a funeral hatchment. At Northampton the Parliament had mustered about 20,000 men, and with this force Essex embarked on his campaign.

Charles was at Nottingham, and thither Essex, without doubt, intended to march. The royal troops were certainly considerably less in numbers than those under Essex. Prudence dictated that an engagement should, if possible, be avoided, and hence, on September 13th, the king marched westwards. On the borders of Wales he expected a reinforcement of some 5,000, and the loyalists of Shropshire and Cheshire were also prepared to join his force. Marching *viâ* Stafford and Wellington, he occupied Shrewsbury on September 20th, and three days later seized Chester. Oxford had been visited by Sir John Byron, with a troop or two of horse, towards the end of August (28th). The Royalist cavalry, however, tarried not longer than twelve days in the University city, starting thence for Worcester with a slight augmentation in force and a small supply of ready money. On September 12th the Parliamentarian troops took possession of Oxford, doing some damage to the ecclesiastical buildings therein. Byron reached Worcester on September 16th, where he made some attempts to repair the tumbledown walls and to place the city in a condition capable of defence.

Essex marched from Northampton on September 19th but though going westward did not, it would appear, follow the king, but advanced nearly direct to Worcester. A small advance guard, under one Nathaniel Fiennes, had been despatched to Worcester, and on September 22nd a rumour reached the Parliamentarian army that this force had engaged the royal troops outside the city. Essex pressed on, and on the 23rd had arrived within five miles of Worcester. Here Byron had come to the conclusion that the city was untenable, and was preparing to evacuate it. Rupert, to whom the post of

Powick Bridge.

covering this movement had been allotted, arrived from the royal army.

While the preparations for the evacuation were going on, the Prince went on a reconnaissance in the direction of Powick Bridge. This bridge is now destroyed, but is represented by a curiously irregular structure of brick which crosses the river Teme near to the electric light station. While the Royalists were dismounted and taking a rest, it is stated that the cavalry of Fiennes were descried in close proximity. To mount and charge them was quickly the order, and a complete rout of the Parliamentary cavalry ensued. Right over the bridge they fled pell-mell, nor drew rein till the Severn had been crossed at Upton and Pershore reached, where some of the troops of Essex then lay. It seems that Fiennes had heard that an evacuation of Worcester was in prospect, and crossed to obtain information of the actual state of affairs. His position on the other side of the Teme was one which Rupert could hardly have assailed even had he known where it was—which he clearly did not. Worcester was at once evacuated, and was occupied by Essex on September 24th. The skirmish between Rupert and Fiennes is remarkable from the fact that the victorious Royalists did *not* pursue their flying enemies. Charles, who had been at Chester, now returned to Shrewsbury, where he remained, endeavouring to equip and organise his army, until October 12th. On the 21st he reached Southam, and the following evening the village of Edgcott near Banbury. Banbury, then walled and held by the Parliament, he designed to capture with all speed, but the news of the near approach of Essex caused a change of plan. Now it must be remarked that Charles was professedly marching on London, and the possession of the City, if it did not completely finish the war, would at least have gone far towards that end. But with Essex in his rear and the hostile city in his front, should the king even reach the walls of London a siege was probable unless he defeated the Parliamentarians *en route*, and the liability of being caught between two hostile forces more than probable. As a matter of fact Charles outnumbered Essex, but was vastly outnumbered himself by the forces at the disposal of the Parliament which lay between him and London or within its walls. Clearly it was the right thing to do to give battle to Essex at once, but it needed a general to select the place and time for the battle, and a general Charles was not. Still, the first position occupied by his army, viz., on the crest of a long steep hill, was a good one—only Essex had no intention of fighting on those terms and fighting a superior force. The Parliamentarian leader drew up his army on the lower ground and at some distance from the hill. Like Surrey at Flodden, he succeeded in drawing the enemy from a strong position to a weaker one. Still there was a reason for this which may be alleged in excuse of Charles. Banbury lay but a few miles in the rear and was hostile. Oxford was held by the Parliament, and the Royalists were singularly uninfluential in the district. Charles's army, which subsisted by plunder, ran thereabouts a heavy risk of starvation long before London could be reached. Starving troops in a hostile country when pursued fare but ill, and this march, though really not so, would practically have been converted into a retreat. Hence it was that Charles, marching from Edgecott, took up his position on Edgehill with 10,000 men, and Essex, advancing from his quarters at Kineton with 14,000, faced him on October 23rd, 1642.

The disposition of the two armies was as follows: Rupert and Lord Wilmot commanded the cavalry of the Royal army, and of this, the force of Rupert (the right wing), was considerably larger than that of Wilmot on the left. The centre was entirely composed of foot. There was also a small reserve of horse posted in the rear. The Parliamentary right (also cavalry) was under the command of Sir Philip Stapleton (two weak regiments), Lord Fielding (one), and Sir William Balfour (one). Sir Faithful Fortescue, an intending traitor, was among the cavalry of the Parliamentarian left, and therefore opposed to Rupert. Two regiments of horse acted as a small reserve. As with the Royal army, that of the Parliament had its centre composed entirely of infantry. Of the

number of guns or their actual position on either side there are no trustworthy accounts.

Early in the afternoon the Royal army descended from the high ground and formed up in the plain beneath. The battle began with a slight but ineffectual cannonade—traditionally Charles is said to have fired the first gun. The small share which guns for the most part took in the battles of the Civil War is somewhat remarkable. Hand to hand fighting was then initiated by Rupert with his cavalry command. The Prince, whose position in the army was somewhat anomalous here as hereafter, appears to have been entirely freed from the control of any superior. Already this strange arrangement had led to bitter reproof from Lucius Cary, Lord Falkland, and to what was worse, viz., the supersession of the veteran, Lord Lindsay, from his position as general. Lindsay, finding that, though ostensibly in chief command, an irresponsible cavalry officer and withal quite a junior in the person of Rupert was to act independently, retired to his regimental command, and was replaced as general by the Earl of Forth (recently created Lord Ruthven).

Rupert began the fight, as has been said, and delivered an oblique cavalry attack. Advancing first in a direction which brought him still more to the right of his original position (a manœuvre he subsequently repeated at Naseby, where it failed), he then wheeled to the left and charged on the left flank of the Parliamentarian left wing. At starting the Prince was immeasurably the superior of his opponents both in the numbers and composition of his force. To render the disparity even greater as his squadrons drew near, Fortescue rode forward and then deserted with his men, joining in the attack on the Parliamentarian left. It is hardly to be wondered that, with a heavy charge of known foes from without and the serious treachery of Fortescue within their lines, the cavalry of the Parliamentarian left wavered and broke, making but a slight resistance. In a brief space it was in full flight, but not before it had almost completely thrown into confusion four regiments of infantry, and these likewise fled. Rupert thundered after the flying cavalry in headlong pursuit, slaying many and chasing them as far as Kineton, where for the purpose of plundering the Parliamentarian baggage train many of the Royalist cavalry pulled up. Others continued cutting up the fugitives till brought to a standstill by a couple of regiments of foot under John Hampden, which, having been outstripped by the main army, were hurrying forward to join Essex.

This prolonged pursuit was fatal, or almost fatal, to the fortunes of the Royalists on that day. Had the Royalist cavalry been but kept in hand after their successful attack, nothing, humanly speaking, could have saved the army of

THE BATTLEFIELD.

Essex from utter discomfiture. Wilmot on the left in the meanwhile had put to flight the cavalry of Fielding, and had galloped off after them bent on a similar mission of slaughter and plunder. But it would appear that while Fielding fled, the horse under Balfour and Stapleton either stood firm or, if shaken, were quickly rallied. This or something like it must have been the case in the face of what followed. In full feather and flushed with the appearance of what seemed like a complete victory, the king's own bodyguard, till then supposed to be reserve horse, begged to be allowed to join in the fray, and with their commander, Sir John Byron, hastily followed in the wake of Rupert. The position was now as follows: Rupert, victorious on the right, had left the field in hot pursuit of the whole cavalry of the Parliamentarian left. Wilmot similarly was chasing Fielding's regiment. The Royal reserve was pursuing Rupert and slaughtering the unfortunates his troopers had missed. Charles with his infantry and guns remained on the field, opposed by the greater part of the infantry of the Parliament and three regiments of horse—these last at a short distance from the extreme left of his centre. The troops Essex had at his disposal, as far as foot went, luckily for him were men drawn from the eastern counties and from London, and were perhaps the most fanatical puritans of the day. One regiment, the "Lord General's own," and the regiment of Holles (Londoners) were particularly conspicuous.

And then the struggle became most severe. Balfour with his cavalry charged and pierced the infantry of the Royal centre, riding through the musketeers and pikemen, discomfiting two entire regiments and penetrating as far as the guns. These he did not spike for lack of proper implements, but did the next best thing as he considered, viz., he cut the traces and then returned to renew the fight. It is strange that he did not use them against the rear of the Royalists as he might have done. For some little time the Royal army was in a condition of imminent danger—nay, the life of Charles himself was in jeopardy. Though early in the engagement he had been placed on the crest of a hill to view the proceedings, he had left that point of safety when things went or seemed to go badly, and at one time was actually mixed up in the *mêlée*. When Balfour abandoned the captured guns they were repossessed—it cannot be called recaptured—by two regiments of Royalist foot, and by these as long as the fight lasted they were guarded. The infantry at the right of the Royal centre stood firm, but on the defensive only; and on another part of the field, cut off from all other portions of the army, stood the Royal foot-guards, above whose ranks waved the Royal standard. This regiment was under the command of the discarded Lindsay, its colonel, and nobly did it resist. Charged in the rear by Balfour and on the left flank by Stapleton, while Essex with the infantry assailed them in front, the struggle could end but in one manner. The ranks first pierced were speedily completely broken. The Royal standard was captured, its bearer, Sir Edmund Verney, being slain. Lindsay fell mortally wounded, and was taken prisoner Some few escaped, but practically the Royal foot-guards were destroyed. Nothing now remained but to dispose of the two regiments which had taken up position around the previously captured guns, and this Essex was proceeding to do. His men were already advancing when the near approach of the returning Royalist cavalry was observed, and the attack was never delivered. It has been urged that Wilmot ought at this juncture to have charged the infantry of Essex, and that Rupert ought likewise to have done so, but it must be remembered that the victorious Royalist cavalry was not in the condition to undertake offensive movements. With horses blown, with no regular formation, and encumbered with loot—a mere mob, in fact, of armed mounted men, what effect would they have produced upon the victorious foot of the enemy, supported as it was by three regiments of cavalry apparently well in hand and certainly in a measure victorious? Wilmot, it is said, flatly refused to charge when begged to do so by Falkland. Whether Rupert was asked to or not is unknown. Moreover the darkness had by this time come on, and the presence or absence of an orange scarf was all the distinction in dress between friend and foe.

All that night—a night of severe frost—the armies lay in close proximity, the Royalists a little drawn off to the higher ground. On the morrow the Royalist cavalry, which had straggled in by parties, had assumed again some appearance of discipline, but the Royalist foot was weak indeed. Essex had received a welcome reinforcement of four thousand men under Hampden, but, with the exception of the regiments of Balfour and Stapleton, he was without cavalry. Charles in his position on the high ground (so steep is the ascent) could have withstood any attack; or at least the chances of any success in an attack on his position were exceedingly small. Lansdown and Stratton are both steep, but the sides of Edgehill are even more precipitous. In truth, neither side felt disposed to renew the battle.

During the day the Parliamentarian army retired, and in the evening occupied Kineton. They encamped there, but not, however, without the rear-guard suffering from a cavalry attack by Rupert. On October 25th Essex retired still further and reached Warwick. Two days later Banbury surrendered to Charles, who on the 29th of October entered Oxford. One dashing exploit which happened on the night after the battle at least deserves mention. A certain Captain John Smyth, a Catholic, the brother of Sir Charles Smyth and an officer in the king's Life Guards, recovered the Royal standard. To effect this he assumed the Parliamentarian badge, an orange scarf, and under the cover of darkness penetrated into the camp of Essex. He found the standard in the custody of the general's secretary. Smyth snatched it up with the remark that it was not fit for a penman to keep such a prize, and straightway carried it back to his royal master. One account tells that he had a hard fight to get his prize, in the course of which he cut down or put to flight several troopers who were on guard. Charles rightly rewarded this brave act with immediate knighthood. Cromwell was present at the battle at the head of a troop of horse, and assuredly did good service there. His son, Captain Cromwell (also Oliver) it was who fled. Through malice or mistake the bad behaviour of the son has been imputed to the father.

The view of the battlefield from the top of Edgehill is much interfered with by the trees which crown its crest and sides. Just below the steepest part of the hillside there is a low green hill known by the name of Bullet Hill, and here many relics of the fight are stated to have been discovered. A long grass-bordered road at the top of the Edgehill ridge is still known as Camp Lane, and here the Royalist army lay under arms on the night following the battle. It seems probable that on Bullet Hill the guns were posted, and that the army, after a preliminary cannonade, advanced over the level plain towards Red Horse, where Essex had drawn up his battle. Far in the distance towards Kineton, in a small bush-dotted field, those slain by Rupert in his cavalry charge and pursuit were buried. Place-names abound on the field. We have Graveground Coppice, Battleton Holt, and Battle Farm. The slaughter at this fight was heavy, and has been computed as high as five thousand. It is somewhat curious to note that the loss on the side of the Parliament was mainly confined to the fugitives, while on that of the king those who stood their ground and fought suffered most severely. Among the slain were several men of note on both sides. Of Royalists Lord Lindsay, Sir Edmund Verney, and Lord Stuart d'Aubigné were the chief.

CHAPTER XXIV.

STRATTON.

May 16, 1643.

TOWARDS the end of April, 1643, the state of affairs in the West of England was as follows: Hopton, after his success at Bradock Down on January 19th, had in succession taken Saltash and Okehampton by storm; the Earl of Stamford retreating before the victorious Cornishmen. The pursuit continued as far as Chagford, where it ceased in consequence of a skirmish there, in which Sir John Northcote gained some little success and where Sidney Godolphin was killed. Probably had the entire Cornish army carried out this pursuit the check would not have occurred; but unfortunately the larger portion thereof had turned off in a vain attempt to lay siege to Plymouth. This step was taken by Hopton, contrary to the urgent advice of Sir Bevil Grenville.

On April 23rd, Captain James Chudleigh, the third son of Sir George Chudleigh, made an unsuccessful attempt to obtain the mastery over Hopton, then lying at Launceston. Two days later, however, he met with better success, and on

Sourton Down Hopton suffered a check which was so serious as to almost amount to a defeat, part of the baggage being lost, and among it important documents from the king to his commander.

The Earl of Stamford now attempted offensive operations against the Royalists, and for this purpose marched into Cornwall with 6,800 men, a force which was more than double the strength of the army of Cornishmen under Grenville and Hopton. Stamford, however, now committed the error of detaching the greater part of his horse under Sir George Chudleigh to overawe the Royalists in Bodmin, who were suspected of intending to muster the trained-bands at that town. The earl, with his foot and the remains of his horse, encamped on the top of a hill near the village of Stratton, and in a very strong position. Stamford Hill, for so it is now named, is an isolated grassy hill on a ridge which runs nearly due north and south. The sides to the east and south are the steepest. The village of Stratton lies south-east by south at a distance of less than a mile, and beyond a brook. On the west side of Stamford Hill the slope is more gentle, and here, at the time of the battle, an earthwork was existing and defended by guns. That earthwork is yet to be seen, but from its appearance gives the impression of having far greater antiquity than the middle of the seventeenth century. Be this as it may, as far as the west side of the position is concerned, the guns ought to have rendered it impregnable. Stamford Hill being, as it were, a peak in a ridge, was capable of being stormed on every side at once, though, as will be understood, the difficulties of the various sides were of different natures. Hopton and Grenville divided their troops into four storming parties. The little army was too small to merit, when divided into such parts, any other designation. In the morning the fight commenced, and continued till noon was past and the afternoon well advanced. At 3 p.m. no impression had been made on Stamford and Chudleigh, all attempts notwithstanding. Powder began to fail the Cornishmen, and it became a question between retreat, *i.e.*, certain disaster or victory. A final and most heroic effort was made—muskets were laid aside, and with pike at push and sword thrust, four attacks simultaneously began. Grenville led the party on the western side, Sir John Berkeley that on the northern. Possibly the gentler slope was in Grenville's favour, but certain it is that his men first reached the crest. When Berkeley prevailed on the north side, the Parliamentarian horse (a few only it will be remembered) fled from the hill headlong down the steep and made off. This had its moral effect on the defenders of the other two sides of the camp, and their resistance perceptibly slackened. Soon the other two storming parties pressed upward, and on the hilltop, the enemy, despite the efforts of Chudleigh to rally them, made off to the adjoining heights. Chudleigh, of whose conduct something will be said later, was taken prisoner while heading an unsupported or feebly supported charge. Stamford, it is stated, had already fled, perhaps in company with the fugitive horse. But the foot, having gained the shelter of the neighbouring heights, appear to have rallied somewhat, and to have shown a disposition pointing to a desire to renew the combat. For a wonder the captured artillery was made use of to disperse them. This act is believed to have been the work of Grenville. Turning the cannon on the men who clustered on the ridge, a few rounds sufficed to dislodge them. Panic ensued, and a general stampede, in which arms and accoutrements were flung aside, concluded the fight of Stratton. Sir George Chudleigh and Captain James Chudleigh, his son, require notice, though merely brief notice. Sir George was created a baronet on August 1, 1622, having served in Parliament as M.P. for St. Michael and also Lostwithiel. He was subsequently member for Tiverton in 1623-4, and again for Lostwithiel in May, 1625. On the outbreak of the civil war he was active in the west, on the side of the Parliament. His sole military exploit was the expedition to Bodmin in command of 1,200 horse. After the defeat of his son at Stamford Hill, he left Bodmin for Exeter, and went thence to Plymouth. When Lord Stamford accused Captain Chudleigh of treachery at Stratton Sir George resigned his commission. He died in 1657, having in his later years become a Royalist. Captain James Chudleigh began his active military career on the side of the Parliament when the civil war broke out. Previously to this he had been mixed up in various negotiations, acting as intermediary between the officers in Yorkshire and the Earl of Northumberland. He was the messenger employed by Jermyn and Endymion Porter to urge the acceptance of Goring as lieut.-general. Chudleigh was also the chief mover in the meeting of officers at Boroughbridge, which led to a circular letter to Goring, then supposed to be in London.

Chudleigh, a few months later, was examined before the House as to his conduct on this occasion. After Stratton, Stamford openly accused Chudleigh of treachery, but this accusation is believed to be false. Chudleigh, however, it is only fair to state, joined the Royal cause ten days after the battle. His life was not a long one. On September 30th in the same year, in a skirmish between the royal garrison of Dartmouth and the besiegers, under Lord Fairfax, he was shot, and died of the wound a few days later. Clarendon says he was "a wonderful loss to the king's service." It is rather curious to note that the baronetcy in this family existed 123 years to the day, having been created on August 1, 1622, and expiring on August 1, 1745.

Sir John Berkeley was a most distinguished Royalist, and one of the Berkeleys of Bruton. His military career commenced against the Scots in 1638, and at Berwick in July of that year he received the honour of knighthood. On the outbreak of the civil war Berkeley's first exploit was to convey in safety from Holland an important supply of arms, &c., despatched to the king by Queen Henrietta. Berkeley fought through the whole of the campaign in the west. His great exploits were the reduction of Exeter, and the repulse of the enemy's fleet at Topsham. When the royal cause was wrecked he was employed with Ashburnham to negotiate terms for the king. In exile, after the death of Lord Byron, Berkeley was put at the head of the household of the Duke of York. In 1658 (by patent, 19th of May) he was raised to the peerage, with the title of Baron Berkeley of Stratton.

266 STRATTON.

On the Restoration Lord Berkeley was made a Privy Councillor. From 1670 to 1672 he filled the office of Lord-Lieutenant of Ireland, and three years later was appointed Ambassador to Versailles. He died on August 28, 1678. The military career of Henry Grey, First Earl of Stamford, is so unimportant that no details thereof need here be given.

WENTWORTH.

BERKELEY.

CHAPTER XXV.

CHALGROVE FIELD.

June 18, 1643.

THE combat at Chalgrove Field—for it can hardly be dignified by the name of a battle—is mainly memorable for the death of John Hampden. Hampden, as a deputy-lieutenant of Buckinghamshire and a Parliamentarian, was active in the execution of the militia ordinance in that county. On July 4, 1642, he had undertaken to raise a regiment of foot for the Parliament, and this regiment, the "green-coats," afterwards did good service. There is a tradition that the first muster of his men took place on Chalgrove Field, the spot where subsequently he received his death wound. On August 10th he performed the exploit of seizing the Earl of Berkshire and the king's Commissioners of Array at the house of Sir Robert Dormer, at Ascot. Sending his prisoners to London, he marched to the relief of Coventry, successfully effecting this exploit on August 23rd. For the remainder of August and all September he remained with the army of Essex, endeavouring to improve the discipline of that hitherto unorganised force. Prior to Edgehill he had been despatched to Worcester to escort the artillery train thence, and arrived, as has been told elsewhere, too late to join in the battle, though in time to check the pursuit of Rupert's victorious horse. Disregarding Hampden's earnest advice to renew the engagement, Essex withdrew to Warwick. At Brentford, on November 12th, after the Royalist attack under Rupert, the arrival of Hampden with fresh troops covered the retreat of the survivors of that engagement. Rupert had fallen upon Holles's regiment, and had driven it back into the town with loss. Brooke's regiment held the town, and these two maintained the combat till they were nearly exterminated either by wounds or drowning. Hampden here designed to retaliate, and by cutting off the retreat of Rupert to in a measure retrieve the fortunes of the day. He started out with this intention, but was recalled by Essex, and the opportunity was lost. It will be remembered that this attack on Brentford was ordered by Charles while negotiations were pending, an act which can hardly be defended on political grounds, though from a military point of view advisable. When the Royalists were faced on November 12th by a Parliamentarian army of 24,000 men at Turnham Green to Hampden was committed the duty of making a detour to Acton with a detachment intended to complete the environment of the Royalists' position. This order was, however, cancelled, and its withdrawal was a blunder. At the time 3,000 troops, under Sir John Ramsay, held Kingston Bridge, and might have attacked the rear of the Royal army. The main Parliamentarian force blocked the way to London, and Hampden's detachment would, one is inclined to think, have (assuming action to have been in concert) finished the war. But the Parliamentarian force was undisciplined, divers and opposite counsels prevailed among its leaders, and there was, moreover, a wholesome dread of Rupert's horse. Ramsay was withdrawn, Hampden's orders were cancelled, and Kingston was occupied by the king. When Brentford was evacuated by Rupert, Hampden at once reoccupied it for the Parliament. For the remainder of the year, and until June, 1643, political rather than military affairs occupied Hampden.

On June 10th, Essex, having been reinforced, left Reading, where he had been quartered, and took possession of Thame. With a fresh augmentation of troops on June 13th he sent his advanced guard thence to Wheatley, near Oxford, the Royalists having then an outpost on Shotover Hill. Whether or not Essex meditated an attack on Oxford does not clearly appear. That he was not, however, strong enough to succeed there is manifest. One thing is certain, viz., that Hampden, ever ready to strike if possible, warned the Parliamentary general not to attack that city. This would point to some such scheme having been discussed. That the Queen was bringing reinforcements from Yorkshire was ascertained, and these would need to be first reckoned with before a siege began. The Royalists held Islip, and a body of 2,500 men sent thither by Essex to take the place withdrew without even making an attempt. Rupert, eager and ready to do something, now started out from Oxford at the head of 1,700 men, the greater part being cavalry. It was one of those raids which, as a cavalier cavalryman, his soul dearly loved. The Royalists had recently been joined by a deserter from the Parliamentarian force, one John Hurry, or Urry, a Scotchman. This worthy, who deserted to the Parliament again after the recapture of Wareham, on August 24, 1644, brought news that a large sum of money, £21,000, was on its way under convoy from London to Essex, at Thame. The king needed money badly, and could this sum have been obtained it would have been more than welcome. This convoy was ostensibly the chief object of Rupert's raid. With such an end in view, silence, and the utmost secrecy, would have been the line taken by any ordinary commander. How did Rupert proceed? In a manner most characteristic. Starting from Oxford he rode through Chiselhampton, a distance of about seven miles in a south-easterly direction. There he crossed the river Thame, and making his way to Stadhampton, turned north-east till he cut the road from Postcombe to Oxford. Keeping to the road for a space in the direction of Tetsworth, he then took to the fields to avoid that place, finding that it was held by a Parliamentarian outpost. Rupert, however, took no other precautions to ensure silence, and his men were heard, an alarm being raised about midnight. Rupert passed on till he reached Postcombe, where he cut up a small post of Parliamentarians. Proceeding from Postcombe he performed the same achievement at Chinnor, a village three miles north-east by east. Here he slew fifty men, and made rather more than double that number of prisoners, likewise thoroughly arousing the countryside. This, it may be observed, was not more than three miles from the road to

Thame by which the convoy was bound to pass—the convoy which was the main aim of his raid. That warning was given to its drivers and the escort is not to be wondered at, and that they took the precaution of hiding in the woods is still less remarkable. Essex, aroused by messengers, called out his men and proceeded to show fight. It appears at length to have dawned upon Rupert that his method had been faulty, that the convoy had escaped, and that beyond the fact that a few men had been killed and some 120 prisoners taken, he had little to show. He was, moreover, compelled to skirmish by the way as he turned his horses' heads towards Oxford beneath the Chiltern Hills and on their northern side. By degrees the Parliamentarian troops were mustered, being summoned from their quarters in the villages and farmhouses roundabout. Hampden, who chanced to be that night at Watlington, a town distant fifteen miles east-south-east from Oxford, heard of the raid—he could hardly fail to do so—and arising from his bed, armed, and rode out to take part in any event which might occur. He on this occasion acted purely as a volunteer. Rupert, by the time he had reached Chalgrove Field, found that the increasing force which was following him might prove inconvenient, and the main body under Essex from Thame might be expected shortly to appear. His pace, unless he abandoned his foot, must be regulated by theirs. At Chalgrove Field, therefore, he turned at bay, and with a view to guarding his line of retreat very wisely sent his foot in the direction of Oxford to seize and hold the bridge at Chiselhampton, over which he had passed a few hours earlier. This bridge is distant about three and a half miles from the scene of the fight, and is about one mile west of Stadhampton village. The Parliamentarian troops were without horse, and were scanty in numbers. They drew up behind a hedge in some sort of regular array. The Royalist horse, with the prince at their head, leaping this hedge—Rupert himself is stated to have been the foremost among them—fell on the enemy. It was with some surprise that the Royalist horse found an immediate rout did not follow their attack. Despite the disparity in the numbers, and the fact that seldom even in later times in the war could foot soldiers withstand a cavalry charge, with dogged courage the Parliamentarians for a space stood firm. At length, however, overwhelmed, they gave way and ran. There was no pursuit, probably because the advent of the main body under Essex was momentarily expected. Rupert retired, picking up his foot and prisoners at Chiselhampton, and without delay returned to Oxford. The story of Hampden riding off wounded from the field has often been told, and need not again be related. After nearly a week of terrible suffering he died at Thame, probably at the house traditionally pointed out and known as the "Green Dragon." He was buried on June 25, 1643, in the church of Great Hampden. That even the reputed grave of this great man should have been desecrated, and his supposed body hacked about to prove or disprove the assertions of contending antiquaries, is a disgrace to civilisation. Such, however, was the case on July 21, 1828, when Lord Nugent and a party of friends opened what was afterwards found to be the wrong grave.

The career of Colonel John Hurry was rather remarkable, and a few details as to the life of this scoundrel may not here be uninteresting. He fought at Edgehill under Balfour, on the side of the Parliament, but having laid down his commission in 1643, when Essex was at Reading, suddenly betook himself to the king at Oxford, bringing information of all the Parliamentarian military plans and dispositions in the neighbourhood. On Hurry's information Rupert started on his raid. After the combat the colonel brought the news at full speed to the king, being sent by Rupert. Charles knighted Hurry on receipt of the news, according to one account, but Metcalfe gives the date as August 13th. On June 25th, at the head of a body of horse, he sallied out on another raid, defeating a small detachment of horse under Sir Philip Stapleton, and plundering Wycombe. The effect of these two raids was to cause great alarm in London. At Marston Moor he fought in the left wing, sharing with Lucas the command under Goring. In October the same year, the day after the relief of Banbury, Hurry deserted under pretext of obtaining leave to go abroad. To the Earl of Manchester in London he made a full discovery of the composition and projects of the King's army, and also an accurate description of the persons and habits of the various commanders. Hurry was sent to Scotland, where, with Baillie, he operated against Montrose. With Baillie he did not agree. At Auldearn Montrose inflicted a crushing defeat on Hurry, who rejoined Baillie with but 100 horse. Late in 1646 he left Scotland and again deserted to

the king. Hurry was taken prisoner after Preston in 1648.
Lastly, presumably having escaped, he was in arms with his
old antagonist Montrose, and was taken prisoner with Hay
and Spottiswood on April 27, 1650. Conveyed to Edinburgh,
Hurry was executed with all the concomitant barbarities on
May 29th.

STAPLETON.

GROSS SPECIAL.

CHAPTER XXVI.

LANSDOWN.

July 5, 1643.

IN the month of June Sir Ralph Hopton—soon to be raised to the peerage as Baron Hopton of Stratton—was in Devonshire, where, with the exception of Plymouth, Dartmouth, Exeter, Bideford, and Barnstaple, the entire county was Royalist. Hopton proceeded eastwards and effected a junction with Prince Maurice and Lord Hertford, at the interesting little town of Chard in Somersetshire. The troops at his command now numbered about 6,000 men, more rather than less. The effect of the past Royalist successes in the west—successes achieved with a smaller force—were soon apparent. Taunton was won, Bridgewater offered no resistance, and Dunster Castle on the north coast surrendered. The only active hostilities were at Glastonbury and at Chewton Mendip, and at both of these the victory, such as it was, lay with the Royal troops. But an opportunity was now at hand for operations on a larger scale, and in this way:

Bristol was Parliamentarian and of great importance.

Waller, to protect Bristol, had been established at Bath. Up to date, notably at Chewton Mendip, the royal troops had prevailed against him, and it was obviously the duty of Hopton to crush, if possible, the enemy, and then to threaten Bristol. Hopton, therefore, marched from Wells through Shepton Mallet, and Frome to Bradford-on-Avon, by which means he got between Waller and the direct road to the metropolis; an important point gained, as Bath could thence be seriously threatened and along the easiest line. Waller's army was encamped on both sides of the river—the main body near Claverton Down on

the south side, and the remainder at Moncton Farleigh on the north.

Still Hopton could neither with safety attempt to cross the river in the face of two hostile forces nor dare to strike at Bath with Waller in his rear. After some ineffectual marches and countermarches, which occupied one day, he eventually started in a north-westerly direction, passing through Batheaston and arriving at Marshfield, a village five miles to the north of the city of Bath.

Waller, however, had not been idle. Suspecting the intention of Hopton, he had marched through Bath and taken up an extremely strong position on the lofty ridge of Lansdown.

LANSDOWN.

There he had raised a breastwork, behind which his guns were posted, and had so distributed his foot and horse as to defend all points of access. Hopton, marching along the direct road from Chippenham to Bristol at dawn on July 5th, came in view of the army of Waller, and at once perceived that only by beating Waller could he get into Bath. His road, or rather the road by which he marched, turns south at Tog Hill, running down into a valley, and then rises till the height of Lansdown is reached, at its north-west end. Hopton and

Tog Hill. The extreme Royalist Right.

Hertford marshalled their troops at Tog Hill in the hope that Waller would thereby be persuaded to come forth and attack them. It was, however, in vain. Waller knew too well the advantages of his position, and declined to be drawn therefrom.

On this, Hopton and Hertford withdrew the way they came, and had reached Cold Ashton when they were overtaken by the horse of Waller, among which were some dragoons and the London Cuirassier Regiment (commanded by Sir A. Hazlerigg), popularly known as the "Lobsters." Hopton's men turned and with but little trouble routed their pursuers, who were chased back to their original position at Lansdown. Hopton now assumed the offensive. It is said that the Cornishmen, under that grand old cavalier Sir Bevil Grenville, coveted Waller's cannon and begged at least to be allowed " to fetch off those cannon." In the result, down from Tog Hill and up the steep height, the Cornishmen went with a rush. The formation of this storming party was somewhat peculiar. The horse formed the right, and correctly, as the ground is more open ; but the musketeers were collected on

Waller's Position on Lansdown. He withdrew his guns behind the second wall when the crest was stormed & taken. Grenville's Monument stands, just to the left of the road : is a culmination of that by which the storming party ascended.

the left, and all the pikemen formed the centre. Waller's guns, it is to be presumed, fired over the heads of the attacking force ; at any rate there were but few casualties till a bend in the road was passed, a bend which was still further sheltered by a stone wall, which received the bullets of the enemy. Near the top this road again bends, and in front of this bend lay the key to Waller's position. At it rushed the Cornishmen, absolutely repulsing no less than five charges of Parliamentary cavalry, charges made down hill ! In a short time the breastwork was reached, surmounted, and won, but the guns had been withdrawn. Waller had even got them again in position behind a stone wall to the rear of the breastwork, and had rudely loopholed the improvised defence.

It may be asked why the battle terminated in this sudden way. Why, having his guns in a position to sweep the Royalists off the height, Waller did not use them? The fact is that the losses on both sides had been terrible. Out of 2,000 Royalist cavalry not more than 600 remained, and Sir Bevil Grenville, the Cornish leader, had fallen. Waller, however, had had enough, or his men had more probably. As

Lansdown. The wall behind which Waller withdrew his guns when the crest was stormed and taken. Grenville monument in distance.

the evening gathered into night a few stray shots were from time to time exchanged, until at eleven there was a final volley of musketry, after which dead silence ensued. A venturesome Royalist soldier stole forward and found Waller's line abandoned; he had retired to Bath.

On the morrow the Royalist army retreated in the direction of Chippenham, stopping there and also at Marshfield. Hopton, who had been slightly wounded in the battle on the morning after the fight, was dangerously injured by the explosion of a powder waggon. This misfortune was indeed serious, as it not only robbed the little force of its commander, but also of almost all the already scanty supply of powder. The passage from Chippenham to Devizes was almost a rout. Waller pressed on behind, and lost no opportunity of harassing the retreating Royalists with his cavalry. The battle of Lansdown, bloody as it was out of all proportion to the number of forces engaged, was, however, practically fought in vain.

It is interesting to note that the monument erected to Sir Bevil Grenville by his grandson, on the battlefield, yet remains, and in fairly good preservation—a memorial of a gallant soldier and loyal man. At this point it may not be out of place to supply some brief biographical notes on both Grenville and Hopton.

Sir Bevil Grenville was born in 1596. His father was Sir Bernard Grenville; his mother Elizabeth Bevil, daughter of Philip Bevil, of Killygarth, Cornwall. Grenville was entered at Exeter College, Oxford, in 1611, and took his degree in 1613-14. He sat for Cornwall in the Parliaments of 1621 and 1624, and represented Launceston during the first three Parliaments in the reign of Charles I. During this later period he belonged to the popular party. As a supporter of Sir John Eliot, Grenville was politically opposed to his father, Sir Bernard, in 1628. In 1639 Grenville had changed his views, and henceforward supported the king. In the Long Parliament he again sat as member for Cornwall, and was conspicuous as adverse to the attainder of Strafford. On August 5, 1642, with others, Grenville was concerned in publishing the King's Commission of Array against the militia of Launceston. Thrice was his arrest ordered by Parliament as a delinquent. His next exploit was the occupation of Launceston, which was effected by the Royalists of the county who had raised the *posse comitatus*. This cleared Cornwall of the forces of the Parliament. On January 19, 1643, Grenville led the van at Bradock Down, where the Parliamentary forces under Colonel Ruthven suffered defeat, losing 1,200 prisoners and all their guns. It was contrary to the advice of Sir Bevil that Hopton undertook the siege of Plymouth—a siege speedily raised. On March 5th a brief truce was agreed to in Devon and Cornwall, but the advent of the Earl of Stamford in the following May at the head of 5,600 foot and 1,400 horse led to a resumption of hostilities. Stamford encamped at Stratton, as has been related, where he was attacked on May 16th by a numerically very inferior force under Hopton and Grenville. The Royalist party were completely successful. The subsequent events which led to the death of Grenville at Lansdown have been narrated. Sir Bevil was buried at Kilkhampton on July 26th. His loss to the royal cause was very great indeed, and it is noteworthy that among all the royal commanders he was most conspicuous in restraining all license and plundering among the soldiers whom he led, and ever led to victory. The coat-armour of Grenville was gules, 3 sufflues (or organ-rests), or (*vide* initial).

Ralph Hopton, the son of Robert Hopton, of Witham, Somerset, was born in 1598, and was educated at Lincoln College, Oxford. He served through a part of the Thirty Years' War, having taken service under the Elector Palatine.

Hopton is said to have escorted the Queen of Bohemia in her flight after the battle of Prague. In December, 1624, he held the commission of Lieut.-Colonel in Sir Charles Rich's regiment—a regiment raised to take part in Mansfield's expedition. Hopton appears to have declined to serve at Cadiz, alleging that the expedition was improperly equipped. He was knighted (K.B.) at the coronation of Charles I. Hopton sat as M.P. for Bath in the first Parliament of Charles I., and for the county in the Short Parliament. In 1628, and also in the Long Parliament, he sat for Wells. Like Grenville, Hopton was at first on the popular side, but, unlike Grenville he voted for the attainder of Strafford. He was also spokesman of the committee named to present the Remonstrance to the king. By 1642, however, Hopton had completely thrown in his lot with the Royal cause ; so much so that he excused the attempt to seize the five members, and so vigorously attacked the militia ordinance that a ten days' imprisonment in the Tower was the result. Hopton accompanied Lord Hertford to Somersetshire in July, 1642, with the title of Lieut.-General of the Horse. His arrest of William Strode, a Parliamentarian Deputy-Lieutenant of Somerset, is well known. On August 5th he was, as a delinquent, expelled from the House. On the retreat of Hertford into Sherborne Castle it was resolved that Hopton should lead the small body of Royalist horse into Cornwall—a body numbering rather more than 220 men. In Cornwall he raised the infantry, which afterwards did such yeoman service for the king in the west. Present at Bradock Down, Stratton, and Lansdown; he was each time among the victors, his troops being only checked at Chagford and Sourton. Wounded at Lansdown, and subsequently maimed by the explosion of powder, Hopton from his bed directed the defence of Devizes, but of course could not be present at the victory of Roundway Down. He was nominated Governor of Bristol by Hertford, but through the influence of Prince Maurice, was deprived of the post, accepting that of deputy-governor under Rupert.

On September 4, 1643, Sir Ralph was raised to the peerage under the title of Baron Hopton of Stratton. Henceforward his military career was unsuccessful, with the exception of the capture of Arundel Castle. In conjunction with the Earl of Forth he was defeated by Waller at Cheriton, though Hopton succeeded in saving his guns. In July, 1644, with a part of the garrison of Bristol, he found Charles in the west, and was in August appointed General of the Ordnance. The intrigues of Goring now affected the power of Hopton, and it was not until the retirement of that cavalier to France that he regained a semblance of command. Hopton was then given the command in chief of the undisciplined mob called an army, which Goring left behind. He ought to have declined the questionable honour, for it was an impossibility to organise such materials. On February 16, 1646, he was beaten by Fairfax at Torrington, and after an unavailing attempt to make his troops stand at Bodmin, was compelled to capitulate at Truro. His troops were utterly insubordinate. Henceforward he was with Prince Charles, firstly at Sicily, then at Jersey, and lastly on board the revolted fleet. Abroad, the intrigues of Rupert and others nullified any good which his wise counsels might have been to the exiled prince. Hopton died in exile at Bruges in September, 1652—perhaps as badly used a man as can be found amid the many who lost their all in the service of their king. His coat-armour was ermine on two bars, sable, 6 mullets, or (*vide* initial Chap. XXIV.).

It is interesting to remember that the Marquess of Hertford mentioned was first Sir William Seymour, second Earl of Hertford, and was raised to the marquisate in 1640. He had married Arabella Stewart in the last reign, and thus incurred the wrath of James I., who committed both husband and wife to the tower. Hertford escaped, but his wife died in prison. At the restoration he was made a K.G., and restored by Act of Parliament to the dukedom of Somerset, as if no attainder of the Protector Somerset had ever taken

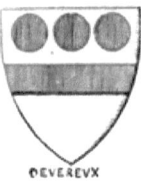

DEVEREUX

place. The marquess married as his second wife Lady Francis Devereux, the daughter of Robert, 2nd Earl of Essex. He died in 1660, and was succeeded by his grandson, William. This marquisate is extinct, the present creation dating only from 1793. Coat-armour: Quarterly 1 and 4 or on a pile gules between 6 fleurs de lis azure, 3 lions of England (coat of augmentation, temp. Hen. VIII.), 2 and 3 gules, 2 wings conjoined in lure tips down, or.

Two other notable Royalists fell at Lansdown. Sir Nicholas Slanning, of Leye, Devon, who was born in 1611, and knighted at Nonsuch on August 24, 1632. After the Restoration a baronetcy was bestowed on his son (also Sir Nicholas Slanning, K.B.). The baronetcy became extinct in 1700. Arms: argent 2 pales engrailed gules, over all on a bend sable 3 griffins' heads erased, or. Also John Trevanion (said to have been a knight, but not mentioned in Metcalfe). He was the eldest son of Sir Charles Trevanion, of Carryhayes, Cornwall, and was born in 1613. Sir Charles received the honour of knighthood at Boconnock in August, 1644, subsequent to the battle of Lansdown, and it is almost reasonable to suspect that the statement as to the knighthood of John Trevanion is erroneous. Arms: argent on a fess azure between 2 chevronels gules 3 escalops, or.

CHAPTER XXVII.

ROUNDWAY DOWN.

July 13, 1643.

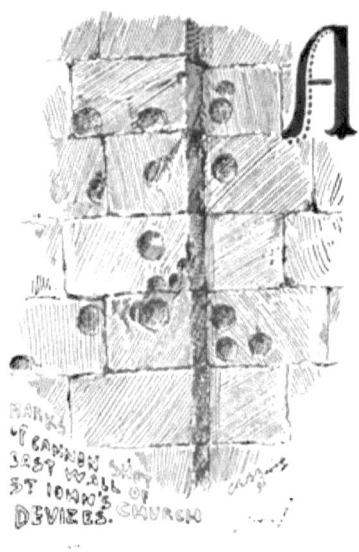

AS has been related, the Royalist army, carrying with it the wounded Hopton, arrived at Devizes after Lansdown on July 9th, and suffered severely by the way, especially after leaving Chippenham. The two days' halt there had given Waller an opportunity. He guessed—and indeed it was sufficiently apparent—that Devizes was the Royalists' goal; and determined, if possible, not only to annoy them *en route*, but to intercept them. Weak as the royal army was in cavalry, it would have been madness to have attempted to reach Oxford. In addition to Waller's army, the garrison of Malmesbury was too near to be pleasant. Their stock of powder was so low as to be practically nil, and the store of match was exhausted. The conduct of the Cornish foot during the retreat between Chippenham and Devizes was magnificent. Under Sir Nicholas Slanning they disputed every mile of the road, and repulsed at Bromham House a heavy attack ; by this means saving the guns from capture. This Bromham House was the mansion of Sir Edward Baynton, and has now almost, if not quite, disappeared. It stood in that part of the parish of Bromham which is called Netherstreet, and almost on the old road to Iron-pear-tree farm. At Devizes a supply of powder had been arranged for, which was to be brought *viâ* Marlborough and Roundway Hill.

Waller, when he failed to intercept the enemy, encamped for the night on a "large moor near Rowde," and this would appear to have been Edith Marsh and Netherstreet. On the morrow his army, from the high ground north of Devizes, blocked the road to Marlborough. Through spies, information reached him of the coming convoy of powder; and his first care was to intercept it. This duty was committed to Major Francis Dowett, who performed his task with speed and success. The powder-waggons, with an escort of dragoons under Lord Crauford, were sighted near Beckhampton and captured, together with 200 prisoners. Crauford escaped with five waggons only. Beckhampton is distant seven and a half miles north-east of Devizes, the old road thence lying beneath the south-west face of Roundway Down.

Meanwhile Waller drew nearer to the town, and observed the Royalist horse drawn up on some rising ground—the ridge of Coate-field, east of Green Church and Devizes. This body was evidently on the look-out for Crauford, and for a time seems to have mistaken Waller's men for the expected convoy. The mistake was discovered in time, and a retreat into the town took place without fighting. Devizes, however, was ill-adapted for defence, and, moreover, according to all accounts, lacked stable accommodation for cavalry. It was therefore decided that during the next night the Royalist horse should cut its way through to Oxford (forty-five miles) under Hertford and Maurice while the foot remained to withstand Waller's siege. With Hopton, who was now better,

COATE-FIELD.

though still unable to leave his bed, there remained the Earl of Marlborough, in command of the guns, and Lord Mohun. Hertford and Maurice successfully carried out this scheme, and with speed reached Oxford, losing, however, a few prisoners.

It may here be observed that since Lansdown relations between the Royalist horse and the Cornish foot had become much embittered. The Cornishmen affected to depreciate the part which the horse had taken in the battle at that place.

This was, however, unjust, as must be conceded when the circumstances are considered. The Parliamentarian horse, notably Hazlerig's regiment, had fought extremely well—better, indeed, by far than any horse which had hitherto been opposed to the army of Hopton and Grenville. The storming of the steep ascent at Lansdown was eminently a task for infantry, and that the Royalist horse did not shirk fighting is to be proved by its enormous loss—a loss sustained not after being repulsed, but in absolute hard fighting.

Devizes, despite its castle, was practically an open town, or at best but scantily provided with works. What these works actually were does not appear to be known, but the probability is that they consisted of barricades across the main and by-roads into the town, with the addition of a few loopholed houses and walls. A large force would not be required to defend it—nay, in this case there was no ammunition for a large force. Hence the despatch of the cavalry was altogether a wise move, especially as jealousy existed between it and the foot. Waller, on the hill at Coate-field, immediately established a battery of seven guns and opened fire upon the town. Hopton, though he could not supply the deficiency of powder, succeeded in roughly constructing 1,500 lbs. of match for the musketeers, by unpicking and boiling all the bedcords to be found in the town. Bullets, it seems, were cast from the lead on the church roof, that fertile source of supply in those times. There is also a tradition in the town that a townsman, one Pierce, had a hidden store of powder, which he forthwith discovered to Hopton. Richard Pierce, a notable Royalist, was an alderman.

On the morrow Waller, who had continued his cannonade, summoned the town, and at the same time informed Hopton of the capture of the convoy. His troops surrounded the place, and it seemed to be at his mercy—at any rate he thought so. Waller had his headquarters in a farmhouse at the foot of Roundway Down. Five hundred dragoons were stationed at Pottern, a mile and a half south of the town, and an outpost of horse was established on the plateau of

"OLIVER'S CASTLE." WALLER'S CAVALRY POST.

Roundway. On July 12th, after a wet morning, Waller and Dowett led two attacks on the town, and were successful in effecting a lodgment after four hours' hard fighting. St. John's Church suffered in its east end on this occasion, being struck many times by cannon-shot. The town was again summoned to surrender, and on this the besieged demanded a truce of two hours—a period subsequently extended to eight hours. Herein Waller acted like a fool. It was obvious that the town must surrender, and any delay could only be intended to increase the chance of relief without improving the possibility of resistance, for of course the construction of earthworks was barred. Waller, however, believed that Essex at Thame would prevent help from Oxford; nay, more, would be active enough to cut off Hertford and Maurice. Obviously Essex, who was well informed as to the state of affairs, should have done so. He was, however, jealous of Waller—the two never agreed —so he did nothing.

The morning of July 13th arrived; Devizes had not surrendered. Waller prepared to storm the place, and during a ride of inspection by a miracle escaped capture. He rode

ROUNDWAY DOWN, WEST.

out with an escort and was perceived. The enemy expected him to return the same way, and lay in wait. Waller, however, separating from a part of his escort, sent them back, and proceeded by a different road. The detachment of his escort was taken or killed to a man. A storm was about to be ordered, when in galloped scouts, who announced the approach of a powerful cavalry force from Marlborough.

Maurice and Hertford had done their work well. They reached Oxford on the morning of July 11th, had an audience with the king, and Maurice started on his return ride the same day, his force being augmented by the Royal Life Guards and the remains of Craufurd's horse. With them came Wilmot, Craufurd, and Byron. On the afternoon of July 13th they were duly drawn up on Roundway Down, and Waller, abandoning the siege with precipitation, went forth to meet them. He marched out intending to fight in the usual formation—*i.e.*, his 1,800 foot in the centre, with the 2,500 horse and dragoons divided into right and left

ROUNDWAY DOWN, EAST, SCENE OF THE FIGHT.

wings. His guns were also dragged out. Waller, however, modified his plan, and wisely, seeing that the Cornishmen within the town and in his rear were by his first disposition unprovided for. To keep these in check he reserved his infantry, leaving the cavalry alone to oppose Maurice and Wilmot. Up the steep and slippery side of Roundway Down charged Hazlerig at the head of his "black lobsters," followed by Sir Edward Hungerford and Captain Baugh, who led the west-country horse. A more unpropitious place for a cavalry charge can hardly be imagined. They were hurled down the steep immediately and with precipitation, being driven right on to the guns, of which the Royalists captured four. Hungerford and Baugh had had enough, but not so Hazlerig. He rallied his men, and with the utmost gallantry returned to the charge, recapturing the cannon and inflicting considerable loss; in fact, it looked for a brief time as if he would hold his own. Wilmot, who on this occasion commanded a reserve of 500 horse, now joined in the fray and completely turned the scale in favour of the Royalists. Hazlerig and his regiment lost heavily, and were

DEVIZES FROM ROUNDWAY.

put to utter rout. Waller joined in the flight, and now the Parliamentarian cavalry, officers and men alike, were off and away. Bagdon-hill (Beacon-Down Hill), down which Hazlerig and his troopers were driven, is so steep that it excites wonder how men and horses ever got to the bottom otherwise than by rolling.

Deserted by the horse, however, the Parliamentarian foot, 1,800 in number, stood fast and fought with great valour —a very frequent occurrence on both sides in the Civil

War. This foot was mainly composed of the London Trained Bands, and worthily they supported their traditions, till overwhelmed. Out from Devizes sallied forth the besieged Cornishmen and attacked them from the south. Down on them from the north rode the cavalry joined with Wilmot, and not only rode, but gave them the benefit of their own artillery, which now had again fallen into the hands of the Royalists. Such attacks they were unable to support, and, after offering a hardy but unavailing resistance, were put to flight. Waller escaped to Bristol, Hazlerig and the rest to Malmesbury. The foot retreated,

though badly mauled, in some semblance of order under the leadership of a Scotch officer. This, however, is the version of their own party.

But little more needs to be said of this dashing cavalry fight, in which the numerically weaker force prevailed. Maurice's men had covered forty-five miles in two days, and though not fresh, were fairly so. Waller's army had for at least a fortnight been continually fighting and marching, and are stated to have been almost worn out with constant watching and fatigue generally. The Royalists had no guns, but captured eventually Waller's entire train

of artillery. To the pikemen of the London trained bands were opposed not only the Cornish musketeers, but their pikemen, the entire Royalist cavalry, and Waller's captured guns; so that, if they gave way, it was not without good reason. On the field itself it is stated that not more than fifty of the Parliamentarian horse fell, so that it would look as if a panic seized them. This might be so, but the chances are that Hazlerig found it difficult to charge home up such an incline, and that in reality the cavalry attack was less sharply delivered than usual. There is a tradition that a body of volunteer horse, some fifty in number, who had hastily collected on the approach of Royalists and joined them just before the fight, either in the battle or in the pursuit managed to get surrounded by the enemy's horse, and perished almost to a man. One volunteer—the Earl of Carnarvon—is named as having specially distinguished himself at Roundway. He fought in the Life Guards under Byron, though one account states that on his arrival the command of that regiment was voluntarily handed over to him— a statement rather hard to be believed. After the battle Hopton remained at Devizes to recover his health, while the Royalist army drew off to Bath and Bristol. Bath, having no power to resist, surrendered; its garrison had been withdrawn to Bristol, which was subsequently besieged in regular form.

CHAPTER XXVIII.

NEWBURY.

September 20, 1643.

ABOUT the middle of August, 1643, Charles, with the Royalist army, was occupied in the siege of Gloucester. At that city the besieged were reduced to great straits, suffering not only from want of provisions, but also from a lack of powder. Essex in London had received definite instructions to relieve the beleaguered place, and was actively engaged in equipping a force for that purpose. On August 22nd his army amounted to 8,000 men, and he held a review on Hounslow Heath. Four days later he was at Colnbrook, in Buckinghamshire, a town ten miles east-south-east of Maidenhead. Reinforcements joined him as he advanced, and his army speedily numbered between 14,000 and 15,000 men; being for those times a large, well-armed and equipped force. From Colnbrook he marched northward by country roads till he struck the main road near Denham, and then proceeded through Amersham and Wendover to Aylesbury, a distance of thirty miles. From Aylesbury he turned westward to Bicester (seventeen miles)

and thence passed to Adderbury (thirteen miles), reaching that place on September 2nd. Essex had thus avoided Oxford, but had nevertheless on the march to suffer frequent attacks from the Royalist horse, under Wilmot. His progress the last few miles was slow, and indeed it had occupied one entire day to move his army from Aynho to Adderbury, a distance of only three and a half miles. From Adderbury he marched direct on Chipping Norton (nine miles), and reached that town on September 3rd. On the morrow, by a cross-country march (eight miles), he arrived at Stow-on-the-Wold, where Rupert's horse fell on him, but was repulsed. From Stow-on-the-Wold, where after the fight an attempt on the part of Rupert to negotiate was declined on the plea of "no power," Essex took to the Cotswold Hills, and proceeded to Naunton the following day. On the next he was at Prestbury, and by September 8th was established in Gloucester, the siege having been raised by the king. The distance covered by Essex in the last four days of his march was approximately twenty-three miles—a slow rate of progress indeed, but provisions were hardly obtainable, to such a degree had the district been foraged by the Royalist horse, and water was scarce.

As early as September 29th, when Essex was but three days' march from Colnbrook, a rumour of relief was current within the besieged city. Matters there were in a terrible condition, the powder supply almost exhausted, and surrender apparently inevitable. By September 5th no more than three barrels of powder remained, and a false notice (shot, it is stated, over the wall attached to an arrow) had two days earlier informed the garrison that the relieving army had been engaged and destroyed. Suddenly the Royalists were observed to be destroying their camp and posts, and from the walls the anxious defenders saw the besieging army retreat southwards. On the night of September 5th Charles slept at Painswick Court House, distant nearly six miles south-east by south of Gloucester. Painswick Court House, where a document which is extant was signed on that day, still survives in good condition. It is an interesting old place, with a fine panelled dining-room. The relieving force marched *via* Cheltenham, resting at that town, and driving thence a small Royalist post, which appears to have been forgotten in the hurry of retreat. Charles from Painswick turned to the north-east, crossed the old Roman road near Whitcombe Magna, and, leaving Cheltenham on his left, proceeded to Sudeley Castle, where he arrived on September 7th, and remained till the morning of September 12th.

The position from a military point of view now offers some peculiarities worthy of notice. Charles, though he had failed in his siege, and appeared, as it were, to have retreated before the advance of Essex, was, through the direction taken by his force, in a far better situation to strike a blow than if he had remained to fight before the walls of Gloucester. That city, reduced to starvation, with the country for miles round cleared of food supplies, had received an addition of 15,000 starving or nearly starving men within its walls. The originator of the king's march is unknown, but its effect was to get between starving Gloucester and starving Essex, and their base of supplies London. Well managed, the Royalist army ought to have crushed both. Essex could not remain within the walls, and must go somewhither. Charles ought then to strike, and strike heavily. From Oxford the king could obtain all needful supplies, as he held command of the district and the line of communication. Having crushed Essex, nothing would have been easier than to have renewed the siege of the unvictualled Gloucester; and this time with an almost absolute certainty of speedy success.

Essex being bound to leave the city did so, and marched to Tewkesbury, taking the route in all probability followed by the unlucky Queen Margaret in 1471. News of this movement reached Sudeley on September 11th, and at once the royal army was set in motion. It was evidently the intention of Essex to get back to London without fighting; his troops being hardly in a condition for a pitched battle after their long march and privations. A five days' rest was, however, obtained at Tewkesbury, and then the Parliamentarian general again set forth. Meanwhile, on September 12th, Charles had removed to Pershore, probably to obstruct some design which Essex was suspected of entertaining on Worcester. Pershore lies about eleven and a half miles north-west by north of Sudeley, and nine miles north-east by north of Tewkesbury. Remaining only a short time at Pershore, the Royalists moved west to Evesham, a distance of six and a half miles, and arrived there on September 14th. Under the circumstances of the case the Royalist scouts ought to have been more than usually active, but as a matter of fact they appear to have utterly failed. On September 15th Essex, with his army refreshed, left Tewkesbury unknown to the Royalists, and, taking a course through Cheltenham and Colesbourne, surprised two raw Royalist regiments in Cirencester, a town distant nearly twenty-five miles from his starting-point. Here he had the good luck to capture a most acceptable supply of stores. Speed was now everything if he was to outstrip the Royalists in the race for the City. On the 16th Essex reached Cricklade by the Roman Road (seven miles south-east), and on the same day the outwitted Royalists started in pursuit from Evesham.

As the crow flies Essex was now fifteen miles to the good, the respective distances from Evesham and Cricklade to London being ninety and seventy-five miles. What he wanted to do was to reach the road to London which passes through Hungerford, Newbury and Reading, in Berkshire. Could he gain this road all would be well. But for the pursuers there was an advantage, in that the cavalry under Rupert could precede the infantry, and, travelling with far greater speed, could annoy Essex on his march, thus gaining time to allow the royal foot and guns to arrive. Rupert reached Hungerford on September 18th, and the king, marching through Stow-on-the-Wold, Faringdon, and Wantage, arrived at Newbury on the following day. Rupert's cavalry march from Evesham to Hungerford was fifty-seven miles; the distance covered by Essex in the same time, marching *via* Swindon and Ramsbury, being nearly twenty-three miles. At

Aldbourne Chase Rupert's horse came into collision with the Parliamentarian forces, and a sharp encounter took place, the consequence of which was to send Essex into Hungerford when he would fain have passed through to Newbury by the direct road. This was now impossible, and if he persevered in his intention of proceeding to London, he was bound to take a southern road beyond the river Kennet, which goes through Kintbury and Enborne, and traverses the town of Newbury. On the north side of Newbury he would regain,

if successful, his original road. Charles arrived at Newbury on September 19th, and sent his army through the town to take up a position on the south side of the river, and thus blocked the Kintbury Road. On the night of the 19th the Parliamentarian army reached the battlefield and encamped, the commander sleeping in a mean wayside cottage, still existing. A reconnaisance on the part of some scouts drew Royalist fire late at night from a post established at the head of a lane.

The site of the battlefield is not easy to describe, owing

to the complicated nature of the ground and the divergence of the various accounts which have come down to us. The river Kennet winds its way along the north; on the south is the En Brook. At Enborne the ground rises and forms a ridge lying north-east and south-west, and from this ridge several spurs project, some towards the river on the north, and others towards the En Brook. The ground slopes down to the brook on the south, and here there was an open space known as Enborne Heath. Beyond this eastward, was Newbury Wash (common land), and therefore at that time open. Nearly in every direction on the position lanes radiated out from the Kintbury Road, and not a few copses and enclosed fields further obstructed the ground. Along such a position as this the army of Essex advanced, their right resting on Enborne Heath, their left a little thrown back on one of the projecting spurs. The Royalists awaited them with their right on the Kintbury Road, which they held, and their left on Newbury Wash. To force a passage Essex required to fight his way through the ground cut up by lanes and obstructed by copses. Any attempt by way of the open ground, *i.e.*, Enborne Heath, would be to court disaster; for there Rupert's horse could act, and this of all things was discreetly to be avoided.

Essex in some respects fought with a halter round his neck. The Cirencester supplies of provisions were now exhausted, and on empty stomachs his men must that day fight to win, or surrender through starvation. Essex was therefore bound to attack, and the king need only act on the defensive. The policy of Charles clearly was to wait and repel till surrender followed. Rupert, stationed on the left—that is, on Newbury Wash—could make safe against any attempt to break through in that direction, so that beyond this, merely ordinary military precautions were needed to be taken in the posting of the foot and the guns. A small part only of the cavalry was stationed on the Royalist right, and under Sir John Byron. Essex advanced to the attack, and, as was reasonable, directed his attention to his centre and left. To advance was not easy, owing to the hedges, lanes, and copses. To have obtained the least advantage would have been impossible had there been ordinary care exercised on the Royalist right. The fact remains, however, that a hill which commanded this part of the field was left unoccupied, and on this hill Skippon promptly seized. An attempt to dislodge the enemy was at once made by foot under Sir Nicholas Byron, and a body of horse under his nephew. Up the hill this devoted band charged, and with them charged Lord Falkland, a volunteer that day in Byron's troop. From behind each hedge the Parliamentarians kept up a constant fire, and offered a most stubborn resistance ; but at any rate at first matters went well with the king's army. It was while endeavouring to turn the enemy out of their position on this hill that Lord Falkland fell. A modern obelisk marks the spot where traditionally Lucius Cary Lord Falkland, met with his untimely death.

In the centre but little progress had been made by Essex, thanks to the lanes and copses. On the left Rupert's horse had nothing to do ; though had that commander only waited he might have been fully employed. Obviously his duty was to bide his time till the main body of the enemy had succeeded in getting through the various lanes, and were in scattered bodies endeavouring to form in the more open ground beyond. One of **Rupert's** charges then would presumably have ended the battle. Rupert, however, **restless as** usual, skirting the right of the enemy, advanced till **within** sight of the Parliamentarian reserves. More than this, he saw what his soul loved, the baggage waggons. The artillery train was also within view, but this was not so interesting to him. Unfortunately, too, the baggage and **guns were too** strongly guarded to be attacked, and Rupert forbore. But the right wing, or what practically made the right wing of **Essex's** army, was drawn up on the Heath—two regiments of London trained bands (foot), flanked by two bodies of horse. Rupert charged the horse, who fled ; the foot, however, stood firm, and, despite all efforts of the Royalist horse, could not be broken. Guns were now brought to bear on the Londoners ; still they would not give ground, though severely punished. Rupert's horse, after suffering heavy losses, had fallen back. Infantry now came up to attack the Londoners, and through the nature of the ground had the protection of a hill till quite close. This foot charged, and then, but not till then, did the trained bands retreat. It is recorded to their honour that they retreated in good order.

Essex still did not seem to be making much progress. The fighting had been severe and continuous, especially in the centre, but no particular impression had been made on the Royalists, none, at any rate, sufficient to justify any idea that they were giving way; on the contrary, they appear to have held the Parliamentarians in check. On both right and left, however, the Royalist loss had been heavy, on the left specially so, and before the day was over on this side something like disaster happened and in this wise. After the withdrawal of Rupert's horse, two of Essex's cavalry regiments under Sir Philip Stapleton rode through a lane and debouched on Newbury Wash, where they were opposed by a Royalist

Falkland Memorial, Newbury Wash.

regiment, which they repelled. Other Royalist horse coming to the support of their broken comrades, charged Stapleton's men, and put them to flight after heavy fighting. During this time the Parliamentarian foot had drawn nearer, and had command of both sides of a deep lane, the hedges of which they lined with musketeers. Down this lane bolted Stapleton's defeated horse, with the Royalist cavalry in hot pursuit. The result may be imagined: hardly a man got back unwounded—few alive. Grafton's ride down and back through the lane at Norton St. Philip in 1685 much resembles this episode.

On pressed the Parliamentarian foot, but still not yet clear from the hedges and ditches. The next phase of the battle was a strong concentration of Royalist forces on the right, and a powerful attack on the Parliamentarian left. This was repelled by Skippon, who left his vantage ground on the hill, and descended into the low ground near the Kennet, where he effected his purpose, and then, having left a guard, returned to his previous position.

Accounts of the battle now vary, but it would appear that the fighting was renewed vigorously along the entire front, its result being somewhat favourable to Essex. Still the passage through Newbury had not been won when night fell, nor was the road to London open to the Parliamentarian army. One enterprising attempt to secure a ford which then existed over the Kennet, and thus to obtain a place to cross the river, was made by Skippon's men, who were left in the valley to guard against attack in that direction. It failed, though it deserved to succeed. When night fell both armies lay down in the positions they happened to occupy at the time, and earnestly, at any rate on the side of Essex, considered the situation. What would be the event of the morrow? Would the battle be renewed? would they surrender? or would they retreat, to be pursued, cut up, or starved? Luck—the ill-luck of the king—settled the question. Late that night a sentinel heard a sound of rumbling wheels, evidently artillery in motion, and concluded that more guns were either being brought up or that some alteration was being made in the position and strength of the batteries. It was the Royal army in retreat — powder had failed them, nay, quite early in the fight the supply had been short. Two days later Essex, unmolested save by one attack from Rupert near Aldermaston, had safely reached Reading, and Charles practically, though not actually, defeated, had withdrawn to Oxford.

BYRON.

KASSERING.

CHAPTER XXIX.

CROPREDY BRIDGE.

June 29, 1644.

THE fight at Cropredy Bridge presents some features which are not without interest, differing as it does in many points from most of the battles of the Civil War. A brief *résumé* of the preceding manœuvres is, however, needful. On May 27th Charles was at Oxford, and Abingdon had two days earlier been abandoned by the Royalists, only, however, to be immediately occupied by Essex. After deliberation in Oxford it was determined that the king should leave a sufficient garrison in the city and start himself with the bulk of the army upon a campaign the objects of which were twofold. His plans were to keep the field in such a manner as to assure communication with Rupert, who had already returned to Shrewsbury; and, if an opportunity served, to defeat in detail Essex and Waller, should these commanders embark on separate enterprises. Hopton had been sent into the west to save Bristol. Maurice was unavailingly besieging Lyme Regis, in Dorset, and the Parliamentarian Massey had just succeeded in taking Malmesbury. In the north the Scots had crossed the border under Leven, and with them Rupert designed to deal.

On May 28th Essex and Waller separated, and the former, crossing the Thames at Sandford, three miles above Abingdon, and avoiding Oxford by a rather circuitous march, took up his position at Islip, a town three miles north by east of that city. Waller remained with an independent command on the Berkshire side of the river. Waller, on June 2nd, having previously left his mark on Abingdon by destroying the beautiful market cross, marched in a westerly direction from that town and crossed the river, forcing a passage at Newbridge, six miles south-west of Oxford, but above it on the river. Charles was at Woodstock at the time, and, with Essex a few miles off on his right flank and Waller unimpeded by any river on his left, found himself in a position the reverse of safe. Essex, luckily, was the other side of the Cherwell, and had been foiled in his attempts to seize and hold two bridges across that stream, viz., those at Gosford, nearer Oxford, and at Enslow, immediately opposite Blechington House.

The position was serious, and there was even talk of a capitulation. In the event, however, Charles retreated into Oxford. His whole force was therefore again within the walls, and, being unprovisioned for more than a few days, must either fight or surrender. But his advisers, probably Patrick Ruthven, Earl of Brentford, planned a manœuvre which was daring and successful. Marching out towards Abingdon early on the 3rd of June, he made a feint as if to attack the place. This, of course, was conducted openly and with the intention of drawing Waller and Essex further apart, by causing the former to return. Waller deceived, did so, and the king's object having been attained, he immediately returned to Oxford till nightfall. Then, the coast being clear, at the head of 2,500 foot and 3,000 horse he marched due west through Witney to Burford, a distance of twenty miles, reaching that place on the afternoon of the following day. Resting here for a few hours only, by another night march he arrived at Bourton-on-the-Water, distant nine miles north-west. Resuming, he marched three miles north-east to Stow-on-the-Wold and then crossed the Cotswold Hills to Evesham, a distance of thirteen miles north-west. Here the bad news reached him that Massey had taken the old town of Tewkesbury, that Essex and Waller were hurrying in pursuit of him, and that a small reinforcement for the enemy out of Staffordshire and Shropshire was on its way southwards. Cities of refuge in those parts were few; Bristol might be reached, but if reached it would be after a battle and not before. Worcester appeared to be the most promising spot to select, despite the fact that its walls were but in a ruinous condition. To Worcester, therefore, the Royalist army went, and reached it on June 6th. On that day Waller, who had recrossed the river at Newbridge and continued north till about five miles west of Oxford, then, turning due north-west, arrived at Stow-on-the-Wold. Essex, starting from Islip, and having obtained a passage across the Cherwell at Enslow Bridge, had passed through Chipping Norton and then bent round southwards, crossing Waller's line of march about two miles from Stow-on-the-Wold.

The two generals met at the last place, on June 6th, to determine on the next move. The upshot of this council of war was somewhat extraordinary. Essex withdrew to march to the relief of Lyme Regis, leaving the task of dealing with Charles to Waller. Obviously this was a grievous error. The king was known to be altogether unable to cope with their united forces, and to be practically in retreat, yet the obstinate pertinacity of Essex in urging his pet project was permitted to outweigh all other considerations, political or military. Waller advanced therefore, taking Sudeley Castle on June 9th, while Essex hastened off in the direction of Lyme. News of the fall of Sudeley reached Charles on June 12th, and caused much discomposure in the Royalist camp. Waller was getting uncomfortably near, and Worcester was untenable. A retreat to Bewdley was therefore decided on, and that town was reached with all despatch.

On the day that Charles received the news about Sudeley Essex had arrived at Blandford in Dorsetshire, where a message overtook him from the Committee in London, commanding his immediate return—a command which the general utterly refused to obey. In his reply he announced that, being ordered to relieve Lyme, he should do so in the way he thought best, and that as commander he should divide his forces and give such orders to his subordinate Waller as he deemed suitable for the enterprise in hand. His further remarks as to his intentions, and his opinion of both Waller and the action of the Committee need not be recapitulated. Suffice it to say that he carried his point, did relieve Lyme, as the siege was abandoned on his approach, and eventually was ordered to reconquer the west.

On June 13th, at Bewdley, the Royalist officers met at a council of war. The separation of Essex and Waller was known to them, and the news came almost in the light of a deliverance; but to stay where they were was hardly possible. What should be the next move? Should the army join Rupert and operate in the north, or should it now try conclusions with Waller, he being completely severed from Essex? The latter course seemed wisest, as it undoubtedly was, with one proviso —that sufficient reinforcements could be obtained to assure success. Where, however, were these reinforcements to come from? Certainly not from the district around Bewdley. Oxford was suggested, and seemed feasible; so back to Oxford the Royalists went with all becoming speed. Starting on June 14th, and marching through Worcester, Evesham, and Stow-on-the-Wold, Woodstock was reached on the 21st, Waller pursuing with as much speed as possible.

The previous movements of Waller after taking Sudeley Castle had been as follows : he was supposed to be in pursuit of the king, who, retreating before him, had thrown himself into Worcester, and had subsequently retired to Bewdley. Waller marched north to Evesham, where he found, on June 11th, that the inhabitants had repaired the bridge which the retreating Royalists had broken down. From Evesham he made his way towards Worcester, and then, avoiding the city, turned north to Kidderminster. It may be observed that though the armies were but two and a-half miles apart the river lay on the east side of Bewdley, and therefore formed a defence for the Royalists.

Charles on his starting for Bewdley had collected all the boats obtainable from Bridgenorth, in Shropshire, and Worcester, and employed them to expedite the conveyance of his foot. His progress to Worcester, at least, was therefore far more rapid than that of Waller. Here he waited a night for the rear-guard to come up, and with all expedition passed on to Evesham, where again he destroyed the bridge, fining the town £200 and 1,000 pairs of shoes for the good reception of Waller at that place. From Evesham several despatches were sent to Oxford to prepare the Council there for his return. The next night the Royalists lay at Broadway, near Stratford-on-Avon, crossing the hills near Camden early on the following morning, and safe from Waller, who was quite outmarched. That night a halt was made at Burford, and on the following evening at Witney the army was met by reinforcements from Oxford, raising the force to 4,000 horse and 5,500 foot and artillery. Such was the strength of Charles on June 21st at Woodstock.

From Woodstock the king proceeded to Buckingham, securing there by his unexpected appearance no small quantity of stores of food—stores in transit from London to Coventry and Warwick. Waller, in the meantime, had not proceeded far—he was in Worcestershire as late as June 25th, on which day he started towards Gloucester, hoping thence to obtain reinforcements. These were refused by Massey, but Waller eventually obtained seven troops of horse, 600 foot, and 11 guns from Coventry and Warwick, his place of rendezvous in Warwickshire being the battlefield of Edgehill.

From Edgehill Waller marched to Banbury, and Charles, on his approach, moved from Buckingham to Brackley in Northamptonshire. The king, whose presence at Buckingham had caused great alarm in London, had wasted time there, and had thereby lost opportunities. At least three plans of operations had been discussed. The juncture in the north with Rupert was of course one of them, and this was rejected. An attack on the associated counties was likewise proposed, and held to be unadvisable. The third, and that which for a time seemed to be adopted, was to make a bold dash for London, between which city and Buckingham no hostile force lay to block the road. But by the time the Royalists had made up their minds Waller was too near. Moreover, a force under Browne was on its way to co-operate with that general, and likewise to defend the road to the city. Browne's force was not, however, of much account, being composed of 2,000 newly-raised foot, and lacking a single troop of horse. To strengthen this a portion of the cavalry occupied around Basing House, then being besieged, was withdrawn and sent to join Browne's foot. After immense difficulties Browne succeeded in reaching Dunstable with a force which amounted to about 4,000 men, but which was composed entirely of raw levies. He never joined Waller.

Leaving Worcestershire on June 25th, Waller reached Banbury on June 28th, and found Charles prepared to give battle, but to give it, if possible, on his own terms. Charles

CROPREDY BRIDGE.

ostensibly, but Patrick Ruthven, Lord Brentford, in reality, now set himself to endeavour to outwit Waller, and the day was occupied in various manœuvres intended to place Waller at a disadvantage. Waller was not, however, to be caught. On the morrow the Royal army marched as if striking out into Northamptonshire, possibly with the intention of seizing Daventry. Waller, on the west side of the Cherwell, marched parallel to the Royalists. This state of things continued until the Parliamentarian army reached Cropredy, where Waller

seized and held the bridge over the Cherwell. The armies were within sight of one another though out of musket-shot, and separated only by the river. Charles's army was in three divisions; the van was led by Lord Wilmot, in the main body was the king and the Prince of Wales with Brentford, and of the rear-guard Colonel Thelwell commanded 1,000 foot, while Lord Northampton and Lord Cleveland had each a brigade of horse.

Now it appears that intelligence came to the royal van that a body of horse, 300 in number, were marching to join Waller, and were less than two miles ahead. Upon this the royal horse in the van were directed to advance and cut them off before a juncture with Waller could be effected. The horse obeyed orders, and the foot of the van, though not ordered, followed in haste. The main body did likewise, apparently without quite knowing why. The rear-guard maintained its original pace, and there was in consequence a considerable gap between the rear of the main body and the front of the rear-guard as they neared Cropredy Bridge.

Waller perceived this, and saw an opportunity which he was not the man to neglect. He despatched a party of 1,000 horse under Lieut.-General Middleton, a Scotch officer of no little repute, to cross the river about a mile below the bridge, where there was a ford. He himself, by means of the bridge, thrust a strong body of men between the royal main body and the rear-guard.

The position was now thus: the royal vanguard and main body were ahead, in quest of 300 horse said to be marching to join Waller. Next, Waller had taken up a

CROPREDY BRIDGE.

position on the Royalist side of the river with 1,500 horse, 1,000 foot, and 11 guns, facing the rear-guard, and in rear of whom were Middleton's 1,000 horse, who were momentarily expected to attack this apparently doomed division of the royal army.

Cleveland appears to have been the first to discover the enemy's intention and to have seized on a small rising ground. From this point he discerned Middleton's 1,000

horse ready to attack his rear. Charles by some means became acquainted with what had happened, and sent off speedily for the royal vanguard, himself taking up a position on another little hill to the north of the bridge. Cleveland charged Waller's horse with some success, but not enough to prevent them from rallying and preparing to attack him. Charles perceived this, and sent his own guards, under Lord Bernard Stewart, to support Cleveland. The combined Royalist cavalry was successful. The attack of Middleton's men now developed in the rear, but was repulsed by the Earl of Northampton, who completely routed the enemy. A renewed attack by Waller, which was resisted by Cleveland and Wilmot, also failed, and cost that general his entire battery of guns, eleven in all. With them were captured one Wemyss, a Scotchman, then general of ordnance, and two "barricadoes of wood, which were drawn upon wheels, and in each seven small brass and leather guns charged with case-shot."

Waller now drew off his army to some high ground on the west side, and seemed hardly desirous of renewing the fight. Charles, in like manner, did not feel eager to engage in more hostilities, and so drew off. Thus ended the curious but indecisive affair at Cropredy Bridge. Thomas Wentworth, 4th Baron Wentworth of Nettlested and 1st Earl of Cleveland, seems to come best out of the combat. He belonged to an old English family, and throughout the civil war was a staunch Royalist. He died in 1667, when the earldom became extinct. Patrick Ruthven, Lord Ruthven of Ettrick, Earl of Forth, and finally Earl of Brentford, was the son of William Ruthven, of Ballindean. Ruthven was a soldier of experience, having served in Sweden, Denmark, Russia, Poland, Prussia, and in the German war under Gustavus Adolphus. He became a lieutenant-general abroad. After the surrender of Ulm in 1632 Ruthven was appointed governor of that place, and most bravely defended it subsequently. His first title was granted in 1639, that of Earl of Forth in 1642, and the English peerage of Brentford on May 27, 1644. This title was derived from the battle outside that town. Prior to the civil war Ruthven was governor for a time of Edinburgh Castle. Lord Brentford died at a very advanced age in 1651, when the title became extinct.

The curious carving which forms the initial letter to this chapter is to be seen on the mantelpiece in the consulting-room at the Herald's College. It evidently represents the augmentation won by an ancestor of Waller's at Azincourt. At that battle one of the Wallers took prisoner a member of the French Royal Family. By the laws of heraldry he in consequence assumed the French Royal Arms. How the carving came into the possession of the heralds is not known. Possibly it was removed from some house or church stall, where it had been wrongly erected by one of the name of Waller, but not of the true family. The real Wallers to this day still bear this augmentation, above which is the word "Azincourt."

CHAPTER XXX.

MARSTON MOOR.

July 2, 1644.

THE military position in the early part of the year 1644 was, in brief, as follows :—Discipline on the part of the Parliamentarian army had already borne fruit. At Cheriton, in Hants, on March 29th, the troops under Waller had achieved a victory of which the moral effect was of the highest importance. The hands of that party in London which inclined to prosecute the war with vigour were immensely strengthened, while the Royalists in the south-east of England were both sadly weakened and, what was worse, were dispirited. On January 19th the Presbyterian Scots crossed the Tweed, and shortly afterwards the Royalists withdrew into Newcastle. Brereton was in Cheshire, shut up, together with Sir Thomas Fairfax, in Nantwich, being besieged by Byron. On January 25th the besieged made a sally, and after hard fighting defeated the enemy. This success was also important, as Nantwich was at that time the only town in the county held by the Parliament.

To retain it, and moreover to seriously defeat the besiegers, was therefore highly encouraging. On February 5th Cromwell signed the Solemn League and Covenant. The next month found him at Newport Pagnell, operating to protect a convoy of stores destined for Gloucester. In Yorkshire, in the West Riding, Sir Thomas Fairfax, though absent in Cheshire, had much influence, and the population was strongly anti-Royalist. Ferdinando, Lord Fairfax, held possession of the East Riding, and was already taking measures to overrun the North Riding. Whitby fell, though Scarborough was too strong to be attacked by the force detached for that purpose by Lord Fairfax under the command of Sir William Constable. Newcastle, strongly garrisoned, was left by the Marquis of Newcastle, who turned his attention to the Scots there in the neighbourhood of Sunderland. Lacking success in this quarter, he withdrew first to Durham and subsequently to York. Prince Rupert, who appears to have been called hither and thither with the utmost importunity, now started for the North, and as usual, with but a scanty force of organised troops. Following his ordinary custom, he recruited a few men here and a few men there from the various Royalist garrisons. February 21st found him at Shrewsbury, *en route* for Chester. Here it became a question whether he should proceed to the relief of Lathom House or make an attempt to raise the siege of Newark, then closely beset by Sir John Meldrum and Willoughby. Lathom House, heroically defended by the Countess of Derby, was besieged by the Parliamentarians of Lancashire. An order from the king appears to have decided the matter, and indeed, gallantry laid aside, the safety of Newark was assuredly of the greater importance.

Leaving Chester on March 13th, in seven days Rupert found himself about twelve miles to the south-west of the town and castle of Newark. Starting about 2 a.m. on the following morning, he proceeded by the Roman Fosse Way till near the town, when he turned rather eastwards to a hill known by the name of the Beacon, his artillery left in the rear, not having reached beyond Farndon. Rupert, by means of one of his headlong charges, supported by the arrival of his infantry and assisted by a sally from the beleaguered place, obtained such an advantage that on March 22nd Meldrum surrendered. By the terms of capitulation his artillery (heavy guns) and all arms and warlike stores remained in the hands of the victors. Thence Rupert marched into Wales to raise more troops—he wanted a "regular" force of his own in lieu of scattered items gathered haphazard. Immediately, however, he was recalled in hot haste to Oxford, on one day, only to have the order countermanded the next. At this juncture the battle of Cheriton, previously mentioned, was fought and lost by Lord Forth and Hopton, and within ten days Andover, Salisbury, and Christchurch had been beaten up by the Parliamentarian forces, Winchester, with the exception of the castle, had been occupied, and an expedition into Dorsetshire was being actively threatened. The king now took the field in person, leaving Oxford on April 10th. His army amounted to some 10,000 men. These he reviewed near Newbury on April 11th, but returned to Oxford the next day. On April 17th the queen, who was near her confinement, started for the "ever faithful city" Exeter, and never saw her husband again. The abortive attempt of Montrose to invade Scotland during the month of March need not be more than mentioned here.

In the North the Fairfaxes had not been idle. Leaving Lancashire and driving the Royalists whenever met with before them, Sir Thomas cleared the West Riding and effected a juncture with his father, then investing Selby. Selby was stormed on April 11th, and on its capture some 3,000 Royalists fell into the hands of their enemies. The Marquis of Newcastle now lay between two opposing forces, on one of which he had already been unable to make any impression. At Durham the Scotch faced him, while at Selby the victorious Fairfaxes, father and son, menaced his rear. Hence it was that within seven days of the taking of Selby he shut himself up in York. Two days later, *i.e.*, April 18th, the Fairfaxes joined hands with the Scots under Alexander Leslie, Lord Leven, at Tadcaster. The situation, therefore, from a Royalist point of view, was in Yorkshire one of the gravest anxiety. Elsewhere things did not look prosperous for the royal cause. For some weeks 6,000 of the royal troops had been occupied, and unsuccessfully occupied, in attempting to reduce the out-of-the-world seaside town of Lyme Regis, in Dorsetshire. A royal force under Sir Charles Vavasour posted near Gloucester had been so weakened by withdrawals that the remainder had failed to prevent a Parliamentarian train from successfully replenishing the stores of ammunition in that city. Charles at Oxford commanded, as we have seen, 10,000 men, and these included Vavasour's contingent. He craved more, and hankered after the now respectable little force which Rupert had with infinite toil collected. To this, naturally, opposition was raised by the prince, who, rash though he may have been in action itself, had the instinct to see that York must at all hazards be saved; and if he did not save it, who would? Charles compromised the matter by mulcting the force of the prince in 2,000 men, whom he insisted should be stationed at Worcester. Rupert then repaired to the headquarters at Oxford, and endeavoured for many days to knock a little military common sense into the irresolute counsels there prevalent. Rupert's design was briefly this: strengthen all the garrisons in the towns round about Oxford, to wit, Reading, Wallingford, Banbury, and Abingdon, and operate between them with a powerful mounted force, leaving to him the task of marching north to save the northern capital. Under the impression that by dint of perseverance he had obtained acceptance for this plan, Rupert left Oxford on May 5th. That he was mistaken will be understood when we find that within twenty-four hours it had been decided to dismantle the fortifications of Reading. Within a fortnight Reading as a walled town and place of arms had ceased to exist. On the day that Rupert left Oxford the Earl of Manchester, operating in Lincolnshire, met with success at Lincoln, taking the city by storm. This success was followed practically by the submission of the entire county and secured the passage of the Trent. By this means, using a temporary bridge at Gainsborough, Manchester started for York, intent on a junction with Leven and the Fairfaxes. It should be noted that Manchester's command consisted of the army of the Eastern Counties Association, that he had originally been summoned to join forces with the Earl of Essex at Aylesbury, but that owing to pressing requests from Leven his destination had been changed. Reading, reduced to the condition of an open town, was occupied at once by Essex and Waller. A week later Abingdon was abandoned by the Royalists, and was at once seized by Essex, while his coadjutor pressed forward towards Wantage to secure a passage over the river higher up than the royal position. Of the results of this manœuvre the previous account of the battle of Cropredy Bridge furnishes details. To return to the proceedings of Prince Rupert, who departed from Oxford on May 5th, and returned to Shrewsbury. Leaving that old town on May 16th, and recruiting by the way, in quick succession he seized and plundered Stockport and Bolton, effecting the relief of Lathom House on the 29th. His march was then directed on York. On June 1st Rupert was joined by a force of 5,000 cavalry and 800 infantry under the command of Goring, and as far as the cavalry was composed, largely made up of troops dismissed from York in anticipation of the siege. It should be remarked that on shutting himself up in York, Newcastle, imitating the tactics of his opponents, had dismissed almost all his cavalry, retaining only his infantry intact, and numbering

6,000, to defend the city walls. From Bolton Rupert turned aside to free Liverpool, an important place at this juncture, seeing that through it the long negotiated for Irish reinforcements must pass when they landed, if they did. On June 7th Rupert attacked the place, which, ill fortified as it was, delayed him until the 10th; nay, on that day the defenders managed to successfully repulse a rather brisk attack. Losing heart, however—and indeed they could hardly hope to prolong the struggle to any extent—the besieged that night sailed away. A remnant of the garrison, numbering some 400, were the next day put to the sword. York, under its able governor, Sir Thomas Glemham, assisted by the Marquis of Newcastle, was now hard pressed. Blockaded on all sides, with famine within and foes without, surrender was but a question of days. Famine also, or something very like it, was abroad in the camp of the besiegers, to such an extent had the country for miles round been foraged for provisions—provisions now nearly exhausted. On June 13th Newcastle made an offer to treat for the surrender, but that offer was declined, chiefly because one article stipulated that the clergy in the Minster should be secured in their "altar service." By means of an intercepted message to Rupert (and this had great weight with the enemy) it was known that on the sixth day at the longest Newcastle must surrender. Jealousy in the camp now came to the aid of the Royalists. A mine prematurely exploded, the firing of which had not been communicated to either Fairfax or Leven, led to the discomfiture of Manchester's troops, who ran to the assault. This gave the besieged breathing time. Three days prior, *i.e.*, on June 14th, Rupert had received a letter from Charles, involved and enigmatical in its meaning. This letter on the face of it could bear the construction—Save York and fight at all costs. If York be lost or you are too weak, march at once on Worcester; if you fail in both ventures, "all the successes you can afterwards have most infallibly will be useless to me." York still held out, not six but fourteen days or more, till on June 28th news of the approach of Rupert, who had marched from Lancashire into Yorkshire, arrived at the Parliamentarian camp. Somewhat aghast, the Fairfaxes, Leven, and Manchester heard that his troops numbered 10,000 horse and 8,000 foot. A council was held, messages for assistance were sent to Denbigh and Meldrum, and replies received that at the earliest no aid could be expected before July 4th. Between Rupert advancing from the west and the garrison the three disunited generals found themselves in a tight place and, unanimously for once, decided on a course of action, viz., an abandonment of the siege and a march westward to bar the way of the relieving force. On June 30th Rupert had reached Knaresborough, the shattered fragments of whose noble, and then almost impregnable, castle still crown the precipitous river bank.

RUINED KEEP OF KNARESBOROUGH.

On July 1st the Parliamentarian army marched from York and took up its position on Marston Moor, distant six miles west of York, and on the direct road, *viâ* Wetherby to

Knaresborough. Rupert had, however, no intention of giving battle on these terms. Marching north-east from Knaresborough he reached Boroughbridge, distant seven miles therefrom on June 30th. Continuing in the same direction for another five miles he crossed the river Swale at Thornton Bridge. Then wheeling, he marched directly south-east to the Ouse, where, having dislodged the guard left by Manchester to hold a bridge of boats at Overton, he on the night of July 1st encamped without the walls of York on its northern side. This last march covered seventeen miles. Here he sent a message to Newcastle, requesting, or rather commanding him as his superior officer to set forth and pay him a visit. Things now looked well for the Royalists, in Yorkshire at least. On Marston Moor, or rather at Long Marston Hall, the situation was the subject of anxious debate on the part of the generals of the Parliament. The siege of York was ended, the enemy, which had avoided conflict, superior in numbers, was in the immediate neighbourhood, and it looked as if a Royalist dash into Lincolnshire with a campaign in the other counties on the eastern coast to follow was the programme. The result of such a series of events none of them dared to forecast. Fighting must come sooner or later, but some effort required to be made, and made at once, to protect this part of England, which was specially Parliamentarian in its tendencies.

Hence, on the morning of July 2nd, the infantry set forth in the direction of Cawood, a town on the Ouse, situated some nine or ten miles south-west of Long Marston, and an equal distance almost due south of York. The cavalry, under David Leslie (afterward Lord Newark) and Cromwell, remained posted on the ridge which overlooks the Moor as far as and beyond York, in order to cover the retreat.

At the time of the battle Marston Moor was unenclosed: a wide flat track of moorland covered with whin-bushes, and in no few places marshy. On the north lies Wilstrop Wood and a moor of the same name, while the river Nidd runs a winding course eastwards towards the Ouse. In those days

MARSTON MOOR, FROM PARLIAMENTARIAN CENTRE, LOOKING DUE NORTH.

Wilstrop Wood was far more extensive than at present. To the south of the moor lay the villages of Bilton and Long Marston. The village of Tockwith lies at the western extremity of the battlefield, and near it is the Tockwith Moor. A wide lane running north-west and called Marston Lane joins the villages of Long Marston and Tockwith. From this lane, and crossing the moor eastwards, are two lanes, Atterwith (with a dyke) and Moor Lane (having both dyke and hedge). The Atterwith Lane joins on to the road to Boroughbridge. From Bilton village straight through Long Marston eastwards runs the road from Wetherby to York. The ridge of rising ground already mentioned lies on the south side of Marston Lane, and at the time of the battle was covered by a rye crop. Parallel to the Marston Lane, and situated about 300 yards on the north side, there used formerly to be a wide ditch with a hedge on its north side. This ditch joined the Atterwith dyke with the Syke Beck, a brook which runs through Tockwith. Beyond this beck, and almost opposite the point where it was joined by the big ditch, is a small hill, known to-day as "the Rye Hill." All accounts point to the supposition that the ditch at the time of the battle was dry, or nearly so. Whether parts of it were or were not filled up remains an open question, but the evidence on examination seems to prove that some portion had been filled in eastward of Kendall Lane, a lane it may be observed which runs due north from Marston Lane, and which at its Tockwith end is nearly joined by another direct from Bilton. Rupert meanwhile had had angry converse with Newcastle, the latter did not want to fight, or at least urged delay. At one time the Prince and the Marquis nearly, if not quite, came to blows. Finally it was resolved to fight. It seems most probable that Rupert, either through a spy or from a deserter, had become aware late on the night of July 1st or early the following morning, that a retreat of the Parliamentarian troops was contemplated even if it had not already been carried into effect. Only on this supposition can the sudden appearance of a body of Royalist cavalry on the moor at the hour of 9 a.m. be accounted for.

This reconnaissance, however, produced great results. Cromwell and Leslie with their cavalry observed the enemy, and moreover observed them wheel about and return post-haste to York. What did this portend? One of two things: either it meant an intention to fight at Marston, or it was a feint to cover some movement against the infantry, already by this time far on their way to Tadcaster. Battle under either case would have been at a disadvantage, and it became imperative forthwith to reunite the divided forces. This might have been done either by following the infantry or by recalling them. Obviously the latter was the course to pursue, and instant messages of a most urgent character were sent after the retiring regiments. Rupert, as we know, meant fighting, and fighting at Marston. The Parliamentarian decision was therefore for him most untoward. Overtaken within a mile of Tadcaster, the half-starved Parliamentarians were hurried back with all speed and placed in position. Food they had not tasted since leaving York, and they had, moreover, marched eighteen miles at least since abandoning their trenches, and by the way some of their siege guns and mortars. The horses, turned out to graze on the moor all night, were, however, in fair condition, though rough grass is but a poor substitute for good forage.

The task of Rupert now was to get his troops to the front, and here he was hampered by something like a mutiny among Newcastle's men, who clamoured for pay, and would not march from York without it. This difficulty was overcome by persuasion, but not until late.

The disposition of the two armies was as follows: Fairfax occupied the extreme right near to Long Marston, his men being drawn up with cavalry on the right and infantry on the left. The cavalry numbered 4,800 in eighty troops of sixty men. Sir Thomas Fairfax commanded the English cavalry in the first line, and Colonel Lambert headed fifty troops of recruits. Eglinton, Dalhousie, and Balgonie formed the second line with three regiments of Scotch horse. The infantry, 3,000 in number, on the left of the cavalry, were commanded as a brigade by Sir W. Fairfax, with the Colonels Bright, Needham, and Forbes. In reserve, and to the rear of these, were posted two Scotch regiments of foot under Colonels Rae and Lord Buccleugh.

The centre, under the command of Alexander Leslie, Lord Leven, consisted of nine regiments of Scotch foot, numbering 9,000, and over them Lieut.-General Baillie; the various regimental commanders being Lord Lindsay, Lord Maitland, Lord Cassilis, and William Douglass. The reserve consisted of three regiments of Scotch and two brigades of Manchester's troops. The left wing under Manchester was composed of three brigades of infantry, numbering in all 3,000 men, commanded in chief by Major-General Crawford, the brigade commanders being Colonels Russell, Pickering, and Montague. These were posted on the right. His left was composed of 2,280 horse under Cromwell (including the Ironsides), and three regiments of Scottish horse under David Leslie. There was in addition, still further to the left, a body of eight troops of Scotch dragoons under Colonel Frizeall and Lieut.-Colonel Crawford (of Nether Skeldon). The cavalry in the Parliamentarian army therefore amounted to about 7,500 in number, the infantry to 19,000. Of the composition of their artillery force no details have come down to us beyond the fact that there were twenty-five guns of various calibres, that these were posted on the ridge, and that they were under the command of Sir Alexander Hamilton, the general of the Scottish Ordnance. Not far from the guns the baggage train, such as it was, was stationed. It will therefore be understood that the extreme right and the extreme left of the army rested on the villages of Long Marston and Tockwith respectively, and that each of these extremes was composed of cavalry. That no attempt was made to either occupy or to use the buildings of those villages for purpose of defence or offence appears strange in these days; but the disposition of the army was in accordance with the military notions of the date at which the battle was fought. How far the result of this battle of surprises would have differed from that which eventuated had some guns been posted on each flank, and the villages occupied by infantry with cavalry to support them it is impossible now to say. As it was, to all intents and purposes the absence of artillery on both sides would not have been felt.

The Royalist army was drawn up on the north side of the ditch on a front which was slightly greater than that of the enemy. It extended from the Atterwith Dyke to the

Syke Beck. Rupert in person commanded the Royalist right wing, 7,200 strong in cavalry, with certain regiments of foot, which were posted on the right of the centre under Colonel O'Neile. The centre was entirely composed of infantry, having on its extreme left Newcastle's famous "White-coats," a body in themselves 3,000 strong, the whole under the command of Lieut.-General Lord Eythin. A regiment known by the name of the Blue Regiment was placed in reserve. There was also a Green Coat regiment, but its position is unknown. Goring's command, viz., the entire left wing, was made up of 1,200 of the "King's Old Horse" under Urry, and Newcastle's cavalry under Sir Charles Lucas, in addition to some troops held in reserve. The united troops of Urry and Lucas amounted to 4,000 men. It appears to be a reasonable computation that the whole Royalist force consisted of 14,000 foot and 10,000 horse. Their artillery numbered twenty-eight guns of various types Demiculverins = 9-pounders, and Drakes = 6-pounders. These were posted along the ditch at regular intervals in the centre, but more thickly at the wings, especially on the left. Musketeers also lined the hedges both of the great ditch and at Moor Lane. Balancing the two armies, it will be seen that the Royalists exceeded in cavalry by 2,400 men, but were deficient in infantry to the number of 5,000 men; the three extra guns, as the event turned out, were immaterial. The disposition of the two armies occupied a considerable amount of time, and it was not till four o'clock in the afternoon that Lord Eythin arrived with the

White-coats. Rupert's line of battle struck Eythin with astonishment. There were the two armies confronting one another, with only a hedge and ditch and narrow strip of ground between them. The older soldier, who had served his apprenticeship in the art of war abroad, and who was a cautious commander, expressed his opinion plainly when asked, condemning not only the marshalling of the forces, but their proximity to the enemy. Rupert desired to attack at once—it was his nature. Eythin demurred and suggested the following morning. Rupert offered to withdraw his troops a space, to be met by the reply that it was too late. Rupert could not withdraw and thus decline battle. Hitherto the Parliamentarian army, which had managed to get into position as early as two o'clock, had made no sign of attack. True, a brief cannonade took place about three o'clock, during which Sir Gilbert Houghton, a captain in the royal army, was slain—some say by the first shot fired. The royal guns replied at once, and four or five rounds were exchanged by both sides. Then quiet again reigned, and in frequent rain-storms the opposing armies faced one another. At four Eythin arrived, no doubt hurried on by the sound of the guns earlier. The consultation with Rupert was held, and time went on till between six and seven in the evening. Newcastle, who had come to the field in his coach and six, then retired to that commodious vehicle to smoke and sleep. Rupert professedly determined to postpone fighting till the morrow, called for food and returned to his division. Suddenly, whether owing to an order from Rupert or as the

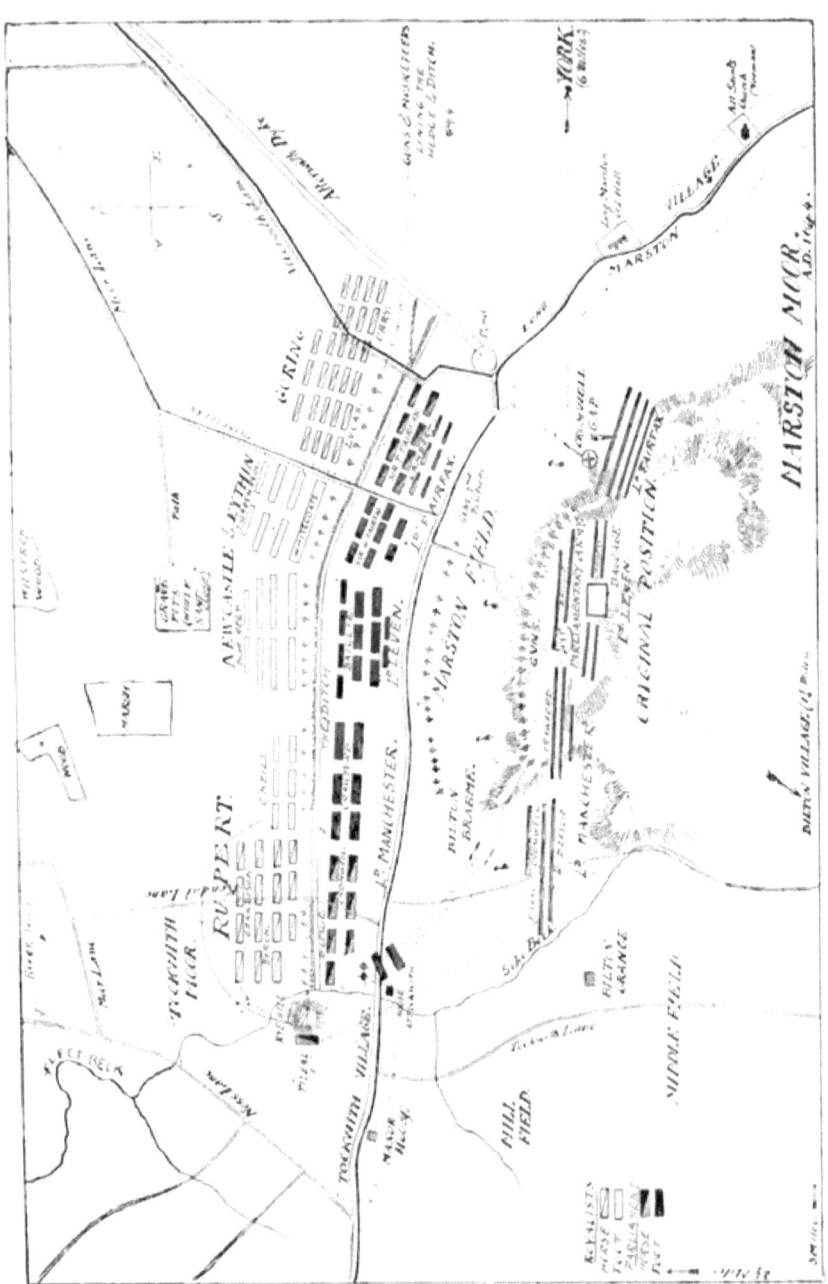

independent action of some subordinate officer, the Rye Hill on the extreme left of the Parliamentarian army was seized by a Royalist regiment and a party of horse. These were speedily dislodged by a charge of the dragoons under Colonel Frizeall, who then occupied the little hill. Rupert, it is said, at once opened with his guns on the left wing, severely wounding Captain Walton, the nephew of Cromwell. Cromwell ordering down two 6-pounders from their useless position on the hill, sent them forward, escorted by two infantry regiments, to silence Rupert's guns. The musketeers in the ditch immediately opened fire on these, and in a brief space the action developed like a quick match all along the line.

The first movement of importance was undertaken by the Parliamentarian army, and was this. The remainder of the guns were brought down the hill, and the entire front was advanced (one account says 200 yards). A bare 40 or 50 yards only now separated the two front lines. The time was now nearer 7 p.m. than 6 p.m., and late though it was, a general engagement, to be fought out on this July evening, became unavoidable. Down the hill from Bilton Breame rode the cavalry under Cromwell in good order, five well-disciplined bodies of horse, and headed by the Ironsides. In the centre the Earl of Manchester's infantry advanced at the double, and attacked the foot of the Royalist centre and right wing. Frizeall on the flank with his dragoons appears to have been permitted almost unopposed to clear the ditch in his neighbourhood of the royal musketeers, and he there captured four 6-pounders. What was Rupert doing at this juncture? or rather where was he? for not until Lord Byron with the cavalry on the right had charged and failed to regain the position is anything definite to be heard of him. Then it was that the great charge took place in which Rupert's picked cavalry and Cromwell's Ironsides met for the first time. Rupert's attack was delivered in front, being assisted on the flank by Byron's command. At first it succeeded, Cromwell's troopers were driven back. Returning, however, to the charge they were met and severely handled by Rupert's favourite lifeguards. Again the Ironsides came on in an undaunted way and actually rode through Rupert's men, but only to be met by a fresh body under Grandison. It was at this period of the battle that Cromwell was wounded in the neck by the sword of Mr. Mark Trevor, of Brinkynall (afterwards Lord Dungannon). The wound was not dangerous, but through loss of blood Cromwell was obliged to be conveyed out of action. He was taken to a house at Tockwith, where his hurt was dressed and then returned to the fight. For more than an hour this desperate cavalry battle continued, till, having obtained an opportunity for delivering a flank attack, Sir David Leslie, at the head of his Scotch horse, charged headlong on the Royalist squadrons. The cavalry of Rupert, caught between two bodies, wavered, for the first time broke, and finally fled across the moor in the direction of Wilstrop Wood. Leslie, who should have been more wary, detached a large portion of his command to go in pursuit, thus weakening his fighting strength, and then returned to the battle.

Meanwhile Crawford, with some of the infantry of the Parliamentarian centre, was hotly engaged with the foot under O'Neile, and here again fortune was unfavourable to the Royalist cause. The noise of the firing, it is said, awoke Newcastle, who hurriedly armed himself and rode from his coach to the field. He arrived in time to find the right wing routed and in full retreat. An attempt on his part to rally O'Neile's foot succeeded for a few minutes, but they ultimately took to their heels.

Let us now trace the battle as regards the Royalist left wing, which was commanded by Goring, with Lucas and Urry as his subordinates. The cavalry of Sir Thomas Fairfax, from the right wing of the Parliamentarian army, advanced over the rough, bushy ground which then lay between the Atterwith Dyke and Moor Lane, but could only pass the Great Ditch at the spot where it is crossed by the latter. The cavalry, however, managed to clear the intervening ditch of musketeers and took their three guns, two sixes and one 9-pounder. The ground there, however, was quite unfit for cavalry through its roughness, and despite a gallant charge against Urry's squadrons in this part of the field Fairfax failed. Seeing that he brought no less than 4,000 men, or nearly the whole cavalry force of that wing, to bear on the 1,200 of the King's Old Horse, failure is somewhat remarkable. Here the loss of officers among the Parliamentarians was very severe. Sir Thomas Fairfax received two wounds and was unhorsed, Major Fairfax was wounded, and Sir Charles killed, besides many others killed and wounded. Three times did the enemy's cavalry charge the Royalist left wing, and three times was it driven back. A small body of 400 men (five troops), under Sir Thomas Fairfax himself, did manage at last to break through, and routing their immediate opponents, chased them in the direction of York. Goring and Lucas now delivered a counter attack with all the forces at their disposal. They fell upon some raw troops, who wavered and were then driven back. Meanwhile Sir William Fairfax, with the

YORK FROM PARLIAMENTARIAN CENTRE, LOOKING DUE EAST.

regiments of Yorkshire foot, was trying conclusions with the left of the Royalist centre. He cleared the Great Ditch of his enemies with little loss, but then found himself face to face with the famous regiment of White-coats, while on his right flank the musketeers who lined the hedge and ditch of Moor Lane were prepared to give him a warm reception. Caught between these two fires, it is not to be wondered that his troops turned and fled back across the Great Ditch. In their flight the infantry became mixed with the demoralised cavalry, just then recoiling after the counter attack of Lucas and Goring. This completed the discomfiture of the Parliamentarian right wing. A few isolated bodies of horse endeavoured to make a stand, but with little effect. One regiment did cut its way through the royal infantry (evidently by an obliquely delivered charge), and continuing its career eventually joined the cavalry of the left wing which was returning from the pursuit of Rupert and his Life Guards;

ORIGINAL PARLIAMENTARIAN POSITION, FROM ROYALIST CENTRE.

but the main body of the Parliamentarian left wing, both horse and foot, fled in the utmost disorder. They were, of course, pursued, and of course the pursuit was too extended. One party followed the fugitives in the direction of Tadcaster; another rode directly through the fleeing mob to the waggons, which they forthwith commenced to loot. Now there were yet near these waggons some of the guns, for all had not been brought into action lower down. A few rounds from these poured into the Parliamentarian centre from the rear and followed by cavalry charges down the hill would have practically won the battle at this juncture, but it was not to be.

After a time the Royalist cavalry indeed did return to the charge, and against the Parliamentarian centre. Their charge, delivered in flank, was directed against the Scotch foot. Hitherto in the centre, though the action had been hot, it had been indecisive. Newcastle's White-coats having now shaken off the Yorkshire foot, were at liberty to try conclusions with the Scotch, and were thus employed when the squadrons of Goring and Lucas crashed over from the hill. The Scotch, with the White-coats in their front, besides the whole of the remainder of the infantry of the royal centre, were taken in flank by this terrific charge of cavalry. Twice they withstood the combined attack by means of lining their musketeers with pikemen, as it is stated, but after a third, save three weakened Scotch regiments, they turned and fled. Leven tried to rally the fugitives—he was even quite pathetic in his appeals—but in vain; so, making the best of a bad matter, he joined in the flight, and played his part therein so well that he never drew rein till safe in Leeds, a distance of 20 miles; nor did he flee in solitude, for a goodly band of officers "of good quality" bore him company. Ferdinando Lord Fairfax, the commander of the right wing, had also fled, and was at the time on his way to Cawood Castle, where he safely ensconced himself in bed. The Earl of Manchester ran away also, but, unlike the others, pulled himself together, rallied a band of some 500 fugitives, and came cautiously back to see what was going on. Sir Thomas Fairfax, who, it will be remembered, was last heard of pursuing a small body of Royalist cavalry towards York, pulled up shortly and returned to the field alone, only to find the right wing and the centre of his friends completely routed. Pulling from his hat the white cockade (the sole Parliamentarian uniform on that day) he mingled with his foes and passed through unharmed.

The position of affairs on the battlefield was now somewhat peculiar. The Royalist right wing had been completely routed, but pursuit of it had ceased, and the pursuers had returned to the field. The Parliamentarian right wing and centre were both scattered to the winds, save a small remnant of infantry under Baillie, and completely beyond recall. Their original position on the crest of the hill was in the possession of the Royalist left wing. All the moor north of the ditch, except the portion held by the White-coats, was then clear of troops and tenanted merely by the dead and wounded. Cromwell, under cover of the smoke, changed his position from the rear of the Royalist right to the rear of the Royalist left, having met with Sir Thomas Fairfax, Lambert, and the Earl of Manchester. How the last got there is rather a mystery, seeing that he had fled in the other direction, rallied fugitives, and then returned towards the hill. It can only be accounted for by supposing that Manchester on rallying his 500 men returned to the extreme left, crossed the right of the former Royalist position, and met Cromwell rallying the pursuers of Rupert's troopers. Cromwell now gathered together his forces and prepared to deliver a counter stroke. His resources consisted of his own cavalry of the left wing and a few rallied troops of stragglers. David Leslie had his cavalry and Crawford had the infantry of the Eastern Association nearly intact and well in hand, while Baillee and the three Scotch regiments, though hard pressed, had not yet fled. The Royalist cavalry of the right wing was well on its way to York, utterly routed, that of the left wing was partly engaged in pursuit towards Tadcaster and partly in plundering the waggons. The infantry of the Royalist centre was hard at work completing the discomfiture of Baillie, and that discomfiture did not seem to be far off. Cromwell's decision was quickly arrived at. From his position in the rear he launched Leslie with cavalry against the White-coats, and sent Crawford to combat the remainder of the Royalist foot and sustain Baillie, now in sore straits. He, at the head of his cavalry, rode through Moor Lane in the track of the Royalist left, now disorganised and occupied either in plundering or in pursuit. Back came presently the horsemen of Goring and Lucas, to be met by a determined charge on the part of the Ironsides, and to suffer utter rout, Goring and Lucas, both unhorsed, being made prisoners. The hitherto victorious cavalry of the Royalist left wing, the King's Old Horse, thus as a fighting force vanished from the field. Through the gap now closed by a gate, but still known as Cromwell Gap, the plundering party fled in a panic-stricken stream and hotly pursued by their exulting foes.

Meanwhile the White-coats, taken in rear, were compelled

to give way. Tradition states that they retreated to a ditched field known as White Syke Close and there made their final stand. The position of this field with respect to the probable position of the regiment at the time of Leslie's charge presents some little difficulty. How, if attacked in rear, could they have reached the traditional enclosure? The story is that the ditch surrounding this field rendered it difficult for horsemen to effect an entry, and that hence the disciplined White-coats were able for a long time to keep their assailants at bay. With pike, and musket while ammunition lasted, this gallant body, nearly 3,000 strong, stood shoulder to shoulder; later, when powder and ball was exhausted, the musketeers with clubbed weapons maintained their share of the desperate fight. Great was the loss sustained by Leslie in his repeated and futile attempts to break in; heavier, in fact, in killed and wounded than anywhere else on the field. Presently the dragoons, under Frizeall, not heard of since the opening episode of the battle, were brought up and attacked the doomed men on the opposite side. A gap was made in their ranks, the troopers got among them, and soon all was over. Of a regiment which at 6.30 went into action 3,000 strong, by 10 p.m. thirty wounded men only remained alive as prisoners. White Syke Close is stated to be full of death pits; if it is not the cemetery of the White-coats alone, it is certainly the patch of ground devoted to the burial of the slain on that memorable July 2nd. Little now remained to be done to complete the destruction of the Royalist army. Crawford and Baillie fought on; Cromwell, having discomfited Goring and

MICKLEGATE BAR, YORK.

Lucas, went to their aid; Leslie, having diverted their most doughty opponents and annihilated them, was also free to assist. The Parliamentarian infantry from acting on the defensive was able to assume the offensive and advanced to the attack. Cromwell charging a green-coated regiment put it to flight, while the infantry, aided by Leslie, completed the discomfiture of the remainder. In scattered bodies the infantry of the Royalist centre fled over the moor towards York. The pursuit was pressed almost up to the gates of the city, the road just without the Micklegate Bar being practically blocked by fugitives and wounded men. Rupert, having had his horse shot under him, was compelled to hide until dark, when he luckily obtained a stray charger and escaped hatless and riding headlong in his flight. He reached York and was admitted. Newcastle also arrived in the city at a late hour. The only Royalist general who retreated in something like order was Lord Eythin, for he went so far as to rally and lead a respectable body of men into the city. The scene between the three when they did meet was characteristic. Rupert knew no reason for the rout save that "the devil did help his servants," and prepared to rally such of his men as could be found. Newcastle, fearful of the laughter of the Court, determined on flight to Holland, and Eythin elected to accompany him.

On the morrow, from the Monk Bar, issued Rupert at the head of some 6,000 men. He marched northwards, through Thirsk and Richmond, into Lancashire, picking up some regiments under the command of Colonel Clavering. Sir Thomas Glemham, who had on the night of the battle closed the gates of York and refused admission to the fugitives, on hearing of the defection of Newcastle proclaimed him a traitor. Nevertheless Newcastle, accompanied by a large number of officers of rank and escorted by a troop of horse and another of dragoons, left York the next day for Scarborough; thence he sailed for Hamburg, reaching that city on July 8th. With him went Sir Charles Cavendish, his brother, the ostensible commander of the White-coats. He at least did not die in White Syke Close.

Glemham with his diminished garrison could not hope to hold York, and surrendered on the 16th, the siege having been renewed on July 4th. He was allowed to march out with the honours of war. By the disaster on the moor and the surrender of the city consequent on that disaster, the royal cause in the north was absolutely ruined. This ruin was rendered all the more complete by the defection of so many influential gentlemen. Two shiploads sailed in company with Newcastle! Plunder in plenty fell into the hands of the victors, the capture of upwards of one hundred colours being a most remarkable feature. The complete list issued from the "Leaguer at York," and dated July 9th "at 10 at night," gives a detailed description of their various colours, fringes, and quaint designs. Rupert's, we learn, was "nearly five yards square, with the arms of the Palatinate and a red cross in the middle." Relics of the fight have been found frequently and in large numbers, particularly between Moor Lane and Marston, and along Atterwith Lane. The ditch surrounding White Syke Close yielded quantities when it was cleared out nearly a century ago. Bullets and cannonballs have been frequent finds, and not a few sword-blades and iron skull-caps. Bones when discovered in most cases have been removed as curiosities. This disgraceful habit cannot be too strongly reprehended. To make a "curio" of the bones of a human being is at all times reprehensible, but to remove and make a show of the bones of brave men who, whether in a good or bad cause, have fallen on the field of battle is, be it observed, a cowardly and blackguardly proceeding.

LONG MARSTON OLD HALL.

The old Marston Hall in which Cromwell passed the night before the battle is a brick house with stone quoins. Originally an E-shaped house, only one wing and the lower portion of the other remain; the central part has been pulled down. Long Marston Church, containing Norman work in its south door, seems but little altered from its appearance in 1644. There were probably burials in the church and churchyard after the fight, but none are recorded. The greater portion of the slain were deposited anyhow, in great trenches on the moor itself. Certain mounds explored when drainage operations were undertaken in 1858 and 1859 proved this; at a depth of about 4 feet hundreds of skeletons were found. One pit, measuring 12 yards by 8, it is consoling to read, was left unexplored.

Contemporary writers, while of course agreeing in the result of this remarkable battle, yet diverge in a singular manner in their narrations of how that result was attained. The reason of this is not far to seek, and is to be found in the conflicting factions which bred disunion among the Parliamentarian leaders. Here was a victory in which heaven alone knows how many generals and colonels, not to speak of subordinate officers and whole regiments, had bolted headlong from the field and spread the news of defeat for miles away from the scene of action. Something needed to be done to save their credit; hence, at the only man among them, viz., Cromwell, who had military genius enough, or, to be more accurate, military insight enough to seize an opportunity and profit by it, mud was cast and cast freely. None in these days will, however, impute cowardice to him on the occasion, as Crawford, of Skeldon, is reputed to have done. But the lessons of the battle were many. Divided commands, *i.e.*, three generals, with no supreme head, were again proved a failure— a failure only retrieved by Cromwell and converted into a success. The "caution" of Leven in not attacking the Royalists before they were fully prepared nearly proved disastrous, just as the lack of caution (usual) of the Royalist horse in pursuit ended in defeat. Why the infantry of the Royalist centre should have been weakest at the spot where the great ditch was least an obstacle has never been explained. To Rupert's method of marshalling, however, this may probably be ascribed. Certain it is that not only was the force there (O'Neile's) singularly weak, but one account states that a gap existed between the infantry and the cavalry on its right—a gap where the ditch was filled and over which Crawford marched, then wheeling attacked his enemy in flank. But the old rules of warfare under which the general fought and by his personal prowess often gained a victory were on this occasion assuredly revealed in all their absurdity. Cromwell wounded, and at a neighbouring house; Rupert, his immediate opponent, horseless and hiding; Manchester off and away; Leven also; Ferdinando Lord Fairfax also—a battle in which more than 26,000 men on one side were fighting and were absolutely without any officer in supreme command. Nor were matters one whit better in the Royalist army. Rupert a fugitive; Goring and Lucas pursuing and plundering while they ought to have been attempting to repair the disasters on the right; Newcastle asleep in his coach till the fight had become general, when, after a vapouring speech, he proceeded to execute a little charge of his own at the head of a "company of gentlemen volunteers." He was no coward physically, as he showed that day; but moral coward he certainly was. With all the faults laid to his charge, and they are many, somehow the rash but brilliant Rupert comes best out of the wreck. Many a general has been badly beaten before, but few on the very morrow of a crushing defeat have recommenced the work of organisation, and singlehanded, as it were, embarked on a fresh enterprise. This action of his involved moral courage of as high an order as his known and proved valour on the field of battle. Critics may say, Why did he not remain to defend York? York was untenable, being without provisions. Far more justly may it be urged, Why did he not content himself with relieving York and avoid a battle; or, if he fought, have done so on ground of his own choosing? The rash temperament of the man and the letter of the king will possibly account, or nearly account, for his conduct. Can there not also have been a feeling of contempt on his part for the utter incapacity of Newcastle? Contempt for an ally, which is almost as fatal as contempt of a foe, has driven more commanders than Rupert into the commission of quite as grave military errors as the fight on Marston Moor.

LEATHER HAT.
LITTLECOTE, BERKS.
STEEL CAP & BREAST-PLATE

GLENHAM.

CHAPTER XXXI.

NEWBURY.

October 27, 1644.

Relics at Donnington

EARLY in October, 1644, the military position was as follows: Manchester was at Reading; Essex in Portsmouth, whither he had gone after his defeat in the far west; and Waller at Shaftesbury. Charles, returned from Cornwall, was at Sherborne, in Dorsetshire, on October 8th. On that day Waller began a march which closely resembled a retreat, falling gradually back as the royal army advanced. When, on the 15th, Charles arrived at Salisbury, Waller retired to Andover. Three days later he succeeded in foiling Prince Maurice, who attempted a surprise. He then made for Basingstoke, where he joined Manchester on October 19th. Essex arrived on October 21st, and the three united armies amounted to between 18,000 and 19,000 men. Basing House, at this time closely besieged, was in great straits. Banbury was also invested, as was Donnington Castle, near Newbury; but the two last were able to hold out. The royal army, numbering some 10,000 men, had trusted to be able to free Basing House, but in the face of an enemy outnumbering them by nearly two to one any such attempt was out of the question. But the effect of the presence of the king's army at Salisbury was speedily felt at Donnington, and the siege was raised. Charles now marched to Newbury, detaching the Earl of Northampton, assisted by Colonel Gage then at Oxford, to succour Banbury.

From Basingstoke Waller, Manchester, and Essex marched to Reading, and there the last-named fell ill. Banbury was successfully relieved on October 25th, and on the same day Waller and Manchester were on the road to seek out Charles and give him battle. They marched by the valley of the Kennet, and were unmolested till they reached Thatcham, a village between three and four miles east of Newbury. From this point onward slight skirmishes took place along the road, but nothing sufficient to prevent the army from camping on Clay Hill, a hill to the north of the river, one mile east of Shaw House.

The royal army occupied a strong position between the Kennet, which flows from west to east, and the Lamborne, which flows from the north-west; these rivers thus protecting the north as well as the east side of the royal camp from attack. Charles's front was facing the east. On the other bank of the stream stood, and still stands, that grand old mansion called Shaw House. This, in 1644, was fortified, as also were its outbuildings. It is interesting to remark that Charles was nearly killed by a shot at one of the windows of the drawing-room—the shot yet remains buried

GATEHOUSE (EXTERIOR).

in the panel. About a mile distant, and on the same side of the Lambourne, westwards, stood Donnington Castle, recently besieged. This stronghold of course added to the completeness of the royal defences. The main body of the royal cavalry, including the King's Life Guard, was posted in two fields, known as Shaw Field and Newbury Field, under the command of Sir Humphrey Bennet. In the rear and on a hill behind, and also in the village of Speen, Prince Maurice was in charge of a strong detachment.

On the side of the Parliament a council of war was now held by the curiously composed committee which then had the direction of the military operations against the king. This committee, from its form, needs a brief description. It had now been in existence for eight days, and its members were Manchester, Essex, and Waller (military), with two civilians by name Johnston and Crew. Action was to be decided on by a majority, and at all meetings the non-military members, who were bound to accompany the army, were likewise compelled to be present. Essex, as we know, had been left behind sick at Reading, consequently the council of war resolved itself into two soldiers and two civilians. A very risky experiment at best was this, and it shows very clearly how petty jealousies hampered the military operations of the Parliament, threatening even to bring all concerted action to a complete standstill. Between all three of the military men there was jealousy, if not absolute ill-will.

Both Johnston and Crew were distinguished men; the first, a Scottish advocate, had been made by Charles a lord of session on November 13, 1641, with the courtesy title of Lord Warriston; this appointment being a concession to the Covenanters. Bishop Burnet was his nephew. Cromwell, in 1657, made him one of the commissioners for the administration of justice in Scotland, and in the following year called him to his House of Peers. On the restoration of the Rump Parliament he was one of those chosen to form a new council of state, and of this he was often president. When the Rump Parliament was suppressed he became permanent president of the Committee of Safety. Charles II. specially exempted him from amnesty on the Restoration. He was in absence condemned to death and forfeiture, by decree, on the ground that, having been king's advocate, he had accepted office under Cromwell and sat in the Parliamentarian House of Peers. Arrested at Rouen, whither he had fled, he was handed over to the English and conveyed to the Tower, being subsequently removed to the Edinburgh Tolbooth. His mind seems to have become affected, but he was, nevertheless, brought before the Scottish Parliament. Johnston was hung at the Market Cross of Edinburgh on July 23, 1663, his head being subsequently placed on the Netherbow. Burnet and Carlyle have both summed up his character, neither estimate being particularly favourable, his fanatical Presbyterianism being the chief point mentioned. Crew, whom Clarendon names as a man of the "greatest moderation," sat as member for Amersham 1625, Brackley 1626, Banbury 1628, and Northamptonshire 1640. He sat again for Brackley in the Long Parliament. In May, 1640, he was sent to the Tower for refusing to surrender certain papers relative to the Committee on Religion, but was, on submission, released in June. He voted against

SHAW HOUSE.

the attainder of Strafford. On the outbreak of war he joined the Parliamentarian party. During the struggle he served in several offices. Disapproving of the avowed intention to bring Charles to justice, he was imprisoned on December 9, 1648, but released about three weeks later. He was a member of the Council of State when the secluded members seized the reins in 1660. Crew was in this capacity the mover of a resolution which condemned the execution of the king. He sat again as member for Northamptonshire in the new Parliament. On the Restoration Crew was one of the deputation which met Charles at the Hague. On April 20, 1661, he was raised to the peerage as Baron Crewe of Stene. Lord Crew died in 1679, aged eighty-one. The brief notices of these two men as here set down are interesting in the consideration of the, to them unaccustomed, duties which they had to perform at Newbury.

The royal position at Newbury was duly reconnoitred, presumably by the committee as a whole, and was, as might be expected, pronounced too strong for an attack in front. The river formed one obstacle, and Shaw House, fortified as it was, assuredly would prove a nasty nut to crack. After deliberation, it was determined to attempt a double assault in combination. A strong force was to be detached to make a circuitous march, and then to fall on Maurice in the rear at Speen. Simultaneously with this attack Manchester was to storm Shaw House, after delivering a sham assault, in order to divert attention from the manœuvre. The plan was good, and if the Royalists remained in ignorance of it, or were deceived by the feigned assault, might prove successful. If detected, however, the chances of failure were great.

By some means, however, the details of the whole design became perfectly known within the royal lines, and measures, wise ones as far as they went, were taken to frustrate the assault in the rear. Maurice was ordered to prepare to meet an onslaught in that direction, and this practically meant that his men faced about and fought in a diametrically opposite direction to that in which they had been posted to fight. Maurice received his orders, but when is not known. He occupied the early part of the day on the 27th in digging entrenchments at Speen, on the hill, and mounted five guns in position behind them. Whether his notice was too short, or whether he delayed beginning operations after the receipt of orders, is not clearly to be understood. The fact, however, remains that when the attack was delivered his works were insufficient in size and incomplete in form.

The march against Maurice was undertaken by the troops

Clay Hill, the site of Manchester's Camp from Shaw House.

which formed Essex's portion of the army, the commanders being Skippon and Balfour. Waller accompanied the force, and Cromwell also. To escape notice a start was made very early on the morning of the 26th, and a most circuitous route was adopted. Marching three miles in a northerly direction, along low ground, till a little beyond Grimsbury Castle, which lay east, they were screened from view by an intervening height. Then, turning westward, they crossed the road from Newbury to Abingdon, passed through Chieveley village, and proceeded to North Heath, in all a distance of rather over six miles. At North Heath they bivouacked for the night. There is no record of the Royalist scouts having attempted to obtain any intelligence. With but little risk, covered as they would have been by the guns of Donnington and Shaw, even a reconnaissance in force along the Abingdon road would have almost naturally suggested itself. Nothing of the kind, however, appears to have been done. Early on the 27th Manchester made his feint on Shaw House with a small body of troops. This attack was made, however, with more zeal than discretion, and the party suffered severely. Balfour, Skippon, Waller, and Cromwell marched from their bivouac betimes, and, proceeding in a southerly direction, passed through the village of Winterbourn. Here they turned westwards for a mile and a half to Boxford, and then, bending to the south-west, reached Wickham Heath about 2 p.m., still unperceived by the Royalists. They were now quite near to the entrenchment—in fact, it was less than a mile distant.

Probably the lanes and hedges concealed their approach, but it seems almost inconceivable that Maurice, knowing what he had to expect, should have thrown out no vedettes in this direction. Half a dozen mounted men would almost have sufficed, and had the hedges by the sides of the lanes been lined with musketeers, and held in a determined manner, the attacking Parliamentarians would have fared but badly. Time after time, too, in the war, the value of lined hedges had been proved. Even the memories of the former day at Newbury, if nothing else, should have suggested some such course. But no! Behind his paltry bank Maurice remained, trusting blindly to the fire of five guns (well posted, no doubt, to command the immediate approach) to beat back a small army of determined men. By lanes and through hedges the Parliamentarians advanced till they came in view of Maurice's entrenchment, which was fronted by open ground, on to which the head of the last lane debouched. The open ground was but narrow, and guns, if worth anything and well served, could certainly do considerable damage to the advancing enemy. The attacking cavalry must needs pass up the lane, seeing that the hedges of the fields on either side were not easily to be negotiated by troopers. Maurice opened a hot fire with his guns, which told on the Parliamentarians on their first appearance and until they had got up a sufficient force wherewith to develop their attack. Then, with one rush of horse and foot combined, they made straight for the breastwork. For a brief time—a few moments only—the defenders strenuously resisted. Over the trivial defence the assailants scrambled, and cut down the gunners almost to a man. These gunners were Cornishmen, and fought their guns well. The pieces themselves were those which had been captured from Essex in Cornwall, near Fowey. Maurice with his men then retreated to the village of Speen, suffering not a little in their flight. Speen, in turn, was carried, and four more guns were then captured. Balfour and Skippon had thus performed their part, and without the arranged co-operation of Manchester. That worthy, for some reason or reasons unknown, never delivered his real assault on Shaw House. During the attack on Speen, the sound of which was plainly audible at Clay

Hill, Manchester was repeatedly urged to order an assault, and with equal pertinacity refused to do so. This very sound, *i.e.*, the cannonade, had been the signal agreed on for his assault, but none the less he gave neither word nor sign. It was now nearly dark. Balfour and Skippon, pushing on through the fields which lay below Speen and the main Royalist position, ran a considerable risk of losing all they had already gained. Hitherto all had gone well with them, but the Royalist horse in Shaw Field and Newbury Field had yet to be reckoned with. If these could be discomfited it must be comparatively easy

either that night or on the morrow to finish off the remainder of the foot, even with or without the co-operation of Manchester. But the ground was not suitable for cavalry, at least on the line of the Parliamentarian advance. Near the river Kennet, on their right, the ground was boggy. Balfour led on this side, but being charged by Sir Humphrey Bennet and Sir James Cansfield with the Royalist horse, was compelled to fall back in some disorder. On the Lambourne river side Cromwell met with similar disaster, though in his retreat he carried off with him a prisoner of note—the Earl of Cleveland. Cromwell could hardly expect to succeed despite his most strenuous endeavours, and for this reason. From Donnington Castle his advance was open to a most unpleasant cannonade, in his front the Royal horse was prepared to charge, and did so, well home, while his ranks were most uncomfortably galled by a continuous fire of musketry kept up from behind every available hedge.

Only the Parliamentarian foot escaped disaster after leaving Speen. They, however, slowly but surely progressed, capturing hedge after hedge and rushing field after field. An hour more of daylight, or at most two, would have given them the victory. But it was not to be. Darkness came on—there chanced to be no moon—and with the darkness the combat ceased. By this time Manchester had so far awakened to a sense of his responsibilities as to order an assault — the assault on Shaw. It was nearly dark at the time, and though pressed with much gallantry by the storming party, failed completely. Success was hardly to be expected in the dark, and when attacking so strongly fortified a post. The only intention of the arranged attack had been to occupy a part of the Royal army while Balfour and Skippon made good their footing in the rear. As things were, the attack, when it did come off, was useless. One alternative has been suggested, namely, that Manchester ought to have marched round to the north of Shaw House, and then, turning west, to have gained the Abingdon road. By this he might have attacked the Royal army in flank and rear, but his men would have been compelled to run the gauntlet of the guns from both Shaw and Donnington, at rather long range, it is true, but a factor to be reckoned in a manœuvre of that kind. Practically, though called indecisive, the second battle of Newbury, as the first, was a Royalist defeat. Late that night Charles made a hasty exit to Bath with an escort of 300 horse. His heavy artillery he left at Donnington, while the army, by his commands, with much caution, immediately withdrew to Wallingford. Again, and at the same Berkshire town, the Parliamentary army was robbed of some indeed of the fruits of a well-earned victory.

GATEHOUSE AND WALL (INTERIOR).

CHAPTER XXXII.

NASEBY.

June 14, 1645

AT the end of the month of April, 1645, King Charles with his army was at Oxford. Cromwell, between April 20th and April 27th, with a body of 1,500 horse, had been actively engaged in the neighbourhood, defeating and cutting up various Royalist detachments, and securing all the draught horses for miles round. On April 23rd, through intelligence received, he left Watlington for Islip, with the intention of attacking the Earl of Northampton, who was there quartered with a strong body of cavalry. Northampton, warned of Cromwell's probable advent, made off, but returned with an augmented force. In the skirmish which ensued Northampton suffered a serious defeat. The object which Cromwell had in view when he possessed himself of all the horses in the neighbourhood was to deprive Prince Maurice, then in Oxford, of the means of removing the Royalist artillery. Maurice was under orders to take this to join Rupert's force, then at Hereford. Following on the skirmish at Islip came the surrender of Blechington House. This mansion, in which a number of Royalist ladies had taken refuge and which was fortified, contained a garrison partly composed of the troops of Northampton lately defeated at Islip. The Governor of Blechington was Colonel Thomas Windebank, the son of Secretary Windebank. Cromwell, whose force was only composed of cavalry and without guns, summoned the place to surrender. He could not have taken it had he made the attempt. It was mere bluff, but whether Windebank was a coward, or whether the presence of so many ladies, among them his young wife, worked on his mind, in the result he surrendered. He was tried at Oxford, and shot in the castle garden on May 3rd. In the State Papers there is a most pathetic letter, dated Campden, April 28th, from Sir Henry Bard (governor) to Prince Rupert, and enclosing another from Oxford. Bard pleads most eloquently for the life of Windebank, to whose bravery and previous good conduct he bears strong personal testimony. From Blechington, Cromwell passed to Bampton, where he defeated Sir Harry Vaughan. Next, at Faringdon, an attempt to rush a surrender of the castle was made, similar to that so successful at Blechington. This, however, failed. Cromwell being unable to enter on a siege of the place, started off to join Sir Thomas Fairfax and the new model army.

There were now several operations under discussion in the Royalist headquarters. One proposal was for Charles to attack the diminished Scotch army, under Lord Leven, which was then in the north. But as the guns could not be got from Oxford this became impracticable. This plan originated with Rupert, who, in a despatch, dated April 24th, begged and implored Charles to join him without delay at Bristol, and to march thence with united forces northwards, beating up all Parliamentarian garrisons on the way; but till Leven had been defeated it would not have been possible to perform this. Charles replied that he had no draught horses, either for guns or baggage; that even with Rupert's cavalry he would not be strong in that arm, and that Goring must be summoned with his horse from before Taunton. Goring was summoned, and started with 2,000 cavalry. Sir Thomas Fairfax left Windsor for the west on April 30th, effecting a juncture with Cromwell and his 1,500 horse at Newbury on the evening of the 2nd of May. Goring, *en route* for Oxford, had on the same night a skirmish with Cromwell's cavalry, in which the Parliamentarians were worsted. He then halted at Faringdon, while the brothers Rupert and Maurice, with 2,000 horse and foot, continued as far as Burford, and reached Oxford on May 4th.

Fairfax proceeded to Taunton as originally intended, but was stopped on May 3rd by an order to halt. Two days later came another order to return with the bulk of his army, but to send forward only a detachment to relieve the besieged town in the west. This relief was accomplished by Weldon and Graves on May 11th. Four days previously Charles had marched out from Oxford with Rupert and Goring, having an army of only 11,000 men. A council of war was held at Stow-in-the-Wold, from the deliberations of which, as usual, unanimity was absent. Rupert and Marmaduke Langdale urged the northern campaign. Others held it best to turn the face of the army westwards and fall upon Fairfax, who was still supposed to be *en route* for Taunton. In the end a most extraordinary course was pursued. Goring was sent back to the west, while the king and Rupert went north, in fact both plans were adopted. With respect to the campaign of Goring nothing more need be said here.

Charles marched north with an army now reduced to between 7,000 and 8,000 men on May 9th. Passing Campden House, one of his garrisons, he withdrew the defenders, and Rupert burnt the mansion. On May 11th the army reached Droitwich. Meanwhile, on May 10th, Fairfax was ordered to besiege Oxford. The Scots under Leven were to be reinforced by a mixed body of troops from different counties, and a force of 2,500 new model troops. These augmentations to Leven's army were expected to effect a junction with him at various points on the southward march which he now undertook. On May 14th the king, cheered by good news from Wales, marched forward from Droitwich. Nor was the Welsh success of Gerard the only piece of good fortune at this time, for Chomley, the Governor of Scarborough, by a successful sally, inflicted considerable loss on the besiegers, mortally wounding Sir John Meldrum, the Parliamentarian commander. Haverfordwest then fell into the hands of Gerard, and Milford Haven was threatened. Brereton, on May 18th, alarmed at the approach of the Royalist army, raised the sieges of both Chester and Hawarden Castle. News of this last success reached Charles at Market Drayton on May 22nd, the very day that Fairfax began the siege of Oxford. Ferdinando, Lord

Fairfax, the Parliamentarian commander in Yorkshire, now made great efforts to hasten Leven in his southward march. He implored the Scotch general to start without delay for Manchester, and thence to give support to Brereton in Cheshire. Leven, however, utterly refused to march by the direct road, and insisted on taking a roundabout route through Westmoreland. The only ground which could be alleged in support of this line was that an invasion of Scotland by the king was, in Leven's opinion, imminent, and that by the Westmoreland route he could equally oppose that, while at the same time assisting Brereton.

Leaving Drayton, Charles turned east, intending to cross Yorkshire instead of Lancashire, and proceed thence towards Scotland. He had, however, but a small army still, viz., between 7,000 and 8,000 men—probably 7,500. A new idea then occurred to him, and this was no other than to summon both Goring from the west of England and Gerard from Wales to swell the numbers of his army. But to effect a junction a retrograde movement was thought requisite, and Leicester, then in Parliamentarian occupation, was named as a place of junction for the three armies. A curious scheme truly, but with this merit, that it was inexplicable to the Parliament. The king's march through Staffordshire created no little alarm in London, and it was believed that a campaign of vengeance in the eastern counties was in contemplation, hence Cromwell was despatched thither, and Leven urged to pursue Charles. Oxford, however, now hard beset, was short of supplies and could not hold out. Much depended upon whether Goring, on his way to Leicester, would reach the besieged city in time enough to give relief—a relief to be accentuated by a sortie of the garrison in force. Consequently to Goring went fresh orders changing his line of march, *i.e.*, *viâ* Newbury, in lieu of Harborough, and these were dated May 26th. On May 28th Charles and Rupert reached the neighbourhood of Leicester. The following day was occupied in erecting batteries, and on the 30th a bombardment of the walls began. Late that night, a breach having been made, a storming party assaulted the town, which was quickly taken and given over to pillage. It is interesting to note that, as at Worcester, a few fragments of the old Leicester walls still remain.

And now in the Royal camp the usual season of intrigue set in. Delay meant that neither of the plans proposed could take effect, and, regardless of consequences, that delay seemed almost to be wished for by the contending factions. To these troubles must be added something very much like a mutiny, which took place among the horse under Marmaduke Langdale—a body of Yorkshiremen. They wanted to return home, and when told to march to Oxford flatly refused. Having been talked into a better frame of mind, on the next day (June 5th) they returned, though sulkily, to their duty. Two days later Charles entered Daventry, and was met by the news that the siege of Oxford had been abandoned. Fairfax, on breaking up the siege of Oxford, marched towards Brill, attacking Boarstall on the way and failing. Boarstall, of which the gate-house and moat remain, was a very strong place of arms during the Civil War, and changed masters at least five times during the troubles. Relics of the batteries are still to be seen, and the little church near, whose tower was then demolished, is still barn-shaped in consequence. Fairfax on June 7th was rejoined by the 2,500 men of the model army, which detachment had failed to meet with Leven. This junction took place at a village called Sherrington, near Newport Pagnell. Meanwhile Charles was still at Daventry, trying to revictual Oxford. Fairfax learnt this, and determined on an attack. At once he sent despatches to all commanders of Parliamentary troops within reasonable distance, calling on them to join him. Cromwell, who had been toiling hard and with great success in the Isle of Ely, whither he had been sent to prepare its defences, was now, on the request of the united Parliamentarian officers then with Fairfax, appointed Lieut.-General, Self-denying Ordinance notwithstanding. Cromwell's work in the Isle of Ely between May 26th and June 4th may be gauged by the fact that he had not only organised the defences, but had raised 3,000 foot and 1,000 horse as a reinforcement for Fairfax. June 10th found Charles still at Daventry, while his councillors in Oxford were squabbling whether to march north or to attack the eastern associated counties.

The same state of things continued until June 12th, on the evening of which day Charles was pleasantly hunting in Fawsley Park, while Fairfax had hours before established himself at the village of Kislingbury, distant only eight miles from Daventry and two from Northampton. That evening a troop of Parliamentarian horse on scouting duty was descried, and for the first time the Royalists appear to have been made aware of the proximity of the despised New Model Army. Charles's hunt was cut short, and the regiments of his army, which, as usual, were spread about in a haphazard fashion in the villages and houses near, were with haste collected on to a hill known as Borough Hill. The same evening Fairfax reconnoitred the position of the Royalists, and towards dawn found that a movement of some kind was in progress. In the early morning it was soon discovered that Charles had marched off in the direction of Warwick, *i.e.*, to the west. Shortly after, however, the line was changed to the east, and the Royalists made for Market Harborough, at which town they halted for the night. On that same morning Cromwell arrived from Cambridgeshire, but with only 600 horse. He had not tarried for the newly recruited 3,000 foot and 1,000 horse—these, in fact, would have been comparatively useless in a fight, owing to lack of training.

That night Fairfax slept at Guilsborough, having sent forward a scouting party under Colonel Harrison (the regicide) towards Daventry, and another under Ireton, to endeavour to overtake the retreating Royalists, and delay them by flank attacks, real or threatened. Hastening onwards in the supposed track of the king's army, Ireton entered the village of Naseby, a village a few miles in the rear of the main force. Here he captured a score or two of troopers who, without sentries, were feasting and amusing themselves at quoits. Fugitives brought the news to Rupert, and the king, who had gone to bed at Lubenham, was aroused with the unwelcome news that the enemy was nigh at hand and in force. Late that night, or very early in the morning, Charles rode into Market Harborough. After a consultation, in which it was abundantly shown that to retreat further north in the presence of the enemy was, to say the least, very unwise, if not impossible, it was determined to march south, to take up a position and there await attack. Charles, with his army, then drew up upon the ridge between Oxendon and East Farndon, "a hill whereon a chapel," *i.e.*, East Farndon Church, stood. Fairfax had himself been quartered the night before at Guilsborough, his van having occupied Naseby, and orders were given for the whole force to concentrate at Naseby in the early morning. Assuming that he intended to push on with speed to Market Harborough, the spot where the Parliamentarian army mustered must have been on the ridge one mile to the north-east of the village, and on the road to Clipston. From this spot the Oxendon and Farndon Ridge is visible; the intervening high ground precluding a view from any spot further north. The armies were now facing one another, but not in full front, the Royalists occupying a position parallel to that of the Parliamentarians, but distant some three miles and to the north-west. Rupert's "scout-master," by name Ruce, was sent out to obtain news of the enemy, and returned saying that he could see no signs thereof. This seems in opposition to the story that the Parliamentarian cavalry had been discerned by the Royalists as early as eight in the morning, moving on a ridge between the Farndon Ridge and Naseby. Ruce could not have gone as far as the village of Clipston without obtaining intelligence, as that place is but two miles distant from the probable rendezvous and is on high ground. It is true that the place of muster was invisible; still the presence of 13,000 or more armed men, even in a thinly populated country, could hardly have escaped report when a battle was expected and the opposing army was drawn up. Fugitive country folks, by the direction of their flight, would at once have told Ruce, had he gone as far as Clipston, how the land lay in those parts. This is a difficulty the only solution to which seems to be that the Parliamentarian army moved in a direction north-west by west to a lower hill, where they formed up—a hill which cannot be

NASEBY FROM ROYALIST CENTRE.

seen from the Farndon Ridge; and that the guard of their baggage train in Naseby village prevented any exodus of the inhabitants. To this may be added a possibility that Ruce did not pursue his investigations to any extent and was content to return at the earliest moment.

Rupert at once, with a troop of horse and some musketeers, set out to obtain information on his own account, and speedily did so. Before he had proceeded more than a mile he heard of the presence of the enemy, nay more, saw them with his own eyes. To him it seemed as if they were retiring, in fact they were so in a measure, in order, at the suggestion of

Cromwell, to take up their position on a range to the south, which was of greater altitude—a range the continuation westwards of their original place of rendezvous. One point also is worth notice. Ruce was sent out to hunt for an enemy supposed to be making for Market Harborough, and naturally went on the left of the royal position. Rupert, who commanded the right wing, on the other hand marched straight ahead. Rupert approached as near to the position as possible and found it exceedingly strong; rough ground, too, inter-

NASEBY FIELD.

vened, and there was an awkward brook. There is, however, evidence to show that a further movement, though but a small one, was made by the army of Fairfax, and this was to retire about one hundred yards over the crest of the hill, so that the final battle array would be invisible to the Royalists until the very moment when the battle was joined.

The question now for Fairfax was this: should he be compelled to attack the Royalists, or would the Royalists advance to attack him? Rupert, on the apparent result of his reconnaisance, determined this for him. He believed the enemy to be in retreat, and according to his nature promptly ordered an advance. The ground over which he needs must advance was, however, of a very unpromising character. In the hollow known as Broadmoor—a wet valley—it was impossible for cavalry to act with success; and that valley being crossed, a steep uphill charge lay before his troops. Hence, in his advance he took ground to the right till the Royalist centre rested on a high ridge known as Dust Hill. To Fairfax this appeared as if an attempt at a flank attack was meditated, and he in turn moved slightly to the left in order to compel a direct attack or none.

The Royalist marshalling was as follows. Rupert, with cavalry, formed the right wing, Sir Jacob Astley with infantry the centre, and Marmaduke Langdale with cavalry the left wing. Charles, in the rear, commanded the reserve of foot and horse, and a weak reserve at best. Fairfax placed his infantry in the centre, and these were under Major-General Skippon; Ireton and Cromwell commanding the left and right wings respectively, and both of course cavalry. The reserve in two bodies was drawn up in the rear, and consisted only of foot. After the final disposition—*i.e.*, after the withdrawal behind the crest of the hill, and the extension to the left, the extreme Parliamentarian left rested on a tall hedge with a bank and ditch, known as Sulby Hedge, which ran at right angles to it. The name Sulby is connected with Sulby Hall, distant about one and a quarter miles to the north-west, and formed the boundary then, as it does now, between two estates. It must be remembered that in 1645 hedges were still comparatively scarce. Behind this hedge Colonel John Okey was posted with 1,000 dismounted dragoons, obtaining thereby the advantage of a flank fire on the enemy's attack.

Just as the battle began Cromwell's cavalry wing received a reinforcement, which arrived under the command of Colonel Rossiter, and consisted of troops from Lincolnshire. This was of course a welcome addition, especially as in cavalry the Royalist strength ever lay. Whether the Royalist guns were ever brought into action is doubtful; at any rate, there are no records of their having produced the slightest effect on the enemy. Little enough, too, was done by the Parliamentarian cannon beyond the discharge of a few shots before the *mêlée* began. Rupert's advance was rapid, and he was soon within range of Okey's dragoons, who, from behind their safe hedge, inflicted some loss. Ireton's men behaved but ill, whether from lack of confidence in their leader, or from lack of courage. A part charged to meet Rupert, but the rest wavered. Ireton, whose business it was, or ought to have been, to have first disposed effectually, if possible, of his immediate opponents, for some unknown reason, on slightly checking Rupert's first attack, turned to the right to attempt a flank charge on the Royalist infantry, who were having by no means the worst of the encounter with the foot of the Parliamentarian centre. Rupert returned to the charge with promptitude, and completely routed the rest of Ireton's wing, pursuing them to the baggage-camp at Naseby. Ireton fared badly in the flank attack, being shot in two places and taken

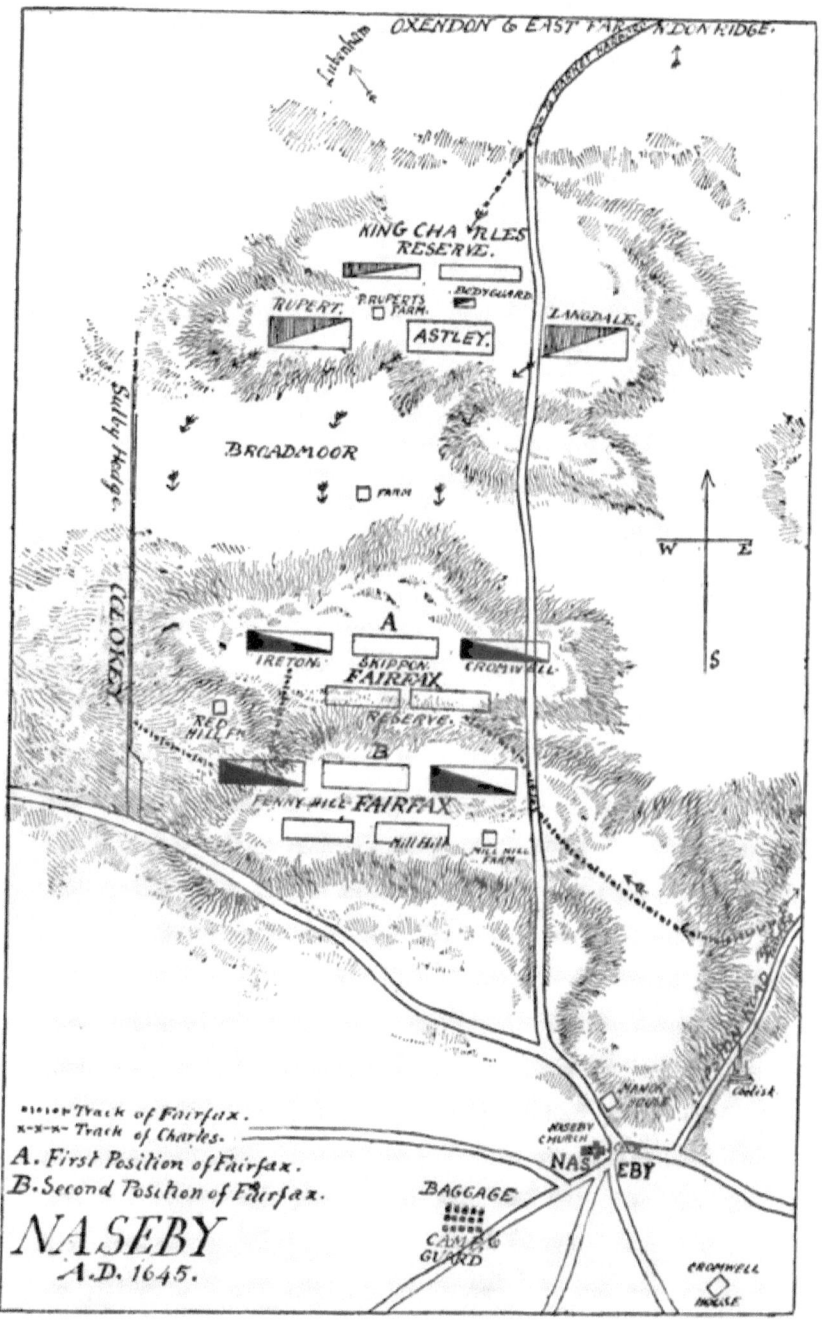

prisoner *pro tem*. Rupert found the baggage-guard prepared to resist, and in answer to a command to surrender received a volley of musketry.

He then wheeled round and returned to the battlefield. Here Cromwell had met with a success as complete as that of Rupert—nay, more so. Charging Langdale—a poor commander this to be opposed to the skill of Cromwell, and with an inferior force of sullen troops—he completely discomfited the Royalist left wing, driving them in on the reserves. Cromwell had now done effectually what Ireton had only begun to do on the left before attempting a flank attack on the centre—*i.e.*, had scattered the Royalist left. How did he employ the opportunity? Dividing his force of 3,600 horse, he despatched three regiments in pursuit of the fugitives, and with the remainder dashed into the left flank of Charles's infantry. Fortune hitherto, if not exactly favouring the Royalist centre, had yet not treated it hardly. Skippon had been early wounded, hence the Parliamentarian infantry had lost its commander. Ireton's flank attack had failed, and Ireton himself was wounded and a prisoner. But now a double danger threatened it with absolute destruction. On its left came Cromwell, thundering down with his Ironsides—nay, more, with the main body of his cavalry, while on the right, Colonel Okey, finding Ireton's men fled, and Rupert's away from the field in pursuit of them, mounted his 1,000 dragoons and cut into the fray on both flank and rear. At this juncture, too, some of Ireton's troops (probably the regiments led by him in his charge) rallied, and also returned to the battle-line. Within a very brief space all the regiments of Royalist foot save one had surrendered. This noble exception needed a double assault before it was destroyed. It was then that Rupert came in view of what had happened during his untimely absence. Meanwhile, Cromwell's detached force was pursuing Langdale's beaten cavalry, and threatened the reserve, under Charles in person—a reserve already slightly disordered by the fugitives. Charles, of whose personal courage there can never be any doubt, gave order to charge the advancing cavalry, and even rode forward to lead that charge. Lord Carnworth seized his bridle to stop him from certain death, and at this moment some one, name unknown, gave the command, "March to the right." Round wheeled the cavalry of the Royalist reserve, taking in their sweep the king

SULBY HEDGE.

and his personal attendants with them, nor did they draw rein till they halted more than a quarter of a mile from their former position. Thence the utter destruction of the centre was visible—a miserable sight indeed. Rupert, when he fully comprehended the disaster, and saw that it was impossible to retrieve the fortune of the day, rode headlong across the field to his old position, and then joined the king. It is somewhat strange that Fairfax refused to permit an attack on Rupert during this curious move. Seeing that the horse of the Prince were without semblance of formation, it would be thought that a charge thereon would have been neither hazardous nor ill-timed. Fairfax, however, occupied himself in re-forming both his horse and foot, and then in battle order advanced towards Rupert, and Charles with his shaken reserve. The combat was declined, and a retreat began, with its usual sequel a rout, till safety from pursuit was obtained in Leicester. Anything more complete than this defeat can

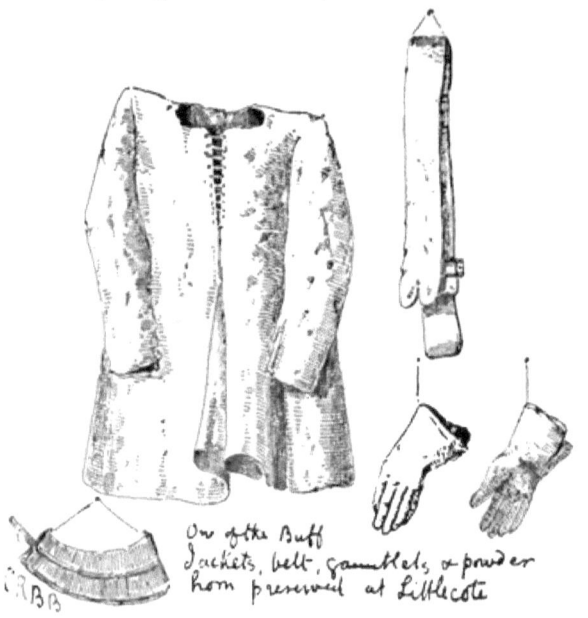

One of the Buff Jackets, belt, gauntlets, & powder horn preserved at Littlecote

hardly be imagined. The prisoners (mostly infantry) numbered 5,000, and might have been replaced, but among them there were no less than 500 officers, and these could not be replaced. Artillery, stores, forty barrels of powder, and 8,000 stand of arms, all were the spoils of the victors. The number of the slain, considering the completeness of the victory, was small; 300 perished in the pursuit, which was

NASEBY.

pressed for fourteen miles, but on the field itself only 700 fell. This is greatly to be accounted for from the fact that the Royalist foot, mainly Welshmen, surrendered on quarter, by whole regiments. Hence also the splendid behaviour of the one firm, though unnamed, regiment deserves to be for ever remembered. On the Clipston Road, though not on the battlefield itself, a large obelisk of modern date commemorates the fight. In the churchyard a massive stone cross of plain design has been erected in memory of the slain there buried.

IRETON.

CROMWELL, FAIRFAX.

PRINCE
OF
RUPERT, CUMBERLAND

LANGDALE.

CHAPTER XXXIII.

WORCESTER.

September 3, 1651.

IN the early half of the month of June, 1651, a Scottish army collected at Stirling, taking up a position at Torwood to the south of the town towards the end of the month (June 28th), with David Leslie in command. Two days later Cromwell marched from the Braid Hills in the north of Edinburghshire towards Stirling. Cromwell's design was to force Leslie to fight, and this course Leslie refused to take. On July 15th Cromwell, detaching a small force, sent it across the Forth to North Queensferry, where it was ordered to entrench itself. Gradually increasing this body of troops by daily reinforcements, by July 20th a small army of 4,500 men, under General Lambert, was there established. Leslie now despatched an insufficient force of 4,000 men against Lambert, and under the command of Sir John Brown.

This force Lambert defeated on July 20th at Inverkeithing, in which fight more than half the Scots were slain and nearly all the rest taken prisoners. Cromwell on the same day reconnoitred Leslie's position in force, but found it too strong to be attacked. A new design now occupied Cromwell, and this was to cross the Forth with his entire strength, capture Perth, and thus cut off the supplies, which Leslie could obtain from the North. This, however, left open the road to England, and there was therefore a danger of a Scottish invasion. To counteract this, or rather to minimise the danger, Harrison, then at Edinburgh, was summoned. His forces were augmented by horse sent for from Nottinghamshire, and he was ordered to take up a position on the border to fight or harass the Scots, should they march south. Cromwell's expedition to Perth was successful, as that town surrendered on August 2nd. But on July 31st the Scottish army had already left Stirling. In numbers they amounted to about 20,000 men. Their line of march was by way of the western border, and consequently led through Carlisle. Prince Charles, into the story of whose intrigues previous or following on his landing in Scotland at Speymouth on June 23, 1650, it would be beyond our purpose to enter, accompanied the Scottish army. Suffice it to say that the Court, such as it was, was established at Stirling in April, 1651. Thirteen months of Scotland had thoroughly sickened the Prince; he looked to England for deliverance, and to England he gladly went, but, to his ruin, led thither a Scottish army. The by no means unexpected news of this southward march reached

Cromwell on August 1st at Perth. On the next day, having meanwhile signed the capitulation of Perth, he started in pursuit of the Scottish army, but detached nearly six thousand men, under General Monk, to besiege and take Stirling. On August 4th Cromwell arrived at Leith, and Harrison had reached Newcastle. After the latter, on August 5th, instructions were sent to muster whatever horse and dragoons he could, and by forced marches outflank the Scots, paying special attention to their sources of supply. Lambert, who had done good work at Inverkeithing, was also detached with 3,000 men to harass the rear of the enemy. Cromwell resumed his march on the 6th at the head of the infantry, and a sufficient supply of cavalry. Harrison left Newcastle on August 7th at the head of 3,000 horse, augmented by infantry, mounted, *pro tem.*, to accelerate their progress. Lambert and Harrison united their forces, some 9,000 men, on August 13th, and conjointly marched to support the Cheshire and Staffordshire militia at Warrington Bridge. Three days later, after a slight skirmish, they fell back on Congleton. Meanwhile matters were not looking well in the Scottish army. Lord Leven, with Lord Crawford, had been left in Scotland to foment a rising. Argyle had refused to accompany the army, and had retired to his home, deeming the expedition, whether successful or the reverse, a certain cause of ruin to himself. The Scots crossed the Border, yet hardly an Englishman joined them. From Lancashire, usually ever loyal, great things were hoped, and messages were sent to the Earl of Derby, then in his kingdom of Man, to come with speed and rouse the county. He came on August 17th to Stoke, accompanied by 250 foot and 60 horse, the latter being nearly all private gentlemen. Derby was sent to Warrington, accompanied by Massey. Next an ineffectual attempt was made to induce Sir Thomas Middleton to head a Royalist rising in North Wales. Middleton did not reply, save by arresting the messenger and sending the letter to Parliament. On August 19th Massey started to rejoin the army, which had remained at Stoke. To it he brought the news of the failure of Derby to accomplish his task. The fact was that the elements which Charles desired to unite were too discordant. Presbyterian mistrusted Royalist, whether Protestant or Catholic, and the mistrust was mutual. Charles, too, by tarrying *en route* in Catholic houses, had kept alive this sentiment. Derby now resolved to raise, if possible, a Lancashire force of 6,000 foot and 1,300 horse by a levy of able-bodied men as of old. Cromwell had by this time entered Yorkshire, and here he sent orders to Robert Lilburne, then serving with Harrison and Lambert, in Lancashire, to remain there with a view to coping with Derby's new force. Lilburne had but few men, still he managed to keep the enemy employed for three days—*i.e.*, from August 22nd to 25th. But on that morning, having received news that Derby, with 1,500 men, was advancing to Manchester *viâ* Preston, Lilburne who had a regiment in Manchester prepared to support him, for which he had sent, retreated before Derby through Wigan in the endeavour to avoid an engagement till his supports had come up. Derby overtook Lilburne, and compelled him to fight in an unfavourable place outside the town. After a sharp engagement the Royalists were defeated, many being slain and some 400 taken prisoners. Derby escaped. By this time Charles and the Scottish army had been established for three days in Worcester, to which city they had betaken themselves, footsore and weary as regards their bodies and utterly despondent as to their prospects. An attempt to corrupt Colonel Mackworth, the Governor of Shrewsbury, had been made, and had signally failed. At Worcester, on arrival, the Prince was received favourably by the Corporation, and a small guard of Parliamentarian horse was expelled not by the army but by the townsmen. Charles now issued a manifesto promising much, especially that, once victorious, the Scottish army should be sent home. Next, a muster of all men between sixteen and sixty was appointed to be held on Pitchcroft (just outside the tumbledown walls of Worcester and along the Severn bank). But few attended this muster. Meanwhile Lambert and Harrison had left Lancashire for Warwick, where Cromwell joined them on August 24th. At Warwick intelligence from various parts of the country showed that matters were safe. Three days later Evesham was reached, and the final stage of the campaign had begun. At Evesham Cromwell divided the 28,000 men he now had at his disposal, with the intention of obtaining command over both banks of the Severn. The marches of Cromwell and Charles are worthy of notice. Charles, leaving Stirling on July 31st, marched southwards in an almost straight course, and took a westerly road, which would have brought his army conveniently near Wales, whence, fallaciously as it turned out, he expected an accession of strength. Passing through Moffat he crossed the border at Gretna, taking the old road through Carlisle and Penrith. Thence he traversed Westmoreland by way of Kendal, entering Lancashire at Burton-on-Kendal, and marching straight on Lancaster. From Lancaster by the direct south road he passed through Preston, Wigan, and Warrington. In Cheshire his march was continued through Northwich and Nantwich, leaving the county for Shropshire, near Adderley. Then proceeding to Market Drayton, he halted at Stoke-upon-Tern from August 17th to August 19th. Resuming his march, he went through Newport and Tong, when the south-west corner of Staffordshire was crossed, Worcestershire entered, and the city reached on August 22nd. The average marching being rather over fourteen miles per diem, calculating the distance as three hundred miles. Cromwell left Perth on August 2nd, and covered the distance between Perth and Leith in two days, at least forty miles. Thence keeping clear of hilly ground he took a south-east course through Edinburghshire and part of Roxburghshire, following the right bank of the Tweed till he entered England at Coldstream, the old crossing. His march continued by the usual way. The Tyne was passed at Newburn; Durham and Darlington touched at in Durham. In Yorkshire, Northallerton, Thirsk, York, Pontefract, and Rotherham. In Derbyshire the road lay through Chesterfield, where it made a slight bend to the south-east, and then resuming its former direction, passed through Derby to Burton-on-Trent, in Staffordshire From this place a long curve was made through Tamworth to Coventry, in Warwickshire, and thence the army passed to Warwick, arriving there on August 24th, where Lambert and Harrison were awaiting the arrival of the troops. The distance from Leith being at least 310 miles, and the total from Perth 350. Cromwell's average march per day was thus about sixteen miles. With his force now augmented to about 28,000 men Cromwell advanced, as has been said, from Warwick through Stratford-on-Avon to Evesham, arriving in that little town on August 27th. On the following morning Lambert was despatched with horse and dragoons to Upton, a village on the Severn, eight and a half miles due south of Worcester, where the Royalists had a post, and where the bridge had been ordered to be destroyed. This order was imperfectly carried out, as a plank was left across the chasm. A small number of Lambert's men (eight it is said) crossed by this plank, forced an entry into the church and barricaded themselves therein. The Scots, occupied in an ineffectual endeavour to dislodge them, kept no look out, and the remainder of Lambert's horse succeeded in fording the river unmolested. The Scots were then driven away, the passage of the river secured, and shortly a reinforcement of foot, sent by Fleetwood, rendered the holding of the repaired bridge assured. During the skirmish the church was set on fire and considerably damaged. The result of this brilliant little fight was that Cromwell now had command of both banks of the Severn, at any rate as far as Powick;

but here the river Teme runs into the Severn, and here the Powick Bridge was broken down. Over the repaired Upton Bridge Cromwell at once sent 11,000 men, and to these the task of making bridges of boats was committed. One bridge was to cross the Teme close to its junction with the Severn. Cromwell then ordered a body of men in position facing the mouth of the Teme, the second to prepare a larger bridge of boats, by which to cross the Severn. At this juncture a welcome addition to his strength arrived from

Fort Royal, from the Commanderies.

the eastern counties, in the form of 3,000 foot. The city of Worcester and its surroundings may thus be briefly described. It stands on the east bank of the Severn, at a spot where the river makes a bend from south-east to south. About two miles below, the river Teme, with a winding course, flows into the Severn from the west. A bridge over the Severn at Worcester joins the city with the suburb of St. John's. North of the city, and on the river bank, was the spot called Pitch Croft. At the time of the battle the walls had been in a measure repaired by the Scots, but they were of little account as fortifications. The most important defence was an earthwork, constructed on scientific principles, on the top of a green hill to the south-east of the city, and known as Fort Royal. A few slight traces of this remain to this day, and the path which led therefrom down the hill to an old house known as the "Commandery," is quite apparent. Opposite to Fort Royal, and distant about one mile, Cromwell posted a large

Ancient house S' John's Newgate between Prwick Bridge + the City

force on the hill known as Perry Wood to keep the defenders of the city in check while he dealt with the Scots posted in the fields between St. John's and the Teme. As will be seen, he held the southern and eastern sides of the city completely, but the river higher up required to be secured. Bewdley Bridge was therefore taken possession of, and other precautions taken to cut off the retreat of the Scots when defeated.

By the afternoon of September 3rd the two bridges or boats were ready and they were then thrown across the river, that over the Severn being the first in position. Fleetwood, however, who was posted opposite to the Teme bridge, crossed first and engaged the Scots, who were stationed to guard the passage. A stubborn fight took place in what were then fields and much cut up by hedges, but which now are hop-gardens and nurseries. Cromwell, who was watching the crossing on the east side of the Severn, then at once led over as many regiments as he had there and took the Scots in their left flank. The Scots were even then hard to beat, but gradually they were forced to retreat, and without disgrace withdrew over the St. John's bridge into the city. Cromwell now had command of both sides of the river right up to the city. Meanwhile his third detachment, *i.e.*, that on Perry Hill, had not been actively engaged; their turn was to come. Charles, according to tradition, watching from the cathedral tower, had observed the large number of Cromwell's men which had been needed across the river to maintain their passage and to engage the Scots on the west bank. To return would involve a march of at least three miles, and this was assuredly

Hiding Place above the Stairs in the Commandery, sometimes called "Charles's Hole"

an opportunity for assuming the offensive towards the Parliamentarian force at Perry Wood. Out through the Sudbury Gate, a gate now destroyed, issued a division of the defenders, and under the cover of a fire from Fort Royal. Charles in person led the sortie, which for a time succeeded, and indeed the Parliamentarian lines gave way. Cromwell with characteristic rapidity grasped the situation, and with all speed recrossed the Severn by the bridge of boats. This timely reinforcement restored the battle, and the defenders were driven back into the town in disorder. Fort Royal, however, remained a thorn in the side of the Parliamentarians and required to be taken at all costs. After considerable difficulty it was successfully stormed, the survivors of its defenders escaping down the slope into the city through the Commandery. Cromwell then turned the guns of the fort on the city, in the streets of which a throng of defeated Scots were surging hither and thither. Into the Commandery the

Duke of Hamilton, severely wounded, had been taken, and there a few days later he died. Refused permission to bury his body in the cathedral, it was until after the Restoration deposited beneath a fireplace slab in the house in which he died. Cromwell's endeavour, the battle being won, was to stop the slaughter. This he accomplished, though at great danger to his life. Alone he rode into the city, right up to the Scots, and offered them quarter on surrender. This offer was accepted. Charles, in the meanwhile, had been smuggled out of the city, passing through the house in which he lodged and gaining a back entrance while the individual sent to arrest him thundered at the hastily-barred door. Most of his chief friends managed to escape for a time, only to be captured by outlying posts. Massey, who was badly wounded, surrendered to Lady Stamford, and was sent prisoner to London. With the subsequent adventures of Charles at White Ladies, Boscobel, Trent, and Charmouth, we have nothing here to do. The most noticeable point about the fight at Worcester is that captured guns were made use of during the engagement and to bring that engagement to a conclusion. It is only at Stratton that an instance of a like nature is to be met with. How effectively Balfour might have employed the Royalist guns he took at Edgehill had he possessed the sense to do so. Similarly at Marston Moor, where both sides captured guns, yet neither attempted to profit thereby. The Royalist sortie was a most gallant attempt, and it was, moreover, well considered in its plan. Probably

Fragment of the City Wall at the back of a Court.

had any other man been in command but Cromwell, success would have attended the Royal arms on that side of the field, at any rate. Worcester of to-day is, however, much altered from the Worcester of 1651. The then dilapidated walls have almost entirely vanished. A few yards remain visible at one spot. Fort Royal, though part of it has been built over, is yet in the main a grassy hill. Perry Wood has been spared, but the view of Fort Royal from it, and *vice versâ*, gives but little impression of a battlefield. Round Powick it is different, especially near the river. The old bridge has been renewed by one of singularly quaint and irregular form, and has been previously sketched. The fields near the Teme and the Severn are fairly open, and south of the Teme a wide flat expanse stretches away eastwards. Here it is possible to realise the advance of Fleetwood's regiments, the manipulation of the bridges of boats and the subsequent fight. Beyond the river, too, in like manner, the ground where Cromwell crossed is still easily to be identified from the position traditionally assigned to it. Such was Cromwell's crowning mercy at Worcester, September 3, 1651.

Carved oak beam above window in house through which Charles escaped.

CHAPTER XXXIV.

SEDGEMOOR.

July 6, 1685.

THE events in Scotland, which preceded by a few days only the insurrection of Monmouth, need not be more than mentioned here. Briefly, Argyle had sailed from Vlie on May 1st or May 2nd, arriving at the Orkneys on May 6th. After various adventures on the mainland he was captured June 18th, and executed, on his former sentence, June 30th. It is only on account of the fact that this attempt in the north was arranged to be in conjunction as to time with Monmouth's landing in the west of England, that it concerns the story of Sedgemoor. Monmouth had pledged himself to start from the Texel not more than six days after Argyle sailed from Vlie. As a matter of fact he did not start till the latter days of the month. It has been alleged that the reason for this delay was a hope that the bulk of the royal

Buttress at Chedzoy Church' used to sharpen swords by Royal troops 1685.

troops would be drafted to the north to cope with Argyle, thus leaving England an easier prey to the rebels. But that the Government would have taken such a course seems hardly probable. Colonel Bevil Skelton, then English envoy at Amsterdam, had for some time, though in a blundering way, been attempting to prevent the expedition from sailing from the Texel. He had represented the state of the case to the Admiralty of Amsterdam, and to the States-General, but nevertheless the *Helderenbergh*, a 26-gun ship laden with arms and ammunition, and accompanied by two smaller vessels, were permitted by the authorities to depart. A request to the Prince of Orange to send to England the three Scotch regiments, then in the service of the United Provinces, was granted, and the regiments embarked, but not until the Admiralty of Amsterdam had placed as many obstacles as possible in the way of their going. That the English Government was on the alert, therefore, is unquestionable, and if Monmouth imagined that England would be left unprotected through the Scottish rebellion, he was much mistaken. Moreover, too, English war-ships, as many as could be got together, were cruising in the channel under orders to keep a sharp look-out for Monmouth's little fleet. How he escaped seems curious, especially as the voyage was long and the weather bad. On June 11th—that is seven days before Argyle's capture—the expedition arrived at Lyme Regis in Dorset, and caused not a little excitement in that borough. A few miles east one of the party, a refugee, by name Thomas Dare, had been landed in a boat. This man had influence in Somersetshire, and he hastened thither, with what results we shall see. Monmouth, with his slender following of about eighty adventurers, put off from the ships in seven boats, and landed on the ancient rough stone jetty at Lyme, known then and now as the Cob. His chief adherents were Lord Grey, Ferguson the fanatic preacher, Fletcher, a soldier of repute, Wade and Anthony Buyse, the last named having served under the Elector of Brandenburg. Certain religious exercises having been performed, the party drew their swords and marched into Lyme, whence the mayor and all authorities had already fled. The Duke was received with enthusiasm, his banner of blue silk was unfurled in the market-place, and a declaration of his intentions read to the assembled townsmen. This declaration mainly, if not entirely, the work of Ferguson, was a most scandalous production, libelling James II. in nearly every line. Monmouth, however, therein, though professing to be able to prove his legitimacy, did not proclaim himself king, but professed an intention to refer that question to Parliament. His line was the line of a champion of Protestantism, and he had come to the west, where his popularity was great and influence considerable, as the best district in which to commence his holy war. But his popularity lay particularly among the lower classes, the better born sympathised with him both on questions of politics and religion, but joined him in scanty numbers. Thomas Thynne of Longleat was perhaps the highest in rank, who at the outset sided with the adventurer. Dare on landing had made his way across country well known to him to Taunton, where he spread the news of the landing and speedy arrival of the Protestant duke. Collecting about forty horsemen, he rode back with speed to Lyme. Here on his arrival a most untoward event occurred. Dare was riding a showy horse, and horses other than plough-horses were rare in the rebel ranks. To this horse Fletcher took a fancy, and insisted on riding it. Dare objected, using unbecoming and abusive language, and finally raised his whip at Fletcher. The latter then shot him dead on the spot. This took place on July 13th. An angry crowd now demanded justice on the murderer, and so pressed their demands that Monmouth was compelled to ship Fletcher off at once in the *Helderenbergh*, which, having accomplished its purpose, was to proceed to Bilbao. This was a great blow to the expedition. Dare, first secretary, and afterwards designed to act as paymaster, was a man of considerable local influence ; he had been a goldsmith and alderman of Taunton, who for political reasons had gone into exile. Andrew Fletcher was the son and heir of Sir Robert Fletcher of Saltoun, East Lothian. A man of many accomplishments, if Burnet is to be believed, his life had been passed in political troubles of all kinds, he being perpetually at war with the Government. He died in London in 1716, and was buried at Saltoun. Had it not been for this affair, Fletcher was designed to have acted as second in command of the rebel cavalry under Lord Grey. Between June 11th and June 14th the party had been engaged in organising, if such a term can be used, the numerous country people who came flocking in to join them. Arms and munitions of war to no great amount, it may be added, had been brought in the ships and these were stored in Lyme Town Hall. On the 14th it was decided to assume the offensive, and to Grey and Wade were committed the duty of attacking Bridport, an old town distant about nine miles to the east, and where it had been ascertained that a regiment of militia had been mustered. This regiment was known as the "Red Dorsetshire Regiment," and had arrived on the previous day. Another, the "Yellow Somersetshire," with its colonel, Sir William Portman, was expected on the 14th. Grey and Wade, with about 500 men, marched out to the attack, and so far succeeded at the onset that the militia were driven back. In the town, however, they rallied and beat off their assailants. Grey and his horse fled headlong to Lyme—as a matter of fact the plough-horses wouldn't stand fire. Wade, more lucky, kept his infantry in hand, and retreated in good order. It is not easy to see how Grey's cavalry are to be blamed for retreating, nor can Grey himself be censured as responsible for their flight. A horse soldier takes more than three days to train; this both Grey and Monmouth knew. Hence, despite all outcry and disparagement, the Duke did not deprive Grey of his command. That Grey was incapable there is but little doubt, and it is questionable whether he was as eager to risk his life in the field as his position warranted.

Meanwhile, thanks to the promptitude of Gregory Alford, the mayor of Lyme, the Government had received intelligence of the rising. Alford gave warning in Somerset and in his own county, and then turned to Devonshire. At Exeter he found the second Duke of Albemarle and 4,000 militia, and these at once set forth for Lyme. On June 15th in the afternoon, Monk and his militia reached Axminster. Monmouth and his force had already advanced thus far, a distance of nearly six miles, dragging with them four guns. The duke got these into position, and lined the hedges on either side of the high-banked lanes with musketeers. Monk approached, and found not only that Monmouth was prepared to fight, but also that his militia showed ominous signs of deserting *en masse*. He at once ordered a retreat, which ended as retreats do invariably with undisciplined troops, and sometimes with regular soldiers, viz., in a rout. Monmouth, who should have ordered a pursuit (an opportunity for Grey), did not do so. Had he given this order Exeter must inevitably have fallen, since the fugitives abandoned arms, and even uniforms, in their flight, spreading dismay throughout the whole countryside among the adherents of the Government. The value of those arms and uniforms in the future equipment of the rebels would have been immense. But in lieu of following up a genuine advantage, Monmouth marched to Taunton, reaching that place on June 18th. Here he was received, as all know, with open arms, and here his forces increased every moment; but that increase was entirely confined to the lower ranks in society—fighters, and good fighters indubitably, as far as their will went, but unaccustomed to arms and lacking leaders. In fact, beyond a few squires of inconsiderable position, not a man of rank gave the weight even of his name to the rebel cause. The adhesion to his party of half a dozen men of weight, nay of a less number even, would have been worth more to Monmouth than all the shouts, green boughs, banners, and Bibles of Taunton. Something was required to be done to awaken enthusiasm, and that something was suggested by Ferguson. It was that Monmouth should assume the title of king. On June 20th the proclamation duly took place in the market-place of Taunton, and it is interesting to note that one house yet remains standing, nearly in its original state, from the windows of which the ceremony was doubtless witnessed by excited onlookers. This house is called the "House of the 5 Gables." On June 21st various proclamations, all of a treasonable nature, were issued under Monmouth's sign manual, which were in due course forwarded by Monk to the Government in the metropolis.

But neither the assumption of kingship nor the proclamations brought the gentry, either neighbouring or distant, to throw in their lot with the rebel duke. Nay more, the contradiction between the first proclamation made at Lyme and the trumpeting in Taunton market-place, looked uncommonly like perjury. On the same day Monmouth set out from Taunton for Bridgwater, where the borough magistrates, the mayor and aldermen, went out to meet and welcome him. The usual proclamation took place at the now demolished High Cross. The army was encamped on the Castle Field, and well cared for by the townsmen, while Monmouth himself occupied the castle. Of the castle, the part of the water-gate alone remains visible, but two vaulted cellars near yet exist, though access to them has been stopped up. By this time his force amounted to 6,000 men, of which the greater part were armed with hastily constructed weapons, scythes on poles, miners' picks and forks. Had Monmouth brought six times as many muskets and pikes with him over the sea, he could easily have found men to carry them. But of scythes and implements of husbandry the neighbourhood was soon drained. Every pike and musket was in use, and the result of course, from a military point of view in the matter of equipment at least, was not promising. Monmouth's 6,000 men were divided into six regiments which, from the presence of old militia red and yellow coats in the ranks, presented some semblance of uniformity. Grey's cavalry, mounted on marsh-bred colts and cart-horses, numbered 1,000, and these horses were many of them unbroken to the bridle, all of them to the sound of drum or shot of musket. To these Monmouth's bodyguard, composed of forty picked young men, mostly yeomen and fairly mounted, must be added. On receipt, on June 13th, of the news of Monmouth's landing, the Privy Council met and orders were at once issued to put all the troops on a war footing. New regiments were to be raised, and a bill of attainder was passed against the rebels by the Houses of Parliament. The forces of the Government assembled with all speed in the counties adjoining the rebellious district, and also in more distant shires. The lords-lieutenant called out every available man and marched towards

Somersetshire. The three Scotch regiments had arrived from Holland, Churchill, afterwards Duke of Marlborough, had marched to the west with the Horse Guards Blue. Feversham was to follow with as many regiments as could be spared from London, and of three of these regiments the recently imported Scotch took the place in guarding the metropolis. Churchill soon got within striking distance of the enemy, and throughout the march of Monmouth from Bridgwater to Glastonbury (eleven miles) he hung on the skirts of the army, and harassed them continually. Had Grey not been supported by infantry, without doubt the rebel cavalry would have ceased to exist as a body of so-called troops long before Sedgemoor; as it was, Churchill's scanty force was unable to do more than it did. Monmouth encamped at Glastonbury on June 22nd, spreading his men over the town, and likewise occupying the ruined abbey. Leaving Glastonbury, the next stopping place was Wells (five miles north-east), from which the army moved on to Shepton Mallet, a like distance, nearly due east. All this while the Government preparations were being completed, and up-to-date Monmouth had given no evidence of a plan of campaign of any kind. He now determined to attempt the capture of Bristol, and for this purpose set forth to cross the Avon at Keynsham (a long way round). The reason for this apparently curious march lay in the fact that while the walls of Bristol on the Somersetshire side were fairly strong, those on the side of Gloucestershire were comparatively feeble. Monmouth reached a place called Pensford, on the direct road to Bristol, and at a distance of five miles to the south of it on the evening of June 24th. The bridge at Keynsham had been broken down, and though a party had been detached and sent ahead to mend it, the repairs were not yet complete. That night his advent was anxiously expected in Bristol, and a rising would have taken place had it not been for the firmness of the Duke of Beaufort, aided greatly, it must be said, by a small body of cavalry which had arrived in the city on that day. Monmouth left Pensford at sunrise on June 25th and marched to Keynsham, a distance of three and a half miles. Here he found the bridge repaired, and here again he halted, intending to proceed to Bristol in the afternoon. At Keynsham two troops of the rebel horse were scattered and severely handled by a sudden charge of a small body of the Life Guards. These numbered but 100 men, and were under the command of Col. Sir Theophilus Oglethorpe. As an immediate consequence, Monmouth then decided to abandon his design on Bristol, and seems to have formed henceforward no deliberate military plan by which to guide his wanderings. Various suggestions appear to have been made as to plans of operations in different parts of the country. Gloucestershire was proposed, to be followed by a march through Worcestershire, Shropshire, and Cheshire. But in no case do we find any anxiety to fight. Nor, indeed, were his men, as far as equipment went, fit to incur such a march as that proposed. Roads were bad, and shoe-leather worn out in the majority of cases. Cavalry attacks on flank and rear throughout their course were probable, nay more, were certain. These attacks in themselves would be sufficient to delay the rebel army till the royal main body came up, even if the rebel army did not melt away under such constant harrying. Finally it was determined to summon Bath to surrender, and then to proceed into Wiltshire. Bath had a garrison, and a strong one; Feversham, with the royal foot, was on his way thither, nay was not far off, and Bath declined to surrender. Monmouth, without firing shot, withdrew to the little village of Norton St. Philip, which lies on the road half way between Bath and Frome, and here he halted on the night of June 26th. His quarters were the quaint half stone, half timber-and-plaster house, which is now an inn. At the window of a room on the first floor the duke was nearly killed by a silver button shot at him from the gun of an assassin. Just north of Norton St. Philip two deep lanes branch off, and at the village end, across one of these, Monmouth placed a barricade. Feversham, with horse and foot, came in hot pursuit of the rebels, and halted between these lanes, in the open fields. A body of the royal horse, under the Duke of Grafton (presumably Monmouth's half-brother) was acting as the advance guard, and at an early hour in the morning of June 27th, entered the lane and neared the barricade. Monmouth had, however, lined the hedges with musketeers, and thus both in front and on both sides Grafton and his luckless troopers were assailed with a shower of bullets. It was the second battle of Newbury over again. Out of 500 men more than 100 fell in that lane before the party could extricate itself. Grey, with the rebel horse, had been sent down the other lane, with orders to work across the fields and hem in the royal cavalry. He in a measure obeyed orders, but either his men declined to charge home or he did not lead them. Anyhow, Grafton's remnant succeeded in cutting their way back to the main body. Feversham drew up his men in battle order, an example which Monmouth followed. The former, however, had no artillery, while there were a few guns in the rebel line. Both, accordingly, after exchanging a few musket-shots, drew off, the earl to Bradford, Monmouth to Frome. At Frome hopes were entertained that supplies, especially of arms, would be obtained. A rising on a small scale had taken place there a few days before, but this, through the energy of the Earl of Pembroke, had been promptly suppressed. Neither arms nor scythes, nor even pitchforks, had been left in consequence. Men there were in plenty, but these, being unarmed, would have been worse than useless. At Frome, on the evening of June 27th, news reached Monmouth of the failure of the Scottish rising and the capture of Argyle. Matters seemed nearly as hopeless as they could be in the rebel camp. The gentry everywhere held aloof, as they had all along. Wiltshire, whither they proposed to march, had given no sign of rising, nor had it been possible to ascertain whether the royal troops would or would not change sides. Monmouth inclined to abandon the expedition, taking refuge in flight while there was time, and heedless of the fate of the men who had risen on his behalf. He absolutely discussed this infamous design with his closest adherents. Grey alone, curiously enough, denounced the idea in the strongest terms. The duke was absolutely at his wits' end what to do next. Feversham, he knew, could not be far distant, and was reinforced with both men and guns; whither should he go? A rumour that the Axbridge country people had risen and were mustering at Bridgwater, decided his course, and thither he bent his way. Taking Wells *en route*, where a halt was made, the Puritan element in the rebel army asserted itself by doing not a little damage to the ornaments in the cathedral. Lord Grey, it is said, drew his sword to protect the altar, and stood over it on guard; he had only his own men presumably to deal with. Bullets, however, or rather the material from which they could be cast, was obtained from the roof of the building. Leaving Wells, none the better for this visit of its Protestant would-be masters, the rebels again returned to Bridgwater, which they reached on July 2nd. Here the thousands of new recruits turned out to be a comparatively small mob armed with flails, bludgeons, and pitchforks. Feversham still not within sight, but known not to be far off, Bridgwater unfortified, what plan was next to be devised? Various schemes were proposed, men to fortify the town were collected, the idea of a march into Cheshire was again mooted; nothing was done, however, beyond digging a few ditches, and time was wasted. On the evening of July 5th, from the tower of Bridgwater Church, with a spy-glass, Monmouth descried the tents of the royal army on Sedgemoor, the camp being three and a half miles distant as the crow flies. Feversham had marched by way of Somerton, which place he left early on that morning. His force amounted to 2,800 foot and 700 horse. Some 1,500 of the Wiltshire militia were also attached to the army, but their share, if any, in the battle is not recorded. The royal artillery was represented by sixteen guns, of which twelve came from the Tower, and the rest from Portsmouth.

It will hardly be credited that the royal artillery lacked both draught-horses and also gunners. This, however, was the case, and, as will be seen, it was not found possible to bring it into action for a considerable time in consequence. Record remains that the coach-horses of the Bishop of Winchester, who accompanied the army, were among those employed to drag these guns when the time came to use them. Volunteers also were called for on the field to fight the artillery,

SEDGEMOOR.

and from a warrant we learn that to Sergeant Weems, of Dumbarton's Regiment, a reward of £40 was paid "for good service" in firing the "great guns" at Sedgemoor against the rebels. The wide plain of Sedgemoor may be thus briefly described: It extends for miles westward of Bridgwater, with its flat surface unbroken only by the three slight eminences on which stand the three villages of Chedzoy, Western Zoyland, and Middlezoy, which are distant from Bridgwater, as the crow flies, three, three and three-quarters, and five and a half miles respectively. These villages form a very flat isosceles triangle, of which the vertex is Western Zoyland, and the base (the most remote from

Bridgwater) the line joining the other two. Behind them, as seen from Bridgwater, the Polden Hills appear, and beyond again still higher ground in the distance. Western Zoyland is the proud possessor of a church with both a lofty and beautiful tower. Of Chedzoy Church mention will be made later. In 1685 the moor was only partially drained; even now, after but a little rain, its peaty grazing grounds are dank and marshy indeed. Fields in these days rectangular in shape and separated only by deep and fairly wide dykes cover the expanse. Here and there a row of pollard willows, or a fragmentary stunted hedge, with now and then a stray bush, breaks the monotony of the scene. Communication between different fields is even now difficult, as the regular passages are few, and the droves even fewer—droves which are more often than not a foot deep in peaty mud. In 1685 the main drainage of the moor consisted of three deep dykes, known by the names of the Black Dyke, the Langmoor Rhine, and the Bussex Rhine. It was beyond the last named of these that the royal army lay. The troops were encamped thus: Near Chedzoy and in the village the regular foot was posted, a part being encamped on the open moor. These numbered several battalions, amongst which were the celebrated 1st, or Royal Foot, then known as Dumbarton's Regiment, and in these days as the "Royal Scots" (Lothian Regiment). On a buttress on the north side of Chedzoy Church the marks made by the troops in sharpening their weapons are yet visible. As another instance of using the stones of a church for a similar purpose, Northallerton may be mentioned, and there, not one or two stones, but several dozens, are deeply scored. Chedzoy Church is an interesting little building apart from its historic memories, and possesses in its external walls four of the largest and the most ornate consecration crosses to be found in the country. At Western Zoyland the cavalry (Life Guards and Blues) were posted, and there Feversham had his headquarters. Middlezoy was occupied by the Wilts militia, under Lord Pembroke. It will thus be seen that the royal army was spread over a very wide front, apparently without connecting links of any kind, and in a country where the means

Middlezoy

of passing from one village to the other was, to use a very mild term, not easy. The previously mentioned artillery, it may be observed, was posted half a mile away from Western Zoyland on the road to Bridgwater, and apparently without a guard. Such, briefly, was the disposition of the royal army when Monmouth, spy-glass in hand, looked out over the moor from the lofty steeple of Bridgwater Church ; and on this army he determined to make a night attack. Nor was his determination in conception other than correct, but to carry it into execution a few requisites were needed, and these were wanting, viz., a good map, a good guide, and implicit obedience.

Monmouth, from his lofty post of observation, and also from rumour, knew to a nicety the exact location of the different drafts which made up the royal army opposed to him. His decision to attack the enemy in its strongest part, as regards infantry, all things considered, was wise, seeing that it lay isolated, and in all other arms his force was weak. Pembroke and his militia in remote Middlezoy might well be left to fight or run away, according to circumstances, their presence or absence being hardly a factor in the case. But that the existence of the third ditch, the Bussex Rhine, should have been unknown to Monmouth seems inexplicable. Still, so it was. At eleven o'clock the rebel army filed out of Bridgwater, in a silence strictly enjoined and absolutely necessary. Those who know the district will know what a Sedgemoor mist is like, and such a mist favoured the enterprise. Monmouth, whose quarters had been in the now vanished castle, rode out at the head of his "body-guard," but in command of the foot. Grey still led his cavalry, though he retained the command in spite of remonstrance to Monmouth on the subject. A supply of ammunition, conveyed in waggons, brought up the rear, and this was under a slender guard. The rebels took their way, not by the direct road, which would have led them to Western Zoyland, but by a branch path, and this none of the best. It is curious to find that the name of War Lane still clings to one part of the road. A space of about two hours was occupied before the force debouched on the moor, and then came the crossing of the dykes or rhines. The first of these was successfully passed by means of a causeway, the second, the

Langmoor Rhine, should have been similarly crossed, but the guide, either by mischance or intention, failed to hit the right spot, and valuable time was occupied in searching out the passage. Considering the fog—it is recorded that men were invisible at less than fifty yards—it is hardly to be wondered that the passage was not to be found at once. Even in broad daylight in these days to hit the causeways over Sedgemoor is not an easy task—this the writer can testify to from personal experience on more than one occasion. At length the Langmoor Rhine was negotiated, and the rebels drew near to what

W. In Zoyland Church from the Grave Mound

they believed to be the royal camp. They were, indeed, near, but between it and them lay the unknown or unsuspected Bussex Rhine. Meanwhile, owing to the firing of a pistol, all hopes of a surprise had vanished. One Captain Hacker is credited with having thus treacherously given the alarm. He was wounded in the fight and taken prisoner, only to be nearly torn to pieces by the furious women of Bridgwater as a traitor the next day. To Grey, with the cavalry, the duty of initiating the attack was confided, while Monmouth, with the foot, formed up in support. This, under the circumstances, seems to have been a rather unwise plan. Granted that real cavalry dashing into a bivouac of foot would, indeed, have been effectual, could Grey's horse be so far complimented as to be termed real cavalry. Possibly also to ensure silence, as the rumble of wheels might have betrayed the rebels, the ammunition carts had been left far behind in the rear on the edge of the moor. A precaution, truly, still one which in its effect in a measure led to the ruin of the rebels. On went Grey to the brink of the dyke, where he was challenged, it is said, by an officer in the foot guards, of which a detachment was present. Amid the rolling of the drums of Dumbarton's regiment beating to arms and the shouting of those despatched to call out the troops from Western Zoyland and far Middlezoy, the battle began. At the first volley, *i.e.*, that from the foot guards, Grey's horse fled, as was to be expected. Far and wide over the moor spread the marsh colts and cart-horses, some with riders and some without; but for this Grey, bad soldier though he was, can hardly be held accountable. Unfortunately some of the fugitives succeeded in crossing both the Langmoor Rhine and the Black Ditch, and they reached the ammunition waggons in full flight, spread terror among the guard, with the result that off to Bridgwater and even beyond the whole train fled. Meanwhile a small body of the horse had managed to rally and hung on the right, though far in the rear. Monmouth, on foot at the head of his infantry, was doing his best to repair the disaster, and indeed on this single occasion during the battle he appears to have behaved as a soldier should. But to cross that ditch himself, or to get his men across, was beyond his power, and hence from its opposite sides rebel and Royalist, at short range, poured volleys into each other's ranks. Soon from Western Zoyland arrived the Blues and the Life Guards, though it cannot have been an easy matter to traverse the old drove which connected the two villages, about midway between which the main fight was going on. At sight of them Grey's rallied horse fled, and, according to one view, it was this body which by its flight struck terror into the drivers and guard of the ammunition carts. With the royal cavalry, or shortly after its arrival, Feversham, who had been aroused from sleep, came on to the field. He found the engagement general along the line of the dyke, and hotly contested on both sides. In the royal army John Churchill, afterwards 1st Duke of Marlborough, had so handled the infantry as to considerably alter their original formation, or rather their haphazard grouping, and it was now in an effective position. Dawn was coming on, the rebel foot held still their own, and seemed likely to hold it while ammunition lasted and provided that the royal cavalry did not get among them. Could the crossing of the dyke by the cavalry however, be delayed or averted? Monmouth probably thought not, and so, considering the battle lost, mounted his horse, accompanied by Grey and one other, and fled the field at full speed. This is no excuse, nor can it be, for the fact that he thereby left some thousands of luckless men to face a fate he feared to face himself. Still the ammunition was not yet exhausted, and the Somersetshire men loaded and fired, loaded and fired, as rapidly as their inexperienced hands knew how. Down on them from the Western Zoyland side, that is on their right, charged the Life Guards. Working round by Chedzoy, the Blues fell on them on their left, and both attacks in the main failed. Sir Theophilus Oglethorpe, who led the Life Guards, was an old comrade of Monmouth, and had been major of the Duke of York's troop of Royal Dragoons when Monmouth was colonel. He was unhorsed, and lay wounded on the moor for a considerable time. Still the rebels stood firm, though falling fast. It was not the end quite, though the end was nearing. Ammunition now exhausted, for offensive weapons the pike or mounted scythe alone remained to them; for defensive the same, and the clubbed musket. Shouting, "Ammunition! for God's sake!" still they fought on, and would have fought on. But tardily and conveyed thither, as has been mentioned, on to the scene arrived the royal artillery, and the end came with it speedily. A few rounds of cannon-shot and a charge of cavalry made fugitives of most of those who remained unhurt. It is recorded that the miners from the Mendip district refused either to flee or to surrender, and that when the royal infantry crossed the dyke perished almost to a man, fighting stubbornly to the bitter end. It is beyond the purpose of this book to reopen the old story of the Bloody Assize, nor indeed need the exploits of Colonel Piercy Kirk be here related at length. A few lines, however, should in justice to him be added, viz., that unenviable though his reputation will ever remain and dissolute as he assuredly was in character and acts, at Sedgemoor, as elsewhere, as far as pure military service is concerned, he deserved well of his country. The man, apart from his private vices, saw much hard fighting in a hard fighting age, and ever behaved on the field with propriety. This his record of service shows. Of his private life nothing here need be recorded. The accounts of the number of the slain vary as regards Monmouth's men. One estimate places it as high as 1,000, another at about half that number. Beneath a low mound between Western Zoyland and Chedzoy a large number of them were buried, and the spot furnishes one of our illustrations. It is disgraceful to find that this mound has recently been rifled, ostensibly for a scientific purpose (of course). The alleged reason being a desire to see whether there had been any changes in Somersetshire skull formation since 1685. And for so paltry a reason as this the bones of the brave Somersetshire lads were disturbed. The grave mounds at Newbury suffered similarly a few years since; at Towton and several other places a like story will be heard. Surely grave mounds on battlefields, whether pagan or Christian, ought to be scheduled and protected by Government. When English soldiers fight and fall abroad, their graves, save in the most savage lands, are respected, though perhaps not kept in cemetery order. The twenty-year-old graves in Ashanti are reported to have been unmolested. Yet, to satisfy the vulgarest of vulgar curiosity, Englishmen are found with the specious pretence of scientific investigation in these late days ready and willing to rifle the graves of brave men of old. Scandalous behaviour such as this merits strong language. The evil is widespread and, to a certain extent, even yet spreading. Clerics spare neither dead warrior nor dead prelate. Restoration leads to a multitude of grave robberies, as more than one cathedral museum case can testify. So much for deans and chapters. Rectors and vicars follow suit, and the results we see behind plate-glass or hear gloated over by enthusiastic pundits at archæological meetings. A man who went to, say, Kensal Green, and exhumed a body to pilfer bones, would be punished, and rightly. Has not the soldier's grave an equal claim for protection?

SEDGEMOOR GRAVE MOUND.

APPENDICES.

I.

MARCHING.

OF two armies *caeteris paribus* the one which possesses the greatest mobility possesses considerable superiority over the other. Now, since the mobility of a fighting force in its entirety, is governed by the rate of progress of its slowest component part, it follows that on the marching power of the foot soldier that rate of progress usually depends. The statement that the more mobile force possesses superiority does not imply that the quickest marchers are necessarily in the best condition for fighting at the end of a march. This need not be discussed, since none would deny that a wearied force is handicapped when opposed to one that is fresher. The regulation of the pace is the province of the general or officer in command. To enter upon any comparison—at least any just comparison—between the marching powers of armies in England in the past with those of the present day is fraught with considerable difficulty, unless, indeed, it is absolutely impossible. Critics, and these are many nowadays, it is true, glibly contrast the marches of old time with the marches of to-day. But, unfortunately, beyond the mention of ascertained times and distances, they are apt to omit any consideration of the widely different conditions under which in various times these marches have been accomplished—conditions as different in the forces which fought at Stamford Bridge and Hastings, at Neville's Cross, at Towton, at Tewkesbury, Flodden, or Marston Moor, as in those which fought at Blenheim, Corunna, or Kandahar. The criticisms, it may be stated, which are passed on the marching powers of English soldiers in these days are in the main unfavourable. That this is unjust, it is the purpose of this section to show. *Primâ facie* the case of the critic is a strong one. He points out that in days of yore men, untrained as far as the parade-ground training goes, were able to cover distances which he asserts the foot soldier of 1896 cannot cover; and quotes history in support of his view. His deduction is that Englishmen in 1896—at least the Englishmen who wear the Queen's uniform—in the ranks lack stamina and physique. Let us examine the question; and for the sake of argument assume that the view of the critic is correct. In that case we are face to face with a curious fact—viz., that while in every other manly and athletic exercise skill has increased, more speed being shown where speed is needed, more dexterity where dexterity is required, and more endurance in feats needing that quality, in marching alone the Englishman has retrograded. But why is it that such an improvement in athletics is manifest? Simply because the younger generation in England exercise themselves. To put it briefly, the cinder-path, gymnasium, and football or cricket-field stand in the same relation to the athlete as the parade-ground or the Queen's highway *ought* to stand to the infantry soldier. But how can the lightly armed house-carl of Harold, or the archer or the billman of Edward IV., as far as equipment goes, be classed in the same category with a late nineteenth century infantry soldier. Can any comparison be justly made between the equipment of the foot men raised by Jack of Newbury who fought at Flodden, the White-coats of Newcastle who were slain at Marston Moor, and the route-march arrayed soldier of these latter days? It were as fair either to expect a Christmas parcel postman to be as speedy as a schoolboy on a paper-chase, or to require the latter to bear the burdens of the former, and to do his rounds. No, the critic is but plausible in his criticisms. His contention is specious but incorrect. Forth to war went the house-carl of Harold assuredly wearing his own private clothes, possibly too bearing his own private weapons, and above all, if lucky enough to own them, with his well-worn but easy shoes—shoes made of good English leather. Later, when feudalism was the custom of the land, the arms in the main were supplied by the feudal lord; the clothing of the foot soldier was, however, private, and bore solely for distinction the badge of royalty or that of a leader of gentle blood. He marched shod in his own shoon, and in nine cases out of ten with his trusty private bow slung at his back, and home-made arrows in his quiver. Evidences of the village bow factories remain to us in the shape of gnarled and hollow yew-trees, alas, now so rare, yet still to be seen in secluded village churchyards. As gunpowder came into use matters changed—arms increased in weight, and were less and less the private property of the users. But their clothing remained their own, and their shoes or boots. Uniform—a notion which in its early days, *i.e.*, before the establishment of a standing army, was hardly on the same footing as it is at present—by its introduction wrought the change. Record remains of the great effect the appearance of Newcastle's White-coats created on the field of Marston Moor. Clad in undyed cloth (hence their name), they went into action 3,000 strong, and but thirty wounded men survived at its close. Present at that fight were also a Blue Regiment and a Green Regiment (both infantry), but neither of these was absolutely dressed uniformly. Hazlerig's "black lobsters" in the same way differed in their clothing, being alike only in their arms and in the fact that they wore cuirasses for breast and back. These were cavalry, as also were the famous Ironsides of Cromwell. Round the hall of that grand old house, Littlecote, in Berks, the seat of the Pophams, hangs what is perhaps the most complete set of accoutrements of the Cromwellian age, viz., the buff coats, steel caps, gloves, horns, and bandoliers, &c., of Colonel (afterwards Admiral) Popham's troop (*vide* frontispiece and elsewhere). But till they were worn out, the foot soldiers in the main of both king and Parliament wore their own boots, and when shoeless begged, bought, or stole others. This may seem to be a digression; in reality it is not so, but merely leads to the conclusion the writer desires to set forth. Uniform in armies, at first partial, became, by force of circumstances and specially when a standing army was established, compulsory. Having become compulsory, contract work was unavoidable. Contract work, in days before advancement in the science of chemistry changed the condition of things, and the invention of machinery destroyed or nearly destroyed hand labour, may have been satisfactory or it may not. Similarly the house-carls of Harold, the archers of Edward IV., or the White-coats of Newcastle may have fallen out of the ranks by scores; it is far from improbable in the case of the first two armies named. But in those times the irrepressible reporter was not at hand to record either failure in equipment or failure in marching. In these days it is different. Times are changed, under the conditions of modern warfare. The bodily burden of a foot soldier must needs be somewhat heavy, despite all the care of the authorities, who are ever on the watch to lessen that burden. To acquire a power to cover the distances marched by the light and unencumbered foot soldier of old, must, in these days, be the result of training: a training carried on under the binoculars of criticism—binoculars of which the lenses are often faulty, though sometimes purposely ground in order to produce a distorted image. The carrying of burdens with comparative ease, comes not to man by nature, but by habituation. The comfort of the soldier during the operation can, however, be increased, or, in other words, his way may be made easier. Unfortunately here the all-important question of cost comes in, and this, in these days of ever-increasing expenditure, is a serious matter. Needless to say the writer is alluding to the English "Ammunition" Boot. Could there not be some improvement in this particular article of dress? Men who attain to special excellence in the use of their feet—for instance, athletes, cyclists, or even acrobats—have arrived at various kinds of footgear which for their respective purposes are as nearly perfect as possible. Men who are in the habit of walking long distances, if they are wise, are shod in such a way as to minimise discomfort. Could not something be done for the boots of the soldier? That the introduction of machinery has ousted "hand-sewn" work is admitted, and in fact any maker in the boot trade will tell you that in England there are not enough men now trained in "hand-sewing" to supply the boots needful annually for Government purposes. Science has so changed the conditions of tanning and leather-dressing that whereas in the past it required from twelve to eighteen months to properly tan leather for boots and shoes, hardly three months are now consumed in the operation. But what leather the old tanners turned out! Boots two centuries and more old, as far as their substance is concerned, are as good as ever. Can we say the same of a nineteenth century ten or even five-year-old boot? Those, however, were made from English, these from Buenos Ayres hides. What is required seems to be a well-fitting boot, machine-made it needs must be, but of English leather, and slowly tanned; in consequence lighter, more flexible, and more enduring. Hardly one-half the iron work on sole and heel would then be needed. An article in these days of heavy contracts not easily to be obtained, and certainly not at the present price. Perhaps there is more variation in the shape of the human foot than in any other part of the human anatomy. This presents another difficulty, and one which it has hitherto seemed impossible to overcome. As is well known, boots ordered and paid for by contract are of necessity made in certain sizes. When served out to the soldier he has to get as comfortable a fit under the circumstances as possible. But in many, too many, cases the results are the reverse of satisfactory. The boots being hard and stiff, which they need not be, if tight, cause great pain; if loose, blisters inevitably follow. A large percentage of men suffer from the pressure of the laces round the ankle—a defect which produces two and sometimes three hard excrescences on the leg above the ankle at the top of the boot. It has been suggested, and the suggestion seems worth consideration—(1) that boots should be made to lace lower down than they are at present; (2) that they should be furnished with tongues lined with felt to prevent friction; and (3) that they should be issued unpierced for laces, the requisite piercing being done by a regimental bootmaker when the two edges have been cut away, so as to ensure a proper fit across the instep and up the ankle, care being taken that the edges should not quite meet when tightly laced. The smart appearance of the boot would not thereby be impaired, its efficiency would be increased, and the comfort of the wearer would be assured. The methods of softening leather and rendering it waterproof (castor oil, by the way, is the best) need not here be touched upon. To the service gaiter there appear to attach two slight disadvantages—one that it has a tendency to rub the back of the leg by working up and down, the other that in hot weather it increases the heat of the foot. This is mentioned not in the spirit of criticism, but from the fact that as a portion of the marching equipment the gaiter must needs be considered in conjunction with the boot. The above remarks on the questions of boots and leather are the result of careful inquiries made by the writer at Northampton and Leicester, both important seats of the boot trade. The statements as to the actual wear and comfort of the boots were derived from some three dozen non-commissioned officers and privates, all encountered separately and fortuitously in different parts of the kingdom. In no case either with soldier or trader was the motive of the inquiry made known.

It may be well here to write briefly on the subject of roads in England in olden time. Practically and for military purposes until the reign of Edward I. the only decent roads in the country were those bequeathed to us by the Romans— Watling Street, Ermin Street, Ikenild Street, and the Fosse Way; cross-roads and roads between market towns being little better than tracks, and a few examples of old drives remain to this day in proof thereof. That this should have been otherwise is hardly to be expected; for, provided that there was a resemblance to a path, more as a guide than a road, it was all that was required for ordinary traffic. A man or horse could pass along it or by the side of it in the days when both wheeled carriages were scarce and hedges almost unknown. Nearly all the battles on English soil have been fought either across one or other of the old Roman roads, or in close proximity thereto. To outstrip an enemy on the march, and obtain the command of a trunk road to London, York, or some great city, was the aim of every commander, and the object of such strategists as existed in those days. To Edward I. is due the widening of some of the roads which united the market towns, but the improvement effected by him in 1285 was more apparent than real as far as affording increased facilities for the transport of troops. Toll for roads we find first levied in 1346. But it was not until rather more than two centuries had elapsed, *i.e.*, till 1555, that any systematic road survey and repair was instituted. Seldom indeed do we find the commanders of old indulging in a cross-country march. To the roads they almost invariably stuck, and probably wisely. Time after time the incursions of the marauding Scots traversed the same paths in England, and with like iteration the English expeditions of a similar character crossed the Border at the well-known fords, and approached the Border by the well-known ways. Along the Roman road in the district known as Redesdale to such an extent had the inhabitants been harried by Scotch invaders, that not even a cottage of any antiquity existed there half a century ago. A map of England on which the Roman roads and the battlefields alone are marked shows this most clearly. In the Great Rebellion the network of roads and crossways had greatly increased. Still anything like a frequent employment of bypaths was most unusual. The infantry generally made their way by the high-roads, along which the guns perforce were compelled to be dragged, and even then in bad weather with the utmost difficulty The cavalry made a more generous use of cross-ways, and some of Rupert's most dashing raids were carried out along the side tracks. There was, however, a reason and a strong one for adhering as far as possible to the great trunk roads or the highways between town and town. This was nothing other than the feeding of the troops. A commissariat train was in ancient days a rarity. Armies marched as often as not subsisting by plunder, and both in and near a town supplies could best be obtained. Camps, whatever may be the popular notion, were as a rule singularly devoid of tents in those days. A few, possibly those of the highest rank, possessed such luxuries, but the rank and file lay beneath the stars on the bare ground. The villages of those times could not accommodate even a moderately sized army, as armies went of old, and either in autumn, winter, or early spring the wise commander halted his men in towns, where quarters sufficient could be obtained, and supplies of food requisitioned. To have provided for the wants of his men in any of the out-of-the-way regions, even in England, would have been beyond the power of any of the commanders of the Middle Ages. On the trunk roads, and between point and point, there was some kind of knowledge as to what to expect. A shift could be made for a day, or perhaps two days, but until the invention of a species of provision train—at best a most imperfect arrangement in its inception—a commander was at the mercy of chance provender seized haphazard as opportunity occurred. Hence it is that we frequently find armies literally starving in the

MARCHING.

days immediately preceding the pitched battles of old; and of these the troubles both of Edward IV. and Queen Margaret before Tewkesbury may be instanced, or the condition of Manchester's army prior to Marston Moor. Of the great marching performances of these three armies, despite their starving condition, on the occasions named notice has already been taken. It now remains only to briefly touch on the question of the age of the infantry of mediæval times as compared with the age of the infantry of to-day. Without entering into the vexed question of long or short service—a question which would be beyond the intention of this book—a few facts may at least be plainly stated. In Saxon times, when all classes from the bondman to the man of rank were liable to be called upon to serve, those of low degree in the ranks, those of higher degree in command, no standard of exemption other than that of physical incapacity was recognised. Side by side marched the boy of sixteen and maybe his grandsire of sixty, the fair-haired youth and the grizzled veteran. In early feudal times much the same condition of things obtained. A man of rank had perforce to supply his quota of men or to pay the difference, and naturally chose the least expensive of the two. Forth then from their usual agricultural occupations marched old and young. Trained troops, according to drill-book notions, they were not—a sufficient acquaintance with the use of sword, axe, bill, or spear being held to be ample military training. Later, when the English archer had become the most powerful factor in the pitched battles at which he was present, skill, marvellous skill in the use of the bow became the pride of the English foot soldier. In times of peace father taught son, uncle nephew, or grandsire grandson. In times of war side by side they marched and fought, perhaps fell. But these were the days when if a man had to go from place to place his mode of progression was in ninety-nine cases out of a hundred by means of the legs and feet with which Nature had endowed him. It was then no age of trains, tramcars, omnibuses, cabs, or cycles. Hence, by an habituation entirely unconnected with military training, the rustic, the small provincial trader, and the London apprentice could with a light heart enter upon a tedious march. It was, as it were, all in a day's work to him. On the road he had the benefit of the experience of his elders, in the fight he had their personal example and moral support. The powerful agency of religious fanaticism so manifest in the soldiers of the Parliamentarian army in the seventeenth century—nay, even in the brave and betrayed rebels of 1685, need not be more than named. The writer has endeavoured to state his case with regard to marching past and present in as fair and unbiased a way as possible. That all will assent to his views he cannot hope, still some may be led to agree with him in this conclusion, viz., that until the infantry soldier of the present day can start on a march, whether in time of peace or in time of war, under the same conditions as the foot soldier of the eleventh, fifteenth, seventeenth, or eighteenth centuries, it is grossly unfair to lay the blame of any shortcomings on his physique. Training, and above all some improvement in footgear, will speedily show the soldier of 1896 to be, as his ancestors were, *but with ease*, able, as he has ever been ready, both to go anywhere and to do anything, with the loyalty and valour which is his heritage.

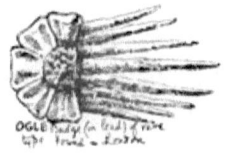

II.

ARMS AND ARMOUR.

THE effect which the introduction and employment of new kinds of offensive and defensive weapons has had both upon strategy and tactics is not a little interesting. The victory of Harold over the Norwegian king and Tostig compared with the defeat a few weeks later of Harold by William is a case in point. At Stamford Bridge two armies equipped with similar arms and prepared to adopt precisely similar methods of attack and defence were engaged. Harold, as we know, was the victor, and his victory was won by the hard fighting of men armed with sword, spear, or axe, and protected alone by the shields they bore. Personal prowess was the factor in the commander which was supposed to conduce to victory, and in those times stood in the place in England of anything approaching to tactics. At Hastings, however, the same personal prowess failed in the presence of novel conditions of warfare. Against the unmailed Saxons were pitted the mailed cavalry of the Norman and a body of archers. As a strategist Harold had taken up a position to which no exception could be scientifically taken. He compelled his enemy to come out and fight, and on ground eminently unsuitable for the employment of cavalry. How the battle developed has already been told in detail, but the fact remains that the crude archery of the Norman invaders primarily was the cause of the Saxon defeat. By means of this weapon, nearly, if not entirely novel in its application to warfare in England at that period, the mailed horsemen of the Normans were, after repeated failures, enabled to achieve victory. But the effect of this victory as regards warfare and weapons was considerable. The horsemen triumphed until some method was evolved by which their onrush could be successfully checked. By the reign of Edward I. the English long-bow had proved its superiority and had become the pride of our infantry and the terror of those against whom it might be employed. But the long-bow passed through many phases before it reached its final pitch of perfection. Originally merely a small weapon, it was pulled horizontally: the Scotch for centuries — nay, never acquired the true English method, and hence their archers were comparatively worthless. Attempts were made to introduce the cross-bow, notably by Richard I., but these, as far as English fighting-men were concerned, never came to any importance. Foreign troops might repel cavalry with pikes and might use the cross-bow in war, but in England neither custom obtained any hold on the people. For purely sporting purposes the cross-bow remained as a weapon down to the days of Elizabeth. Seldom do we meet with a recorded use of the cross-bow in the field of battle in England, save at Stoke. The case of the boy at Towton is specially mentioned, he, seated in an elderbush, shot Lord Dacre, his cross-bow being probably his private sporting engine. But English arrows having been found capable of piercing any mail as worn by knights in early times, and the deadly volleys of shafts which were poured into the ranks of an advancing army proving able to stop any charge whatever, whether of cavalry or infantry, it became needful to increase the defensive gear. Plate armour succeeded the original chain mail, gradually increasing in weight and thickness till the limit of human endurance was almost reached. Man and horse alike were at one period so heavily defended as to render anything like flight impossible. Still, however heavily a man might be armed, a direct shot from an English bow would, if delivered at not too great a range, pierce his armour. A side shot would glance, but the direct hit penetrated through helm or corselet alike. Of the deadly arrow the range may roughly be taken under ordinary circumstances as anything up to between 350 and 400 yards With a favourable wind, as at Towton, it might be greater. This explains how in many cases anything in the shape of a charge failed to reach the line of archers. The effect, especially on infantry proper, was terrible; witness the slaughter of the Galwegians at Northallerton, and that of the men of Cheshire at Blore Heath. But another curious change was wrought by the power of the arrow. The very mailed cavalry which by means of archers had prevailed against the Saxon infantry as a fighting unit almost ceased to exist in absolute battle. Popular notions of a mediæval fight consist of a turmoil of men charging on horseback, riding roughshod over and slaughtering wretched beings with spears, maces, or swords, while here and there an archer shoots at no particular object. The reality, in England at least, was somewhat as follows: A front rank of archers, a second rank of men armed with spear, bill, or kindred weapon, and light defensive armour (perhaps); lastly, the man-at-arms and the vaunted knight of chivalry, but on foot, with their war-horses carefully sent to the rear. Mounted troops, if any, in a battle were reserves, and sometimes the bodyguards of royal persons were cavalry. Neville's Cross and Northallerton are cases in point. Flodden, the last archers' battle, shows us how far gunpowder had brought about the employment of genuine cavalry. No, the knight in armour fought not on horseback. He mounted when pursuing the enemy and when himself pursued. Half the long death-roll of the bloody Wars of the Roses was owing to the fact that either your knight was unable to move sufficiently quickly to reach his horse before capture, or, seeing the day lost, his page had ridden off thereon himself. Truly in the glorious days of chivalry the unfortunate knight fought under more disadvantages than fall to the lot of most warriors.

The application of the use of gunpowder to the practice of warfare came in due time, and the result, though inevitable, took centuries to bring about. At first confined to the curious engines of war which passed for cannon, and which by their noise did more to rout an inexperienced enemy than by the loss they inflicted, the new departure had little effect either on arms or armour. A few rounds shot off at the beginning of a fight and sometimes at its termination was the sole use to which the revolutionising gunpowder was put. And as far as cannon is concerned this custom may be said to have almost invariably obtained until the end of the Great Rebellion. On shipboard and in besieging a town or castle it was another matter, but with this we have here nothing to do. Your hand-gun, the progenitor of the modern rifle, made even slower progress. The 300 men with hand-guns imported by Edward IV. on the occasion of his last and finally victorious effort to win the kingdom are not recorded as having achieved anything. At Flodden one man (Borthwick, the Scottish gunner) was killed by a cannon-shot, and a round or two on the morning after the battle dispersed the Scots gathered on an eminence. Beyond this, however, artillery played a most unimportant part in the struggle. Meanwhile arms and armour had changed in form and fashion. The up-to-date knight of the time of Henry VIII. resembled in no way the mailed horsemen of William I. That a certain uniformity existed in the arms and equipment of the Normans who fought at Hastings is probable, but that anything approaching to uniformity was ever seen afterwards, either in arms or armour, it is difficult to believe. Weapons of all ages and of all kinds formed the equipment of the lower ranks. Arms and armour which had hung for centuries on the walls of castle or manor-house hall were taken down time after time, as occasion required, and made an appearance in the field. A knight found it sufficiently costly to equip himself, his squire, and his page in the latest fashion. Only the wealthy could afford to fit out even a small troop according to the most modern style. This remark does not apply to the great houses, such as the Nevilles or the Percies. Their immediate retainers were, of course, clad and armed with some tolerable amount of uniformity, but the common herd of their vassals, beyond being armed somehow, and wearing a badge, were otherwise a motley crew. How in the days of the Great Rebellion manor houses, nay all places, were ransacked for arms is well known; and that the finds occasionally appeared in the field seems clear—at any rate at Marston Moor the son of Sir W. Slingsby, a Colonel Slingsby, was killed by a battle-axe which cleft his cap and head. But gunpowder prevailed in the end, not, however, without a severe fight for supremacy.

In his infancy, the unfortunate handgun-man, with his clumsy, slow-loading weapon supported on a fork, the handle of which was stuck into the ground, was the sport both of archer, pikeman, and knight. Liable to be smitten hip and thigh by an easily portable weapon, which was effectual at a far greater range than his own ponderous machine, it was not difficult to throw the line into confusion, specially if a charge of horse came down thereon. Back on to the second line of pikemen the handgun-men were thrown, in nine times out of ten producing confusion and causing disaster. Invention came to the aid of the military man in due course. The bayonet was evolved, but at first was clumsy and almost useless. Slowly it passed through the stages of plug, rings, and socket till it became what it now is; but its invention practically made the handgun-man or musketeer his own pikeman. The bayonet, more than any other invention, may in a way be said to have revolutionised infantry, and for these reasons. It ensured victory for ball over arrow, it practically, as far as English armies are concerned, caused the adoption of two lines of men in lieu of three, while retaining an opening on occasion for that system of fighting which has ever been popular, viz., the resort to cold steel. Cavalry, as cavalry, practically dates its expansion from the Great Rebellion. Tactics, strange no doubt to modern eyes, were employed, still the germ of the cavalry service of to-day is to be looked for in the wild rushes of Rupert's horse or the steadier charges of the Ironsides of Cromwell. Quaint indeed are some of the methods employed by opposing bodies of cavalry in those days. They would ride up to within pistol-shot of one another, discharge their pistols, and then retire to reload and repeat the operation. This being done swords were drawn and they fell to work in earnest. At Marston Moor, after the first discharge, the pistols were mutually flung at each other's heads. An interesting feature in the cavalry performance at Naseby is the use made of dismounted dragoons by the Parliamentarian commander. These, 1,000 in number, lined the historic Sulby hedge, from behind which they fired on the flank of Rupert's charge. Later on they remounted and did good service as actual cavalry. Such then in brief are the changes, their causes and effects, which have taken place in the English armies of old. Changes gradual, but eventually far-reaching—

changes ever going on, though in these latter days with far more rapidity than of yore. Warlike engines have varied and are varying daily, and may vary; still, while national spirit remains there will be but little to fear as to the future of English horse, foot, and artillery.

GORING.

III.

STRATEGY AND TACTICS.

STRATEGY, for which the term "generalship" is often substituted, is the science which enables the commander of an army, or the commander-in-chief of several armies, so to manœuvre them, either singly or in combination, that—

1. He can select his own battle-ground or grounds.
2. He can compel the enemy to fight on terms disadvantageous either in entirety or in detail.
3. He can avoid engagement for either the whole or a part of his forces.
4. He can practically enforce the surrender of armies or divisions of the enemy without fighting.

The term "manœuvre" includes the marching of large or small bodies of troops, the seizing of positions, bases of operations, sources of supply, and lines of communication.

The science of tactics is subdivided into two parts, viz., major and minor, and may be thus defined :—

Major tactics are concerned with the general disposition of troops immediately before a battle, and the method with which, as a whole, they are employed during the engagement.

Minor tactics rule the employment of subdivisions of an army, either according to the regulations laid down by masters of the science of war, or by the special exigencies which may arise during the course of the engagement. Briefly, by strategy a general takes up the most favourable position he can obtain. According to the laws governing major tactics he arranges the plan of battle, but by the exercise of minor tactics the subordinates fight their troops, having in view the best advantage of the army as a whole. In its most extended sense, therefore, minor tactics may be defined as the strategy of the non-commissioned officer.

A study of the battles fought in England, despite its geographical limitations, and the exclusion of reference to battles elsewhere, opens up various considerations both interesting and curious. With the exceptions too well known to need enumeration in detail, the majority of English battles resolve themselves into combats the outcome of civil strife—battles in which Scotch, Irish, and Welsh, or foreign mercenaries played usually but an unimportant part. The first point for consideration is how far did the social and political condition of England in old times affect the methods of war, the conduct of campaigns, and the results of battles. That the social system obtaining in a country and the political condition of its inhabitants should, as it were, control the strategy and tactics of the commanders engaged in its wars does not appear clear at first sight; still on examination it becomes manifest. That a country in which bondage exists should be liable to military disaster is not perhaps to be wondered at. But that the political system known as the feudal system—a system established for purely military purposes in the main—should have been the cause of more warlike disasters, from a scientific point of view, in England is somewhat remarkable. These conditions being stated, it is hardly surprising that the military operations of the Great Rebellion were, from a military point of view, unsatisfactory. Protracted, exhibiting instances of personal bravery of the highest order side by side with incompetence, not to say cowardice, on almost every occasion the battles of the Great Rebellion and their results are indeed a puzzle. But serfdom had then ceased to exist, feudalism was practically dead; an interval of something politically akin to despotism had intervened, and no social system had arisen to take the place of either serfdom or feudalism. Practically the armies of Charles I. fought, or endeavoured to fight, guided by the fragmentary traditions of feudal days; fought, commanded in the main by quasi-feudal lords whose military experience was comparatively nil and with a scanty leaven of professional soldiers, trained in foreign service, accustomed to foreign methods of warfare, and rigorously excluded for the most part from any real authority. On the side of the Parliament a similar condition of chaos obtained at the commencement. Private jealousies and political enmities, divided councils, and intentional cross-purposes either paralysed military operations or rendered their results the effects of chance, not skill. The Parliamentarians began the struggle unprovided with any system, failed, and after weary years of warfare formed a system, organised its details, and the upshot we know. Another point needs mention, and it is one which appears rather in the light of a paradox. Bravery, by which here is meant personal prowess in actual fight, among commanders (both great and small) led more often to defeat than to victory. To support the views embodied in these remarks it will be only needful to instance actual battles and their results. Harold, after his victory at Stamford Bridge, starting southwards from York to repel the Norman invasion, could and did call on Edwin and Morcar to follow him with their hosts. Their political position enabled them to disregard his command. Strategically, even with his thus crippled army, he proved himself the superior of the Norman William. His position at Hastings, and the major tactics by which he intended the battle to be fought, cannot be adversely criticised. But two causes led to his ruin. A personally fighting commander, unless so in the direst emergency, loses his control over the troops under him as a whole. Thus it was with Harold. Obedience to previous orders cannot under such circumstances be enforced, with results that are obvious. William the Norman, inferior as a strategist—at least there are no grounds to credit him with superiority—excelled his opponent as a tactician. Hence his victory. Ruled at first by the customary methods of warfare of his country, the Norman attack failed, and failed more than once. A genius for tactics showed him the weak spots in the Saxon defence, and discovered to him the means of victory. Northallerton, though not strictly English, is a curious example. Strategically neither side had the superiority. The English, posted on a hill, awaited attack, acting on the defensive. The

Scottish king, tactically correct in the original disposition of his forces, was, owing to the jealousy among his followers, compelled to change his battle array; the social conditions obtaining thus outweighing the exigencies of the military situation. Lewes and Evesham are only remarkable from the fact that the strategic movements which enabled De Montfort to win the first were applied against him by his vanquished enemy and with success in the second. Boroughbridge, like Northallerton, was one of the most striking proofs of the superiority of archers over any troops, mailed or unmailed. Nevilles Cross is important from the fact that the tactics of Baliol, in command of a reserve of horse (the earliest instance of a reserve proper), practically won the battle. His post was one which, in that "personal prowess" age, it was almost an insult to offer to him, an ex-king. But his skilful handling of that body of horse entitles him to a high place in the list of tacticians of the Middle Ages. The defeat at Otterburn shows Percy both as a strategist and, all things considered, as a tactician, also to have been inferior to Douglas. Percy knew, or ought to have known, the power of the English long-bow. He should also have remembered that the lesson of the long-bow the Scots either could not or would not learn Blindly he attacked at night, hardly knowing what he was attacking, and with wearied troops. His detachment under Umfraville sent northwards was well planned, but for reasons failed in its object. Douglas, on the other hand, took up a naturally strong strategic position, and strengthened it artificially. Tactically, his great stroke was the flanking movement by which he fell on the extreme English right. This movement was conceived on the instant and during the turmoil of a night attack on the baggage camp beneath. Shrewsbury is a good instance of a victory thrown away by personal prowess. The strategic position of Percy and Douglas was excellent, so much so that the very formation of the attacking force had to be entirely changed. In lieu of right and left wings and centre it attacked in two bodies, that on the left being in the usual line, that on the right in a mass, an exaggerated species of column. Ordinary precautions and an absence of the "hew Agag in pieces" order of fighting on the part of the rebel commanders would, in all probability, have ensured a Royalist defeat, specially, too, as the confederates included in their ranks the deadly Cheshire bowmen. As it was, Hotspur and Douglas failed; the former fell the wrong side, scientifically speaking, of the enemy's line, and cut off from assistance, the latter wounded, was eventually compelled to take flight. Blore Heath was the triumph of Salisbury the tactician over Audley the personal prowess blunderer. Wakefield was a curious departure. Richard of York, outnumbered and ill-supplied, was shut up in the impregnable Sandal Castle. That he was outnumbered he was well aware, yet without investigation, and contrary to even the expressed opinion of his associates, he marched directly forth into a trap to give battle. His opponent, making use of somewhat similar tactics to those employed at Blore Heath by the victors, crushed York within the hour. York's sheet-anchor was personal prowess. At this time distrust, begotten of treachery, and savagery the offspring of political hate, had all but killed scientific warfare. Edward IV then arose with the military genius of a great commander and the hideous vices of a "sans coulotte." Strategist and tactician, wherever he took the field he stood a head and shoulders above his opponents as a soldier. His brilliant military gifts were displayed in all branches of the then existing science of war and on all occasions. Ever victorious and, save in one instance, ever with an inferior force at his command, he showed masterly qualities as a leader of men in battle. The vaunted Warwick, the "king-maker," when pitted against him, was but as a pigmy warring with a giant. True, the evils of treachery and the feudal system were in league against Warwick on the field of Barnet, but this does not detract from the abilities of Edward in the preliminary manœuvres, both as strategist and tactician. Mortimer's Cross, a small but dashing exploit, was followed by the great victory of Towton, to which the minor tactics of Falconberg, in command of the Yorkist archers, greatly contributed, and the late flank attack of Norfolk put the finishing touch. To these, years later, succeeded Barnet, the series being completed by the final but clever victory of Tewkesbury. The whole conduct of the Barnet and Tewkesbury campaign on both sides is of unexampled interest. For the first time the science of seizing and guarding lines of communication for strategic reasons and by strategic methods takes really definite form. Edward, Prince of Wales, had given some proof of a glimmering of light on this subject in the operations preceding the battle of Evesham, but it was reserved for Edward, his namesake, King of England, to practically reduce chance inspirations to actual science. Tewkesbury, too, from a tactical point of view, is worth consideration. That Somerset was out-generalled, as he was out-marched, is undoubted. Still, in the strategic struggle he managed to choose his own fighting-ground, and that a strong one. He improved his opportunity by entrenchment. As a tactician he was a miserable failure, and paid the penalty therefor by defeat and death. Tactically the attack of Edward on the Tewkesbury entrenched lines was faultless, his dispositions being far in advance of those usually employed in the wars wherein his experience had been gained. On the question of the "200 spears" in the wood some doubt arises. Could these have been 200 "lances" according to the Hawkwood unit? If so, their effect as a flank attack is easily explained. It is somewhat strange that the unit of "lances" introduced abroad by that great general, Sir John Hawkwood, has not the honour of mention in any chronicler's account of any English battle. Hawkwood, "free companion," freebooter, mercenary, or what you will, was the first English scientific strategist. Naturally, in consequence, not even a biography of him existed until recently. Famous throughout the length and breadth of southern Europe, he died honoured in a foreign land. His body lies beneath a magnificent tomb in a foreign cathedral, while in the church of Sible Hedingham, in Essex, his native place, a miserable, much-mutilated and uninscribed cenotaph alone exists to perpetuate the memory of the fine old warrior.

Bosworth, the battle which decided the fate of a dynasty, was a compound of blundering and treachery. Richard, with a strong strategic position and opposed to a man known to be of a timorous nature, left his commanding ridge, impelled by hate and a belief in the prestige of personal prowess. Treachery worked its worst, with the results that we know. But through his tactical blunder Richard deserved to lose the day, and did so. Feudalism, then in the last years of its existence as a power in the State, gave on this occasion an eloquent instance of its dangers, both from a political and a military point of view. Flodden shows us Surrey, an astute man of the world rather than a scientific soldier : a strategist sufficient to out-general James, who was neither strategist nor tactician. The conditions were strange. Feudalism in England was dying, if not dead ; chivalry, in the old acceptance of the term, was not only dead but buried. In Scotland, on the other hand, feudalism, with all its evils, was as powerful as ever, and the invading Scotch army was commanded by a king brave to the extremity of his finger-tips, but a fool—a fool quite impregnated with the sentiments of that exploded farce chivalry. Surrey, the man of the world, played upon his weakness, enticed him from a strong position after having, according to the laws of that defunct code chivalry, tied his hands as to fighting, in order to gain time and thereby strength. Feudalism, with all its defects and with also, it is fair to say, its doubtful virtues, was manifest on the Scotch side. Even its dying embers emitted a spark on the English right, where the Cheshire archers, feeling aggrieved, fought but feebly. Tactics, specially the tactics employed by Lord Dacre, who commanded the reserve, practically won the day, coupled, however, with the splendid work of the English archers all along the rest of the line. Truly the last bowman's fight on English soil was glorious in its terrible results. The rush of the clansmen on the English line at Flodden, in 1513, was the counterpart of the rush of the Galwegians at Northallerton in 1138. Three hundred and seventy-four years, and the bitter experience of Neville's Cross and Homildon Hill had taught no military lesson to these brave but doomed men. A careful consideration of the battles of the Great Rebellion leads to the following conclusions. As strategists the Royalist commanders, so far as design and intention went, were far superior to the generals of the Parliament. But owing to the disastrous system of independent commands by which the right wing, may be, either knew little and often cared less for the operations of left wing or centre, and *vice versâ*, constant tactical errors were committed which resulted in failure in almost every important fight. Charles, personally brave as he was undoubtedly, but vacillating and uncertain in council, whether civil or military, may have believed himself to be by divine right a general. No great movement, strategically, can absolutely be traced to his initiative. Whether Rupert, young, rash, and brave, was really the strategist of his party does not exactly appear, though evidence seems to point in that direction. Practically, however, it matters little, seeing that the scientific strategic designs which were conceived were, with but few exceptions, abandoned. As a tactician Rupert was the veriest tyro—a commander with one idea beyond plunder and one method of carrying it out, viz., to charge at sight, and this generally by taking ground more to the right of his position and attempting to deliver an oblique flank attack. Boldly and brilliantly executed, and usually with success, though this was, it never seems to have occurred to him, or indeed to any Royalist cavalry commander, to reflect that troops are engaged to win battles as a whole, and that such a thing as unselfish warfare conduces to victory. Seldom or never, save at Marston Moor, did the Royalist cavalry return after success to deliver a second attack. The details, remarkable indeed, of Marston Moor, have been already treated at length. Cropredy Bridge, a battle initiated through a quaint blunder and nearly a defeat, was converted into a victory by the tactics of Cleveland. Of a different class were the exploits of Hopton and Grenville. Their little armies were composed of different stuff from that which furnished the usual Royalist rank and file. Witness the silent storming, pike in hand, of the smooth steep Stratton Hill by the Cornishmen, and the even more difficult feat of carrying the entrenchments on Lansdown. This exploit, which, considering the numbers engaged, was as bloody in its results as any in the course of these long years of bloodshed, was another triumph for the same commanders. Turning to the other side, we find far above his comrades Cromwell stands forth : at Marston Moor—that battle of runaway generals—as a tactician, at Naseby as both strategist and tactician. The ill-omened campaign of Sedgemoor, aimless, apparently, from a military point of view, in the details of its various episodes, might yet have terminated in a rebel victory had but a man of real talent been among the leaders. Strategically, it calls for no remark. Monmouth had to fight or to run. His night attack, if proper precautions had been taken on his part, might well have succeeded, considering the absolute lack of military skill shown by Feversham. The Royal army, spread out over a great front with seemingly no patrols, and no links between its three bivouacs, courted disaster. A bare dozen sentries would have rendered even the chance of a surprise impossible. In these days the personal prowess of old, a physical quality concerned merely with lack of fear and a desire to slay, has given place to a moral quality, nay, a virtue, which is therefore of a far higher order of excellence. Side by side with the undiminished physical courage of the warrior of old has grown up the moral courage of the scientific soldier. Far harder is the task of command, far wider are its duties extended, far greater are its responsibilities now than they were in the years gone by. Then, too often, alas, the pitiable spectacle was seen of the private enmities of separate commanders and troops under their command, extending even to the field of battle, when those who fought on the same side were sacrificed to petty jealousy, class feud, or supposed injury. In these days, regiments may have professional rivalries, and colonels may be on cool terms in private life, but the half-hearted support of one body of Englishmen for another in battle is unknown. Under the feudal system, or in the days of the Great Rebellion, the former vice could, nay, did, exist. In these days, and under our present social and political conditions, such backsliding is impossible. Opinions may differ as to standing armies, armaments, military expenditure, and scientific soldiering. The discussion of such subjects may safely be left to those who delight therein. None can deny the truth of the saying, " Pax potior bello "; as a political motto, however, it were better to remember " Paritur pax bello."

INDEX.

A.

Abingdon, feint at, 309
Abraham's Bridge, 217
Alan de Percy, 32
Apsall, Sir R., 136
Atherstone, 214
Audley, Lord, 118-122
Aymer de Athol, 84

B.

Barnet, battle of, 192, 197
- ,, dispositions of armies, 191, 192
- ,, Edward's flight to Holland, 182
- ,, Edward's foreign preparations, 183
- ,, Edward leaves London, 191
- ,, Edward reaches London, 190
- ,, landing of Edward, 185
- ,, manœuvres prior to battle, 187-191
- ,, march of Warwick, 191
- ,, position and precautions of Warwick, 183, 184
- ,, Yorkist march to Sandal, 185, 186, 187

Berkeley, Sir J., 265, 266
Bewdley, King at, 312, 313
Blechington House, surrender of, 364, 365
Blore Heath, Audley Cross, 122
- ,, battle of, 121, 122
- ,, captives and slain, 122, 123

Blore Heath, preliminary manœuvres, 118-121
- ,, Salisbury's dispositions, 121

Boarstall taken by Fairfax, 369, 370
Boroughbridge, dispositions of Harcla, 61-62
- ,, Hereford's attack, 63
- ,, Lancaster's attacks, 63, 64, 65
- ,, negotiations, 63
- ,, proceedings prior to battle, 58-61
- ,, site of battle, 61, 62
- ,, truce, 65

Bosworth, battle of, 219, 220
- ,, captives and slain, 220
- ,, Richard's preparations, 215-217
- ,, Richard's Well, 221
- ,, Richmond's expedition, 212-215
- ,, site of battle and camps, 217, 218

Bossall Churchgarth, 9-10

C.

Chalgrove Field, convoy expected, 270, 271
- ,, Essex at Thame, 269
- ,, Royalist lack of precautions, 270
- ,, Rupert's raid, 269-272

INDEX.

Charles at Fawsley Park, 370
Chudleigh (Sir G. and Captain J.), 264, 265
Clifford, death of, 152
  ,, notes on, 152–153
Cock River and Ford, 155, 156, 160, 161
Cromwell, 259, 332–350, 358–361, 364, 366, 368, 370, 371, 374–379, 382–394
Cropredy Bridge, battle of, 315, 318
  ,, preliminary manœuvres, 308–315

D.

David, King of Scotland, 25–29
De Vere, Earl of Oxford, 188–197
Devizes, 286–295
Donnington Castle, 352, 353, 354, 362, 363
Dunstable, Browne at, 314

E.

Edgehill, Byron's pursuit, 255, 256
  ,, death of Verney, 257
  ,, Parliamentarian dispositions, 253
  ,, preliminary manœuvres, 249–252
  ,, recovery of standard, 259
  ,, refusals to renew fight, 257, 258
  ,, Royalist danger, 256, 257
  ,, ,, dispositions, 252, 253
  ,, Rupert's charge, 253, 254, 255
  ,, site of battle, 252, 253, 254, 259, 260
  ,, treachery of Fortescue, 253, 254
  ,, Wilmot's charge, 255
Edward (IV.), arrangements for Towton campaign, 150
  ,, junction with Warwick, 149

Edward (IV.), march from Mortimer's Cross to London, 149, 150
Edward, Prince, at Lewes, 42–48
Edwin and Morcar, 1, 2, 16, 17
Evesham, battle of, 55–57
  ,, campaign of, 50–55
  ,, proceedings prior to battle, 49, 50
  ,, slain and captives, 57

F.

Falconberg, archery tactics, 157, 158
Fitzwalter, death of, 151
Flodden, attack of Huntley and Home, 231, 232
  ,, battle of, 231–236
  ,, Borthwick the gunner, 230, 231
  ,, captives and slain, 236
  ,, challenges from Surrey, 224, 225
  ,, English dispositions, 229, 230, 231
  ,, Ford Castle, 223, 237
  ,, Scottish camp burnt, 228
  ,, ,, dispositions, 229, 230, 231
  ,, ,, invasion, 223
  ,, ,, preparations, 222, 223
  ,, ,, want of precautions, 227
  ,, Surrey's march, 223, 224
  ,, ,, advance from Wooler, 226, 227
Fulford, events preceding and battle of, 1–4

G.

Glemham, Sir T., 326, 347
Gloucester, Clare, Earl of, 40, 44, 46, 47, 49, 54
Graham of Montrose, 241

INDEX.

Grenville, Sir Bevil, 261-263, 278, 280, 281
Gurth, proposals of, 17, 18

H.

Harald Hardrada, 1, 3, 5, 8
Harold II., 1-25
Hedgeley Moor, battle of, 169-171
  ,, ,, events prior to battle, 166-169
  ,, ,, Percy badges, 171
  ,, ,, Percy Cross, 171, 172
  ,, ,, site of battle, 169
  ,, ,, treachery, 170
Henry (Scottish Prince), 28, 29, 32, 33, 36
Hertford, Marquess of, 275, 277, 284
Hexham, captives and slain, 179-180
  ,, flight of King, 176, 177
  ,, legends of Queen Margaret, 174, 177, 179
  ,, place names, 177
  ,, site of battle, 174
  ,, Yorkist attack, 175-176
Homildon Hill, battle of, 99-100
  ,, ,, site of battle, 98, 99
Hopton, Sir Ralph, 261, 262, 275-279, 281, 284, 286, 308

I.

Ireton in Naseby, 371

J.

Jack of Newbury, 224
John Hampden, 267, 269, 272
John Hurry, 270, 273, 274
Johnston and Crew, 355-357
Junction of Cromwell and Fairfax, 366

K.

Kenilworth, 37, 50-55, 59
Kennet River, 301, 302, 306, 353, 361
Key Field, 114, 115

Kineton, 252, 255, 260
Kingsland, 147
King's Life Guard, 354
  ,, Old Horse, 334, 339, 344
Kingston, 40
King's Stone, 237
Kingstone or King's Mill, 46
Kintbury, 301, 302
Knaresborough, 328
Kyrielle, Sir T., 144

L.

Lancaster, Thomas of, 58-67
Lansdown, determination to storm, 278
  ,, preliminary manœuvres, 275, 276
  ,, Royalist advance, 277, 278
  ,, Royalists retire, 278
  ,, Royalist retreat, 279, 280
  ,, site of battle, 278, 279
  ,, Waller at, 277
  ,, Waller retires, 279
  ,, Waller retreats to Bath, 279
Leicester, Charles at, 369
Leven's march south, 368
Lewes, battle of, 42-48
  ,, events preceding battle, 37-42
  ,, Montfort's dispositions, 44
  ,, Royalist dispositions, 45
  ,, site of battle, 43, 44

M.

March from Bewdley, Charles's, 313
March of Charles to North, 367
March of Waller from Worcester, 313, 314
Marston Moor, absence of Parliamentary Infantry, 328, 331
  ,, battle of, 337-346
  ,, cavalry combat (Goring's), 339, 340, 341, 342, 344

INDEX.

Marston Moor, cavalry combat (Rupert's), 338
,, disposition of armies, 332-334
,, flight of Newcastle, 346, 347
,, fugitive generals, 350
,, movements of Fairfaxes, 323
,, Newcastle at York, 325, 326
,, Newcastle's Whitecoats, 335
,, night before battle, 327-328
,, Rupert's proceedings prior to, 321-323, 324-327
,, Rupert's reconnaissance, 331
,, site of battle, 329, 330
,, the fate of the Whitecoats, 344, 345
Millfield Plain (fight at), 226
Montague, Lord, notes on, 180
Mortimer's Cross, battlefield, 147-148
,, captives and slain, 148
,, preliminary manœuvres, 145-147
Mullet (badge), 194, 197

N.

Naseby, battle of, 376-380
,, preliminary manœuvres, 364-371
,, Royalist dispositions, 372, 374, 375
,, various Parliamentarian positions, 372, 373, 375, 376
Neville's Cross, Baliol's Reserve, 76
,, battle of, 74-77
,, captives and slain, 77
,, English advance prior to, 70-73

Neville's Cross, English dispositions, 73
,, notes on warriors, 77-80
,, Scottish advance prior to, 68-70
,, Scottish dispositions, 73
,, site of battle, 73-74
Newburn, battle of, 243-247
,, dispositions of English and Scotch, 241-243
,, Leslie's guns and tents, 240, 241
,, Scottish preparations, 238-241
Newbury I., battle of, 303-306
,, dispositions of armies, 302, 303
,, preliminary manœuvres, 296-301
,, site of battle, 301, 302
Newbury II., attack on Maurice, 358-360
,, battle of, 360-363
,, Parliamentarian designs, 357
,, preliminary manœuvres, 352, 353
,, Royal position, 353, 354
,, Royalist preparations, 357-358
,, War Committee, 354, 355
,, Shaw House, 353, 357, 362
Norman attacks, 20-24
Northallerton, battle of, 32-35
,, English dispositions, 30, 31
,, English leaders, 27
,, Scotch dispositions, 31, 32
,, Scotch leaders, 32
Northampton, 38, 39
,, battle of, 128-130
,, preliminary manœuvres, 124-127
,, Royalist camp, 127-128
,, site of battle, 127
,, Yorkist advance, 128

INDEX.

O.

Otterburn, battle of, 89-93
,, Bishop of Durham's marches, 93, 94
,, English advance, 87, 88
,, English attack, 88, 89
,, English leaders, 88, 89
,, from Newcastle to battlefield, 84, 85
,, graves and cross, 94, 95
,, Scottish leaders, 82, 83
,, Scottish march to Newcastle, 81-84
,, site of battle and Scottish camp, 85-87

P.

Painswick, 298
Pembroke (Jasper, Earl of), 145-148
Percy, Henry, 2nd Baron, 70, 72, 73, 78
,, Hugh de, 39
,, Sir Henry, 83, 84, 86-96, 102-108
,, Sir Ralph, 83, 92
,, Sir Ralph II., 166, 170, 171, 172
Perry Hill and Wood, 390, 391, 393
Pevensey, 11-13
Pitchcroft, 386
Plymouth, 261, 281
Pontefract, 133, 150, 151, 152, 153, 224
Ponteland, 84, 85
Postcombe, 270
Powick Bridge, 389

R.

Relief of Lyme Regis, 311
Riccall, camp at, 3, 4, 5, 8, 9
Romans (Richard, King of the), 38, 42, 45-47
Rosa Spinosissima, 163
Rose-en-Soliel (badge), 148, 194, 197
Roundway Down, battle of, 292-295

Roundway Down, Hopton's retreat to Devizes, 286, 287
,, Royalist horse leave, 288
,, Royalist horse return, 291-292
,, Waller arrives at Devizes, 287
,, Waller attacks, 292, 293
,, Waller besieges Devizes, 288, 289, 290
Royalist successes, 367
Ruthven, Lord, notes on, 318, 319

S.

Sedgemoor, advance of Monmouth, 411-412
,, affair at Axminster, 400
,, affair at Bridport, 399
,, affair at Norton St. Philip, 405, 406
,, attempt on Bristol, 403
,, battle of, 412-415
,, Bridgwater, 401, 407, 411
,, Frome, 406
,, Government preparations, 399, 400
,, landing at Lyme, 396
,, preliminary events, 395, 396
,, proclamation, 397
,, Royalist position, 407-411
,, Taunton, 400, 401
,, Wells, 407
Senlac, site of battle, 19, 20
Simon de Montfort, 37-47, 49, 51, 52, 54-57
,, (junior), 50-55
Shrewsbury, battle of, 106-108
,, captives and slain, 108, 109
,, events preceding battle, 101-104
,, King Henry's march, 103
,, memorial church, 109, 110

INDEX.

Shrewsbury, negotiations, 105–106
,, site of battle, 104, 105
Slanning, Sir N., 285, 287
St. Albans I., captives and slain, 116–117
,, events preceding battle, 112–114
,, Yorkist attack, 115–116
St. Albans II., battle of, 143–144
,, captives and slain, 144
,, Lancastrian leaders, 142
,, preliminary manœuvres, 141, 142
,, Warwick's "gynnes," 142
,, Yorkist dispositions, 142–143
Stamford Bridge, events preceding and battle of, 4–10
Stratton, preliminary manœuvres, 261, 262
,, Royalist attack, 263
,, site of battle, 262, 263
,, Stamford encamps at, 262
Sudeley Castle, fall of, 311
Sulby Hedge, 375, 376, 378
Swan (badge), 122

T.

Tewkesbury, captives and slain, 210
,, Edward's march from London, 199, 201, 203
,, events prior to battle, 198–203
,, Gloucester's tactics, 207
,, Lancastrian dispositions, 205
,, Lancastrian failure at Gloucester, 202
,, Lancastrian flight, 208, 209
,, Lancastrian marches, 198–199, 200, 201, 202
,, site of battle, 203, 204
,, Yorkist attack, 206, 207
Tostig, 1, 2, 3, 5
Towton, battle of, 157–160

Towton, captives and slain, 161, 163, 164, 165
,, Lancastrian flight, 160, 161
,, Lancastrian position at, 156, 157
,, Lancastrian retreat from Barnet, 150
,, Lord Dacre and his tomb, 162, 163
,, marches of the campaign, 153–155
,, passage of the Aire, 151–152
,, site of the battle, 155
,, Yorkist advance from London, 150, 151
,, Yorkist position at Saxton, 153

W.

Wakefield, battle of, 135–137
,, chapel on bridge, 137
,, knights made after, 138
,, Lancastrian dispositions, 135
,, Lancastrian leaders, 132
,, peliminary manœuvres, 131–133
,, Sandal Castle and battle site, 133, 134
,, slain at, 138
"Wakefield" Tower, 139–140
Welles, Sir Leo de, 163
William, Duke of Normandy, proceedings prior to battle, 11–14
White Hart badge, 99
Woodstock, Charles at, 313
Worcester, bridges of boats, 389, 390, 391, 392
,, Cromwell's march, 384, 385, 386, 387, 388
,, Fort Royal taken, 392
,, Lambert at Upton, 388
,, preliminary manœuvres, 382–388
,, Royalists at, 310
,, Royalist defences, 389, 390
,, sortie by the prince, 391, 392

www.ingramcontent.com/pod-product-compliance
Lightning Source LLC
Chambersburg PA
CBHW051857300426
44117CB00006B/428